Times New Romanian

Times
New
Romanian

Edited by Nigel Shakespear

Matador
9 Priory Business Park
Kibworth Beauchamp
Leicestershire LE8 0RX, UK
Tel: (+44) 116 279 2299
Fax: (+44) 116 279 2277
Email: books@troubador.co.uk
Web: www.troubador.co.uk/matador

ISBN 978-1783064-519

British Library Cataloguing in Publication Data.
A catalogue record for this book is available from the British Library.

Typeset in Aldine by Troubador Publishing Ltd
Printed and bound in the UK by TJ International, Padstow, Cornwall

Matador is an imprint of Troubador Publishing Ltd

MIX
Paper from
responsible sources
FSC www.fsc.org FSC® C013056

A sincere thank you to each and every contributor for sharing your thoughts and reflections on the land of your choice. Thanks also to Rosalind, co-traveller and co-editor.

ROMANIA

Contents

Omnia mutantur, nihil interit – everything changes, nothing perishes.
   Ovid

Introduction

On a wet day in May I found myself heading up Finchley High Street, passing a charity advertising itself as giving aid in Romania. I went in, and the girl unearthed an old flyer that elaborated on how they provided much-needed social welfare in the country. Like any other high street charity in the UK, it was a shop full of books, clothes and bric-a-brac going for a song. There was nothing special about it other than its purpose. I don't imagine the Londoners in there browsing the shelves gave it much thought – they were looking for bargains. But why?

The short answer is that it was set up in the early 90s, when hundreds of charities responded to the need for help in the post-Ceauşescu period. This leads to the idiosyncratic situation today whereby charities in the UK are funding the welfare of another European Union country.

Romanians have a sense of being different, of living in a country that is different. And it is. Well, all countries have their unique qualities, but this one and its people raise the temperature. They don't leave you unaffected or unmoved; they invite a reaction.

For millennia, foreigners from west and east have been crossing this place, the land of Romania. The poet Ovid, banished to the Black Sea from Rome, died miserable in 17 AD in Tomis – now Constanţa. Today the position of the foreigner, a Western one at least, is privileged and limited. Privileged because most of us are usually treated kindly; limited because Romania is a deep well, difficult for an outsider to plumb.

'They can always outsmart us,' I was told by an experienced Western immigrant. They certainly played the Russians cleverly in the heyday of the USSR, and some would have it that they've played the European Union likewise in the last ten years.[1] This is a country quite used to dealing with outside powers and their representatives.

They can be their own worst critics. They will accuse themselves of 'a lack of civility, a lack of respect, exhibitions of frustration, a world of excess'. They will do themselves down like the Romanian commenting in a Trip Advisor travel posting about Bulgarians being 'a bit more civilised and open-minded than us.' Self-absorbed introspection can look like self-flagellation – witness a well-known author writing on the Romanian feeling of hysteria, when he talked of those who'd been abroad for a long time returning to the abnormality of life here. There's a recognition of the dark side of life here that can outshine flickers of hope.

As an Englishman not integrated into Romanian society but on the outside looking in, I had gone there to work and found it a country of character, a long way from the anonymity of developed consumer societies. From my first night staying in Bucharest's Hanul lui Manuc hotel in 1996, I was engaged by the incongruities and the strangely inexplicable, although it wasn't difficult to understand the young lady who knocked on my door at midnight, asking for a light. In the 90s I was always being asked, 'What do you think of our country?' In time the question more or less disappeared, but I was still looking for an answer.

Working with the public administration, mostly on EU-funded social projects related to the Roma (also known as Gypsies), the real benefits to their communities weren't easy to see. Involvement in so-called Structural Fund projects in the social sector was akin to wading in the Danube delta – slow and murky. Projects are a ready

---

[1] See David Floyd – *Rumania: Russia's Dissident Ally*. Frederick A. Praeger, 1965 and Tom Gallagher – *Romania and the European Union: How the Weak Vanquished the Strong*. Manchester University Press 2009

source of money and resources, subject to the manipulation of the undisclosed agendas of others. Much of my time was spent working out who was after what; we were a long way from 'what you see is what you get'. Unforeseen blockages were the rule. Expectations slid into oblivion, leading to cynicism and disillusionment. Romanians were clearly better adapted to deal with this, but for me the environment became discouraging. Notable exceptions were the educated young people who were my colleagues, in almost complete contradiction to the problematic world with which we were dealing.

Bureaucracy can be painful anywhere, and Romania provides its fair share of pain. You learn that to get anything done you need a lot of energy or good friends. It took two and a half hours and 37 signatures to open a bank account. Often enough, officials just don't know the answer. Eight calls to different individuals in the local administration, just to sort out a local community problem, left one friend giving up on it. Sometimes it's worth going back the next day to find someone else to talk to; it could all go smoothly.

I heard about corruption, although I lived protected from it. My wife had met Cristina, an ex-teacher reduced to begging outside our local supermarket, and we took her on as a language trainer. She told us stories about the area we lived in and about her hard life. In one memorable instance, she had taken her granddaughter with a deep, bleeding cut to the Emergency Hospital, where she had to scream and shout that she had no money before an Indian doctor sewed the girl up – with 36 stitches. In June 2010, the newspaper *Evenimentul Zilei* gave a breakdown of the extra payments required to lead a life in Romania: about €20,000 – for a lifetime, presumably. This didn't include unofficial payments that sometimes need to be made to get a job as a teacher, lawyer or doctor, about which Cristina waxed lyrical. Wages and salaries are low, and most people aren't financially well off, but there can be money to go round when needed. The subtleties of the black economy in the country remained byzantine to us.

Consensus can be hard to come by, and the default mode is to contest. A casual glance at the politics of the country will suggest that politicians are extremely aggressive, continually aiming to destroy each other. It may be a game, but a secretary of state told me that all political parties were in the same boat, being the most conservative institutions in the country. In his party he had little chance of promotion on merit. To get on you have to pay. The more you pay, the bigger the role. And having paid for the position, you get your money back in power. You go into politics to make money. The politics are not ideology-driven but formed around circles of interests.

In her books, the Romanian-born Nobel Prize winner Herta Müller hasn't painted a pretty picture of the place as it once was. She also criticised the EU for not paying more attention to the communist past of its new states. She was well received in Bucharest in September 2010, where she was asked if there was nothing she liked in Romania. Her answer – that she liked some very extraordinary people who she knows and who are her friends and if there were more of them in Romania, things would go better – suggests that her feelings haven't changed.[2] She had been in permanent conflict with the *Securitate*, and remained at odds with them and their successors even after she'd left the country.

Fear of state authorities is still there. Less than five years ago we met a woman who'd been subject to a *Securitate* recruitment effort in the 80s, when she was called down to their local headquarters. They tried to persuade her to report on her colleagues. Saying she wasn't suitable for this work, she had to sign a letter declaring she would never tell anyone about their request. Of course she spoke to her parents, and her mother remains nervous today.

Her mother was an elegant lady, with hair tied back, her face showing traces of refinement. She remembered the interbellum years well, recalling the days of horse and carriage, of men dressed

---

[2] *Adevărul*, September 2010

in gloves and carrying canes, as if those were the days when people behaved better. Essentially, she was an imperfectly preserved specimen of the local bourgeoisie. More than once she and her daughter referred to being unable to trust people. However, the behaviour of the Germans when they came in 1941 was irreproachable, she said, unlike the Russians who stole watches and thought nothing of raping women in front of their children. As the afternoon wore on she showed warmth and humour and opened up, but early in the conversation she had asked me not to tell anyone that I'd been talking to her, as if the *Securitate* were still in operation. I asked her later if they were. 'Rumour has it so,' she replied cautiously. Both women had an attachment to the heavy steel bar that secured the door leading to the street.

Romania today reflects the history of its people over centuries, and of the state since its birth in the 19th century. Its communist legacy cannot account for the way everything works, or doesn't work, but it remains a powerful influence. Behind the political show there are shadowy networks of influential people, a layer of power brokers formed from the communist elite that never intended to hand over the baton in 1989.

We went to the Peasants' Museum in 2011 to see an exhibition set up by the Institute for the Investigation into Communist Crimes and the Memory of the Romanian Exile, the executive president of which is appointed by the prime minister. It showed photographs of archaeological digs around the country disinterring the bodies of people murdered in the late 40s and early 50s. A large Romanian flag covered a plinth in the centre of the room, and laid flat on this was a rough wooden cross. No mention of the repression that continued right up until 1989 but perhaps those are to be found elsewhere. There are associations working to uncover the truth, but the ruling elite will have to cede power before there is any real reconciliation with the past.

For the moment, those who authorised, organised or engaged in the harassment and repression remain secure enough.

The expression *tardo comunismo* (late communism), borrowed from one of the contributors here, appeals to me – it conjures up the lingering presence of the past and an awareness of what lies under the deep pile carpet here. It has coloured my feelings, imparting a sense of tension about the country. This, as well as my provenance from northern Europe and the ordered world of my upbringing, have put me at odds with the place.

Over time I did get more used to the way things went, but I also started to look for an antidote to the frustrations and pessimism. I found it amongst Romanian friends and colleagues in their hospitality and their humour, irony and laughter at life's absurdities; in their ability to enjoy life and also in some who live selfless lives working for others. Many of those we knew living ordinary lives were impressive people and full of spirit. Life was difficult for them. As a well-qualified and successful doctor once told me, 'It's not easy to be born Romanian.' And I'd obviously crossed a line one day when I was told firmly, 'If you faced what we face, you'd be the same!' They have developed coping mechanisms.

You can find glossy photographic books on the country representing a singularly uncommon reality, and I wondered how a number of voices might present a more genuine picture of the place, and answer the question, 'What do you think of our country?' So I looked for foreigners from different walks of life: individuals, not corporate people; those more integrated than myself. When my last contract came to an end, I set off to talk to them individually, following a haphazard and engaging trail that took me through Bucharest, around Transylvania, to Maramureş and the Banat.

To understand some subjects that come up in this book one needs an idea of the context, so for those who don't know Romania's history the following should help: Romania joined the European

Union in 2007; the Kingdom of Rumania had come into being in 1881 with the coronation of Carol I, who had been invited as a German prince to rule the recently joined principalities of Wallachia and Moldavia in 1866. Transylvania became part of Romania soon after the First World War, previously being part of the Austro-Hungarian Empire – hence the large Hungarian minority found in the country. The Communist Party forced the King to abdicate on 30th December 1947 and proclaimed the Rumanian People's Republic – that day marking their total control of power until the regime of Nicolae Ceauşescu was overthrown in the Revolution of December 1989. After this, once the borders to the West had been opened, huge numbers of Saxons left Transylvania in the early 1990s for Germany. Saxons had been living there since the 12th century. As for the Roma, around the turn of the 14th century they arrived in what is now the present-day territory of Romania. And it was here that slavery was only abolished in the middle of the 19th century. Most of the slaves had been Roma.

The following chapters are a series of individual perspectives, observations and stories taken from interviews during the period November 2011 to October 2012. It is the Romanian world seen through foreign eyes, a multi-vocal picture painted as a frieze, each chapter offering something of their reality in the country – there's no consensus and no complete story. This diverse society affects us all differently. These voices speak of the underlying vitality of the people and of the strength of family, as well as the effects of ethnic diversity. There's mention of wine, music and film along with social issues and justice, and of the disappearing heritage of a traditional rural life. Also, of just the way things work in this country. There's good and bad here, as there is everywhere. It is not a full portrait, nor a drawing with hard visible lines, but more a finding out, a seeing of a surface here, a faint edge there, sometimes sublime, sometimes sinister – from this different existence on the eastern periphery of Europe today.

Walter Friedl

Bucharest

'This is Eastern Europe; it smelt like this, it looked like this. It's not any more. It's more modern probably than most places in Vienna.'

I was here in the last six months of the regime, and then during the Revolution; I saw what happened in the streets. And I saw this new Romania coming up in the two years until 1992. I left the country, and came back in 2002 for the Austrian government, as commercial counsellor at the Austrian Embassy for seven years. This was the time when most of these big investments happened, between 2002 and 2007. The big privatisations. We established 5500 Austrian companies here, which was fantastic. In 2009 when my time came to an end, I decided to stay here. I'm working now for a big Austrian insurance company, and I've set up a winery. We're three investors from Austria: two financial investors and myself. We're producing premium wines in quite a quantity. My wife is Romanian and she's with the winery, but she was with me all over the world. We've been married for over 20 years now.

In the last century Romanian wines were some of the best in the world. On the Orient Express from London to Istanbul they were drinking Romanian wine, not French wine. But these premium wines were lost in the communist period. Today this country is the sixth biggest producer of wines in Europe, but of course there's a lot of mass production: 70 or 80 per cent of this production is big wineries. Enormous sizes, up to 3500 hectares.

There's a small group of premium wine producers. We're about ten to twelve, which entered in the last seven or eight years in this sector to sell premium local wines to the Romanian people who can afford these wines – and to experts of course, and then to tourists and foreign business visitors. With premium wine, you start with the grape production. You have to treat the grapes very gently; you have to select them at different stages. We have a potential of six kilograms of grapes per plant, and we reduce them during the year to one kilogram. So through this reduction all the minerals, the water – all the good stuff – is concentrated on a small number of grapes. It's a very expensive way to produce grapes, but at the end of the day the aroma and the quality of the wine is completely different. Then of course you have to have very modern, state-of-the-art production, because of all the hygiene standards which have to be implemented in the winery. We invested €7 million in our winery to be able to produce wine to the latest modern standards. There are non-premium wines which are delicious, but I'm talking about the premium sector.

Under communism, the state thought the more wine you produce, the better it is for the economy – which is wrong. It's the quality and price of the wine that counts. They thought in terms of quantities of wine, of selling to Western countries to get Western currency. This destroyed the image of Romanian wines abroad. Of course in the backyard, for themselves and for their neighbours, people continued producing very good wine, because the conditions are world class and they have the knowledge. They've produced wines for 6000 years, so they know very well how to make good wines! When we started in 2002, we thought we'd have to tell the people we hired how to produce premium wines. But they said, 'Of course we know that. You allow us to do that? Fine, we do it.' It's of course super to have the manpower; from the first day we had brilliant people. We now have 43 people in the vineyard and in the winery and in sales and administration – all of them Romanians, doing very well. They're super-specialists.

We knew that Dealu Mare, this area where we are, is world class because it's on the 45th parallel. It's exactly on that parallel where the conditions for wine in the northern hemisphere are perfect… it's Bordeaux, it's Toscana, it's Dealu Mare. This is the latitude for wine, and we have the southern sun, we have the minerals from the Carpathians, we have the rainy springtime. From June to November we have practically no rain, only sun. The soil is perfect for it, too. We have a small hill which is necessary; like in the cinema, all the leaves can see the sun. It's world-class conditions, especially for red wine, but also for white. The Romans came from Constanța because of Dealu Mare. They saw this and said, 'Wine!' and there was wine. That's why we chose to invest in Romania and the people, in combination with a long tradition of wine agriculture. Also, of course, European money helped us in the project. I was working here as a commercial counsellor, and I could support the whole project from the very beginning.

When do you make an investment, when do you make a company? When you have clients. I was one of these clients in this time, in the seven years when I was here, mainly to help Austrian investors. I went out three to four times a week in the evening with these guys for dinner. They said, 'Walter, can I invite you for dinner? Tell me more about Romania. Help me to invest, what to do and where and what. Give me your experience!' They told me to choose a good restaurant, and in the restaurant they gave me the wine card and said, 'Walter, choose a good Romanian wine!'

If I go to Spain I would drink Spanish wine; the same with all these people, they wanted to have a decent Romanian wine. It was very difficult to find a good Romanian wine at that time; it still is today. The market is big, the demand is enormous and there's not enough good wine from Romania, nicely promoted and so on. So we decided that the best opportunity was to sell the wine here. Of course we're exporting also. We're now one and a half years in the market, and we already export to Germany, we export to France –

but randomly. When asked, we send a quantity, but we don't want to do that actively. Because of the heritage of 45 years of communism, it's not easy abroad to sell premium Romanian wine. You can sell the cheap wine. But good wine, with a premium price of course, is difficult to market.

Austria is by far the largest investor here. It was always present in Romania. I think for people from eastern Austria or from Berlin, people who know what Eastern Europe means, for them it's easier to work here than to work in Switzerland. The mentality of the people in Zürich, it's more difficult for me to understand than the mentality of the people of Craiova.

I don't think it has a lot to do with history. Of course this part here in Bucharest was the Ottoman Empire. This wasn't the Austro-Hungarian Empire; that ended in Braşov in the north of the Carpathians. It has a lot more to do with the courage and the experience of people in the 90s, and also the strategical mind-set of individuals who convinced their supervisory board in Vienna, saying 'Let's buy an insurance company in Romania. Let's buy a bank in Romania. Let's buy the minerals or the oil business in Romania! Let's go there, open a company there, open a factory. Let's invest there, I trust them. We get our money back, we can do a good business and we gain a new market. It's not some bad mafia people coming to you and taking it away from you, or that this country will break apart and you lose your investment.' It was hard for them to convince their supervisory board to say, 'Okay here, you have ten billion, go there and buy it, do it!'

Personally, I could see it was individual people; it was a personal engagement – and of course the situation that our Austrian companies were already located on the southern side of Hungary, on the Romanian borders. They'd already invested there, so they were very close when it opened. They saw new times coming in Eastern Europe and that it will be part of the European Union. I remember in 2002, when I spoke in front of 200 people in Innsbruck. I told them that in five years Romania would be part of the European Union. Half of them laughed, and the other half left the hall. It happened, and it was very successful for many of these companies. And still today, whatever you do here, you can do it by yourself. If you come from Ireland or Italy, you can do it without a local partner. Nobody gives a damn whether you have a local partner or not. You can act freely. Your enemies are the bureaucracy and the taxes, the Ministry of Finance and infrastructure – but no mafia. You're fine here. You have a good local market for your product. These are the bases of a good project.

During the 45 years of communism, the Romanians kept their identity inside the families. They remained what they are, practically a Roman island in the Balkan region; a very rich country full of raw materials, energy, with a wonderful natural world and their own culture, their own food, their own language, their own history. They're very artistic. They're super musicians, architects… they're a very special group of people, these Romanians. They could preserve that over these years. It *was* preserved; it was kept from the outside world. Then right after the Revolution, this came back immediately. But even in '89 I had Romanian friends here. I could see when I entered into their private environment it was completely different to this North Korea on the streets. In the house they had wonderful books, they made music, they had these discussions and these friends. And they stuck together. It's a very rich culture, the Romanian culture, and thank God this didn't change.

We meet Romanians abroad and I tell them I'm from Vienna and I'm living here. And they say, 'What did you do that you have to live in Romania? This is sick, this is absolutely sick! You're coming from Vienna? What did you do wrong in Vienna that you had to leave and go to Romania?' Confidence has been completely destroyed; self-confidence has been taken away from them. To regain it will obviously take more than 20 years, but it's getting better.

I see massive changes. I see it from my business friends who don't come on a regular basis, who didn't come for the last one and a half years. I meet them here and they say, 'Oh, incredible!'

And I say, 'What?'

'When I come from the airport and there's this and that, it looks completely different, the city, no more dogs.'

If you go to the big companies, when you enter there, there's not any more a smell of Eastern Europe. This is a development of the last five years. Even five years ago, wherever you went, in every company, office or ministry you always had this immediately. This is Eastern Europe; it smelt like this, it looked like this. It's not any more. It's more modern probably than most places in Vienna.

How about old attitudes in the ministries?

Look, it's 22 years ago, this Revolution, we mustn't forget that. We have ministers today of 34, so they were 12 during the Revolution! How can they have this old attitude? This is ridiculous. They were raised in a completely modern, new world, with Internet, with Sat TV, with travelling abroad easily. They know very well and they don't have this attitude. Older people, of course, had their function in the communist time and you can see them. When I see an old communist who is behaving like one, he cannot do modern marketing. But the minister of 35 or a state secretary of 32, how can they be communist minded or old-fashioned? I don't believe it. They're modern people, have a good education, a modern education.

And corruption? Corruption you have in Germany, corruption you have in Austria, you have in Italy and Spain. You have it in Romania. But if you ask me about corruption, we're ten years old now with the winery. I never paid any money for European Union funds; I never paid any money for any stamp in the construction. I didn't pay any money for getting land, and for licenses for registration. I don't pay any money to sell the wine, even. Okay, if something happened in privatisation… but look at the projects happening now in Europe, or in Asia, Africa or in America… the daily corruption? I don't see it.

I have challenges, heavy challenges. The only fair system that exists, giving back land to the pre-communist owners, makes it very difficult to buy 82 hectares. I had to deal with 60 different owners and their papers weren't in order. I had to hire our lawyers to bring their papers in order, and then I could buy the land. I paid more for my lawyers than I paid in cash for the land! These are real challenges.

When I enter a restaurant, a newly opened restaurant, and I come with a Romanian wine and they say, 'No, no, no, we buy Italian wines because we're now open,' I say, 'Self-confidence! Look, you won't get good customers if you don't have Romanian wine.' I invite them to the winery; I show them how we produce it. And then they realise something is happening in this country that they can be proud of. Then they sell it, of course. But this is a lot of work, it takes a lot of convincing. The best thing is to show it to them here, in their own country. You show them how it works here, then they say, 'Why can these Austrians do it and we can't?' Then they start thinking and seeing this is possible.

Through this Ottoman Empire, of course, came an oriental way to think and to act, and it's extremely important that the guy you're dealing with, doing business with, you're in a relation with him. You have to know him personally. You have to know who he is. His company, his documents, his titles don't count at all; it's the person. 'Do you have kids? How do you think about this… ?' It's very important to start the conversation with questions which aren't related to the subject. To know the person, to trust him. If he says he can deliver, you trust this person, you don't trust the company. This is extremely important. It's the way to survive in all the difficult times. You have to see from 20 metres if he's an enemy or a friend. There's an instinct in the Romanian, which is the way they've survived. They immediately check you personally. Can I trust you? How are you? Are you thinking the same? Or will you surprise me with stupid ideas or actions? This is the most important thing. That's why, when I'm looking for a new driver, I ask the current driver, 'Do you know somebody? Can you recommend me somebody?' I wouldn't go immediately to the new Human Resources office as I would in Denmark, probably, or in Germany. This attitude is super-important.

The first thing the girls in our insurance company or the banks learn from their relatives is: be careful, look at the people. Just because you're sending a beautiful email and you sign with a super name, this isn't enough. They want to see you. Then you have to go on a regular basis to these people, have a coffee. As a foreigner he'll probably ask you, 'What do you want from me?' Then you say, 'Nothing. I just want to have a coffee with you.' This is the first step. Then he starts trusting you. I have a lot of coffees and a lot of glasses of wine too. In my case, wine. The Romanians don't drink hard drinks, very rarely a whisky or a vodka. They also drink some beer nowadays, but not in the quantities like the Slavs where they really want to get drunk. They're like Italians with food, nice wine… They're 100 per cent more Latin. This is clear. They're totally from the Romanic world.

The 90s were practically lost for the development of Romania, but it was an important phase, it was an important time. Where were they going? It wasn't clear. In 1997 and 1998 it wasn't clear on which side of the world they would be. The Black Sea is a Russian lake – this was Băsescu as mayor here. Since they stopped laughing at the European Union and applied in 2001 for EU membership, it was, 'Okay, then you have to privatise everything!' They really did it in one and a half years. This was of course the most important step in the development of the last 22 years; when they really decided, 'We do everything to join the European Union. Give us the rules and we will implement them: the first five points today; the next five points tomorrow. Till we're through.' That's what they did. This is a very important part of the history of Romania. How fast it went afterwards was incredible! Today Romania is doing very well. The basics are super.

The politics, yes, thank God this isn't so important. The politicians in Romania, like in Austria or in Denmark or in Portugal, these politicians cannot decide. They can't make big switches or changes in policies. Yes, they can raise taxes or they can do this and that – small measures – but they cannot change dramatically the whole appearance of the country. So it's not that important.

So it's turned towards the West?

Yes, and it will remain like this. The direction was super-clear... stronger every day.

Frans Brinkman

Vizureşti

'It's nothing you have, and it's very quiet to have nothing. Another life.'

After 18 years in social work, in psychiatry and crisis intervention, I made a decision. In two years I go take a break, I go travel. So it has not been impulsive. I had no programme, I had no plan where to go; I only quit my job, quit my house, left my country. I had a good life you can say, and the question was at that moment, do I like to continue this life for the next 20 years, or do I like to find something new, different? I just wanted to stop for a moment at least the life I was used to. I was a little bit bored by it.

I had a good meal with friends, and then left in the evening in my van. For sure I would not drive far at that time. I'm from the Netherlands. I stopped somewhere in Germany, in a forest, and the sun was going down. There I was, alone. I had some music of Bob Dylan with me, and some Dutch gin. I travelled on and I had no destination. I had long hair also, by the way. In Hungary I thought I would go to Turkey and then I found out I have to travel through Romania, because in Yugoslavia there was a war.

I knew nothing about Romania. The people in Hungary said it's very dangerous there. It would be crazy to visit the country on my own. You will be dead after one week or sooner, seriously! I thought, what do I do? Because I would not stay in Hungary. In the first place Hungarian is a very difficult language for me. Second, I was travelling. I had the idea to go on; so I take the risk to go to Romania.

When I crossed the border it seems to be very dangerous

because the people at the border were not very friendly. It was 1996. And then after the border there were immediately people changing money and they looked a little bit dangerous. But after one or two days I was helped by someone when I was stuck with my van in the mud. We spoke without words. But the day after I thought, I go take hitchhikers. There were a lot of hitchhikers, also old ladies, and I thought, well, let's give it a try. So I give it a try and then I met only friendly people. They asked me also to go home to eat something, or to drink. I did not do that in the first week, but later I did. And then they offer you also a place to sleep. I said, 'I go further on with my van.'

I came to Bucharest which was awful at that time. I had a hitchhiker and he understood nothing about what I'm asking him. I thought, in Bucharest I have to find a youth hostel or a tourist office. He let me drive around in the city. We find nothing and then in the end he left me in the railway station, saying, 'Good luck!' Well, I drive around and I went in one shop where I asked for a city map and the girl spoke a little bit of English. She said the city map doesn't exist.

And I ask her, 'Where is the centre?' and she said, 'The centre is here.' I was very surprised because there were only blocks, nothing to see, no tourists. I decided to leave the next day.

So I hang around a little bit and then went back to my van. In that time you could leave your van in Bucharest anywhere, and you also could sleep in it. Maybe a policeman came to ask you what you are doing and then you say, 'I'm just sleeping.' He was looking, and mostly he didn't understand you but you give him some drinking money, he said, '*Mulţumesc* – Thank you' and then you could sleep without any trouble. But before I reached my van I met Somna. She was selling flowers at that time. Because I was alone and had no girlfriend with me, she said, 'I cannot sell you a flower but I think you can give me a lemonade.'

I said 'Yes, that's possible.' So we met – and we stayed together.

Somna's from this village, Vizureşti?

Yes, she's born here. She has a lot of family here. Before I really came to live in the community, they knew me already because we were a long time married. I'm well known as the Dutchman who's married with that Gypsy girl, and the other 'white Romanians' in the village know me because I'm a Dutchman in the Gypsies' area. To start the relationship, and to marry as well, was not a problem. But they checked me out. At first I was two weeks with Somna camping in the van, in Bucharest centre, now and then giving a policeman his drink money. We went out to eat in that time because I had no cooking equipment. Then a boy showed up. He said, 'Hello, I'm Robert.'

I said 'Oh, good.'

Somna then said, 'Ah, he's my brother… by chance passing by.'

It's a big family. So I had this some more times. The oldest brother made an appointment to go out for pizza. He wanted to see me. Then I was good enough – with the obligation of a big wedding party. After six weeks we had a big tent in the courtyard of my mother-in-law.

We have three groups in the village. One Roma, or Gypsies; and another part, the white Romanians, as I call them; then we have a group of former Roma – called *Pocăit* – because they take another religion, Reformed Church. I think shortly after the Revolution evangelists came in with help and with their bible. They asked the people to choose, 'Do you like our help? Then you also take our religion.' They left the Romanian Orthodox Church.

Here in our Gypsy part of the village I know more people because part of them is family of course, so that's easy. And these families have neighbours, and these neighbours you also learn to know. I don't know everybody's name and also I do not know exactly who is living in which house; or who is related to another one. I'm not very interested in all these relationships, who is married with the sister of who, who are nephews, who are neighbours. Amazing how my wife always knows what I am doing, with whom I spoke. For me I am greeting everybody because you never know who is family!

What about bars and shops in the village?

Bars *are* shops, and yes, these are different. With one, there's a little bit more luxury you could say, because they have heating and a coffee machine and a terrace as well. The others are small. Sometimes you can sit there, sometimes they have no chairs. But even in the winter time people are drinking there.

And the shops are all little grocery shops. They have things you need for daily food and drink, and a lot of alcoholic drinks. For different things, for a brown bread, I have to go to another place. You will not find that here, and not blue cheese – important for me as a vegetarian! When I came the frequency of the regular public transport, going to Bucharest, was once a day. And now it's three times a day, so that's better. There is also a train. When you have a car it's easy to drive there of course, it's just three kilometres to the railway station. Many people have no car, so they walk, and they try to make it by hitch-hiking; by horse and carriage also.

Most people are working, or have worked, in Bucharest. It's nearby, 40 kilometres, so within one hour you are there. They are in construction working, and guards, taking care of shops, factories, especially in the night. Many people are doing this because it's an unqualified job. You only have not to be afraid and a little bit strong. Or you have to look strong, at least. And the garbage business in Bucharest, including cleaning parks and streets. When you see in Bucharest somebody who's cleaning streets, it's a big chance it's a Gypsy person. Some people are also in Bucharest selling things in the street. They're going around with goods and clothes shouting in the street, '*Ciorapi, avem ciorapi* – Stockings, we have stockings.' It is one of the daily sounds here as well, together with cows, sheep, ducks and dogs.

So how are you making a living?

I have two main activities. One is a small tourist business. We have with our family some places for bed and breakfast, like a guest house. But you live more or less with the family itself. We have a special exotic thing of course, because I can advertise myself as the Gypsy neighbourhood and you're living with a Gypsy family. My sister-in-law, she's a really great hostess. People ask, 'It's not dangerous with these Gypsies then, how does it work out?'

Well, I can give them a clear answer that everything is okay, I'm still living here after years and most people that visit us are also enthusiastic. I'm promoting Vizureşti as a village where nothing is happening. You have no discotheque, you have no traffic, you have no theatre, cinema, you have nothing. It's nothing you have, and it's very quiet to have nothing. Another life.

The second activity is correcting, editing for websites or text books, mostly in the domain of social work and psychiatry, or in supporting homeless people. Of course for me that's more theoretical now. I do this with colleagues in the Netherlands, by Internet.

You've got some experience in project work too, haven't you?

I've enjoyed the projects. In one project on mental health care, I had to do a survey on education of psychiatric social work and nursing. I had contacts with nurses and a board of nurses. They were very willing to give interviews and to let me hear their meetings. All the people I met, they are willing and interested and many of them had a good theoretical background. But their main complaint has always been: we don't have the tools, we have no money, we have no time. So what do we do with your interesting stories? They were not angry at me. They spoke more about themselves. They have no possibilities. If you like to work more professionally, with better quality, with better money, you go to another country.

There were some conferences in that project. Sometimes it was a bit boring because when Romanians start to speak, they forget they have only 20 minutes and they take 40. The programme is a little bit chaotic after two hours already. Another project organised with Dutch colleagues, a four day seminar with healthcare workers and municipal officers, has been a very good four days. We had a lively programme with short speeches, power point presentations and discussion groups.

A problem with all these projects is that they are top-down. Somebody in Brussels or the government here brings an idea to the professionals. The professionals, you could say, eat it, and that's it. For sure there's no follow up. For sure the government are not giving support to the follow up. Then it will fade away. I believe in projects that come from the professionals themselves because then it's their project.

Has it been easy to establish relationships with people in the village?

In a way the people here are not different from everywhere in the world. When you meet someone in the bar or in the shop you can speak with him. Or you can make a joke, and you can drink something, a coffee or a beer. With friendships it's more difficult. When I lived in Holland I was more oriented on my friends than on my family. I would not go every weekend to my sister to go out for a dinner, but with friends I would do this. Here it's the other way around. People are more oriented on their families. To be honest, Romanian people are more reserved. When you are not family and there is no profit, it takes time before they invite me home, or call me. They go visit their families, and that's it. So it's another level of intimacy as well. With Dutch friends I can speak about very personal things, here not.

People are very friendly to foreigners, besides being curious. 'How is it is in your home country?' they start saying, then 'Oh, that's a beautiful country and it's better than Romania.' Before the European Union, when foreigners had a bit more money here, you were also a wallet and a way out. Especially when you were a man and a nice girl came to you, maybe she's thinking about your money and your passport and your visa-potential. You still have a certain privileged position. You are very welcome and people are wondering a little bit when you come as a tourist. And when you go live here, they think you are crazy. How you can leave the paradise, the Dutch paradise, the paradise of even Italy, Spain or Germany? Nobody will do this.

And are you still the same Dutchman?

At the beginning I came here as a real Dutchman, with time schedules and appointments, agenda, calendar. Then I found out for many Romanians it was not very important that you have an appointment at eleven o'clock because they came maybe at 1 p.m. or they did not come at all and didn't tell you. This made me, in the beginning, very angry. When you do this in the Netherlands and also in England or Germany, the people do not think you are serious. Another example is when people come to visit you. You're not sure what time they come, but worse maybe, you're not sure what time they will leave.

At home we have a Dutch regime of eating breakfast, lunch and dinner. Also our children have to go to sleep early, to go to school. But not all these visiting families are the same. They can come at eleven o'clock and expect a warm meal. They do not ask for it maybe but they make some suggestions: 'it would be a good idea…'. In the evening, they're still there, they are sitting and drinking. I don't say you have a bad time but you're not used to it. Maybe they say, 'Oh, it's already late, I missed the last train, we stay to sleep.' So in the morning they like to eat again. You can hope they do not stay for a week. A day in this way, it's very unusual for the Dutch. Now I'm more used to it. People come and go.

It's good to tell you they also learned something from me, in the way that I don't like it when they stay the whole day. They try to respect that. They got the message. My brother-in-law came to help me repair the toilet and then he was hanging around here. We had some wine and then my wife offered him some food. Then he was eating. I was drinking a glass of wine. And then it was finished. We were speaking a little bit. Then I said, 'We drink one wine more, and then I go to work again.' I had nothing urgent to do at that moment, but I cannot tell him, 'Now you have to go.' I have to tell him a reason. Now he will respect this.

Some people speak about the clans of Roma. They are very different because you have groups that are traditional. These traditions could also include arranged marriages between young people. Others are completely assimilated, and you have clans or groups between these two extremes. There are also groups that do not have special clothes, that are more literate, but they still speak the Roma language. The people here are bilingual.

They also have their own kind of judges, a kind of a court, called *stabor*. When there is some trouble between two Gypsy families they can go to the police or the official court, but you can also ask the committee of wise men and they do a mediation. They hear both parties. It's a public affair on the street. The wise men discuss the situation, they come back, they have other questions, and they do this ten times, whatever. Then they say what one party has to do for the other. The end of the story is that one party has to give some money to the other. That's also the only punishment because a committee does not have the power or facilities to put somebody in prison, so you have to resolve the conflict in another way. The conflicting parties say they are satisfied because the third party, the committee, made a decision, and that's it.

Not all Gypsy children will finish primary school in the first place. Some Gypsies will think, why do I have to learn, because I won't find a decent job, I'm a Gypsy. Many times the parents, they are poor, think – now you have done six years in the school, it's enough. You are 12, 13 years old, you can do some work and you can help us with the family income. That's also why children leave school earlier.

Many children in our village, after their school career, when they are 18 to 20, are busy with having a friend or girlfriend to make their own family. It means they do not really have adventure in their life. They do not go out of the country, they do not go around in different jobs or different educations. In the city it's different – students are always different. But let's say it in this way, at this lower level it's traditional and people are also not experienced. They are not experimental with relationships, with different girlfriends or boyfriends. They have one, and with this one they stay. And they will have a child – and maybe after two, three years, they are divorced. That's also possible.

Some Gypsy clans will arrange marriages, but here, in Vizureşti, they're not arranged. It's possible your parents will introduce to you a girl, but you can say no. One case I know, the boy said to me, 'I have a wife.'

'Is she charming, beautiful?' I said.

'I have not seen her yet.'

These things you have to get used to. Although sometimes youngsters trust me: they'd like more adventure. I am saying: please go and do it, don't listen to your parents! But I have zero success until now. Not with further education, not with birth control.

The people share the church, the shops, the bars, and there are no special difficulties. In the community we have our multi-cultural school. But there is segregation in the way we are living in peaceful co-existence. It's not very common for people to marry each other and cross over between different groups. We are staying apart together. You are together in the classroom, but it does not mean you play together outside the school. Everybody goes to his own sector in the village, and that's it. If a classroom has 25 children and maybe there are eight Gypsies, then you would expect you would have four invitations a year for a birthday party from the other ones. Not so. Last month Franco, our son, has been to a birthday but that's maybe the first one in three years. And the other way round. When we have a birthday party here, the children from 'there' find it difficult to come here. I say it in this way: there is a wall of glass in the village.

Jerelyn Taubert

Harghita County

*'I know many women here that are so successful. They're really smart...
and really should be proud of themselves. But no one gives them a hoot
because they're not rolling in the dough with some kind of business.'*

I met Andras in Danbury, Conneticut. I met him in a restaurant.
He wanted to know what am I eating. He was very charming and
friendly and talkative, and I liked his accent; I liked it a lot.
Anyway, we chatted a bunch and then he asked me on a date. Two
nights later we went out to dinner. He had gone to the States to
work, to make some money, like everybody else. He had a tourist
visa so he wasn't really supposed to be working. It was illegal.

When he got into New York City, he didn't know anybody.
Nobody. He just had a backpack and enough money for a week at
the YMCA. He needed to get a job quick, so he went to the phone
book looking for Hungarian names and started calling. He said,
'I've just got here and I'm all alone, I'm Hungarian, can you help
me?' One guy said, 'Yes, I have a friend who has a painting business
in New Fairfield, Connecticut. I know he hires a lot of young
Hungarian guys and he has a place they can sleep and they work
for him.' Some kind of good opportunity for the boss, not for the
people.

He went to work painting with them and it was ridiculous pay,
way below minimum. But they took care of them and he got a
place to sleep. Andras saved every penny he made, he didn't spend
it. Finally, what he started doing was taking cheap cars and fixing

them up with some friend he knew that had a garage, and then he'd sell them. With every car he may only have made $100 or $200, but it was more than he was putting away with this crappy amount the guy was paying him.

He was working on a very beautiful home and the owner was watching him every day, seeing how he was working, just to check up. He was impressed with Andras really working, not sitting around. This guy liked Andras, his personality, and said to him, 'You know, I'm just starting up a new company, and I really need somebody to work where we ship out the clothing in big boxes.'

So Andras started out in his warehouse, folding the clothing, putting them in boxes – did that for a while and this guy's watching him. Andras could do double, triple the amount anybody else did, was always working, working, really hard. Then he got the supervisor of the warehouse position, and within maybe two to three years he was in an office over ten, twenty employees. He just… boom, boom, boom… worked himself right up, because of his total initiative. He took on everything. Didn't have to be told what to do, worked every minute, hardly sat down… The guy was just so impressed with him he ended up as production manager.

He ended up with me as well. I met him down the line a few years. He had a pretty good job and he was doing very well. I went several times to the company where he worked. They wanted him to stay. They hired a lawyer to get him immigration working papers. In the meantime, there was a guy that was quite a bit older. First he was Andras's boss, and then Andras was his boss. He was angry Andras was making double what he was making. He was at least ten years older and felt pushed over that this foreigner, this immigrant, was taking his job and this wasn't fair. Well, he called up immigration, complaining to them. The lawyer, the woman that was doing Andras's legal papers, she said, 'I don't know if this will work, but maybe if you guys got married it would help.' We quickly got married, in March 2000. Didn't work. The company screwed it up. Andras was sent back to Romania.

We'd bought a big rental property together, and it was Andras's savings that went on the down payment and my credit rating that got him the mortgage. The house was 30 minutes from where we were living, with eight apartments in it. Every month we got unbelievable rent. His friend bought it from Andras so he got his money back. I'm the one that went to the closing and did everything, because Andras was already in Romania. When he got back here it was a couple of months and then he had a nice big lump sum.

I really thought the marrying thing would work. If I'd met Andras when I was, let's say, in my late twenties or middle or early thirties, I don't know if I would have moved to Romania. I might have just said, 'See you later, alligator.' When I met him I had already done 15 years at the hospital and I felt like I could move somewhere; I could learn another language. I was ready for an adventure, like something different in my life.

Before I met Andras I'd been working at a state psychiatric hospital for the state of Connecticut. I was a rehabilitation therapist, a state employee. It was a live-in facility for psychiatric patients, not a day programme. Before that I was a pilot. I went to school to become a pilot at 18, but was finished with that at about 25. My mother got ill and I went home to take care of her.

What was it like when you first got to Csíkszereda (Miercurea Ciuc)?

Andras had kind of glossed it over. I had all these photos of pretty fields where I could ride, and of course there were no pictures of all these beat-up fences, rundown houses and potholes. The best buildings in the town, of course those were in. He found a few, the *városház*, the town hall… and I thought, oh, the town looks okay.

Anyway it was really funny. He made a huge effort to fix up the family house because it was pretty much a disaster – he retiled everything, repainted everything, new kitchen, new bathroom before I arrived. I sent my furniture over and it was put into the home. Then I came later. When I arrived all my pictures were on the wall and it was my things, which was really a smart move of that guy. I'm not kidding you, I walked into everything being mine and it was all sparkling new. The whole inside of the house and outside was all painted.

The yard was typical Romanian style. That means like nobody had a lawnmower in this whole town. I don't even think Romania had a lawnmower ten years ago. We had a container and you could put everything in there. We brought over the lawnmower. Oh, is that the thing! All the neighbours looking: what is this machine? We had the only nice lawn. Everybody else's would just get really high and then they would *kossa* it, meaning with a scythe. They would cut their lawns with a scythe, can you imagine? Then, of course, what do you think? Everyone wanted to borrow our lawnmower. Now they're running around with their lawnmowers all the time and it looks great. There were funny things like that. Big difference in the way it was when I moved here and the way things are now.

Csíkszereda is in Transylvania in the Carpathian Mountains, and it's considered the coldest spot in all of Romania – another thing he didn't tell me; I didn't know about that one either. God! The town is 85 per cent Hungarian, Székely. This area was Austro-Hungarian Empire at one time. It was given to Romania and all the people became Romanian citizens, although they're really Hungarian.

What's Andras up to now?

He builds homes. He has big tracts of land and he builds two-family homes and also four-family buildings, apartments. That used to be the major thing he did; now it's a minor thing. Now he's involved in hydro-electricity and solar, green energy. He has contracts for several rivers to make hydro-electricity plants. That's what he does now.

He must be very busy. What about you?

When I got here, well obviously I couldn't be a therapist. That was out of the question. I'd been a part-time aerobics instructor in the States, totally a hobby. Before I went to work in the day I was teaching an aerobics class. When I got here, I asked around. 'Is there some kind of class here? Step or aerobics; do they do that here?' One of Andras's friends said, 'Yeah, I know this girl that's a teacher.' The first class I showed up to was on a Friday night. I'll never forget this. At seven o'clock I go in and there's at least 15 girls there. I think I arrived at ten to seven, and then it was seven, and there was no teacher.

Nobody shows up to teach the class. I went up to one of the girls and said, 'Does anyone speak English?' Several girls did. I said, 'Where's this teacher?'

'She's always late,' they said.

'She is? So what do you do?'

'Oh, she usually shows up,' they replied.

And then one of the girls, about ten after seven, went up to the reception and said, 'Where's M?'

'I don't know, I haven't heard from her yet.'

But then at a quarter after she announces she's not coming. Of course several girls are really angry because they took the taxi there. It was winter, February. They're all complaining. So I said, 'Well, you know, I taught aerobics classes in the States. Are there any discs here? I can't speak any Hungarian but I think we can figure, you know, follow along.' So I taught a class. The girls were thrilled.

So when I'm back on Monday, M showed up five after seven. She knew I'd taught her class, but she never said, 'Oh, thank you for teaching for me, I had a problem on Friday night,' which a normal person would do, or anything. She totally didn't even say hello to me or acknowledge me. That was really strange. The next night comes along and again she doesn't show up, and I teach the class. Never acknowledges me, never thanks me, never pays me. I'm thinking: this is a frickin' weird bunch here. That summer came along, and this girl M finally approached me and wanted to know if I would teach over the summer. But still she never offered to pay me, never even thanked me for teaching those classes.

What I realised about the people here is that they just don't open their mouths. I was always amazed by the fact that nobody complains. I also started to realise that the whole group of them is never on time. Even when I was teaching. It was supposed to start at seven. Well, they were all in at five and ten after. I mentioned this to Andras and some friends. 'That's how they are here.' Just like a natural thing, that everybody can expect they're 15 minutes late. That was odd for me.

And riding, which was really my hobby in the US. That first summer I bought a horse in Hungary, in Debrecen. Rigoletto. There was a stable nearby owned by a wealthy man, the wealthiest guy in town, who's another story himself. We had no place to keep Rigoletto, so he stayed there. This kept me really busy, because every day I'd go to the stable on my bicycle and I'd help out with their horses. I would teach the guys a lot of things. They didn't know so much, just the real basic Romanian-Hungarian style. We made a lot of changes, and I rode their horses and mine.

I had pretty full days and I went to aerobics at night, but it wasn't the ideal situation for me. I was used to being busy in the States. I felt like I went from 100 miles an hour down to 20. It was kind of nice at first because I was overstimulated in the US. It was pretty, go, go, go. I really felt like I was going backwards in

Csíkszereda. It was a different lifestyle for me completely. Slowed down.

And Andras built your house?

That house was after we'd been there a couple of years. Andras had found a piece of property. The first thing we did was just build the stable, no house. At the beginning of the summer we moved Rigi in. We have the riding ring, and we have hectares and hectares of nothing, fields that are called grazing land. Each town has designated grazing land for their cattle, for the cows and the sheep and goats. They have shepherds that take the groups around all summer long. They start out May 1st, the first day they're allowed to go. They're allowed three dogs, this is the law. They all break the law and have about eight. So what happens sometimes when you're riding is the dogs come after you. Beautiful land for riding – great fields that stretch on endlessly, no fences anywhere, incredible views – but sometimes you're attacked by these dogs, which is really not nice at all. There are some shepherds that I've tried to be friendly with when they come by the house, so they can help me out a bit. But most of them are pretty low-functioning people, or drunk. It's a big issue here – a lot of men are alcoholics; they're laying on the ground drunk. They don't care that their dogs are running all over. You're just going along thinking this is the life, this is better than anything, and then eight dogs come after you! I had children fall off because the horse would run; they were scared.

How much has Csíkszereda changed in the time you've known it?

When I arrived here, there were only mom-and-pop little grocery stores. You couldn't get fresh chicken, only frozen chicken. You couldn't get a turkey, you couldn't get a goose. Pork, pork, pork, that's all you could get. And veal. You couldn't find a mango, only in-season things. Only once in a while did you see broccoli and cauliflower. Cabbage, cabbage, cabbage; potato, potato, potato… you felt like you were always cooking the same thing. It's very different now. Now you can get fresh chicken everywhere. Every person in Csíkszereda has a chicken. How come you couldn't get fresh chicken before? I'll never know.

When I first got here, you never had to look for a parking spot. Two Mercedes in that town, maybe five BMWs. Within five years the population of cars at least doubled – Mercedes, Bentley, Porsche Cayenne, everything. Lots of Audis. I could see the economy changing a lot. Lot more private enterprise. There were two restaurants when I first came here. Restaurants and coffee houses popping up everywhere now.

Where I grew up, every school was involved in Earth Day; each classroom with children had one road to clean up, or they'd plant trees. Here I could ride along the most beautiful country and there are cigarette boxes and plastic bottles and beer bottles everywhere. Nobody picks up and nobody cares. They don't care at all about their land here. People are always throwing stuff out their windows. There's garbage everywhere; they just dump it. They don't want to pay the garbage man or have it picked up, so along the rivers and everywhere you ride, there's all of a sudden everything dumped in one big pile. If you're going on a hike and every half a mile you see a big pile, it's not beautiful. It's natural beauty that's ruined by humans.

I think they have no respect for their country. They don't like their country; they're ashamed of their country. They have no pride. I don't know if you've ever met a Texan, but boy, there's nobody prouder than a Texan. There's none of this pride here. I don't feel it from the Hungarians and I don't feel it from the Romanians. The Hungarians are pissed because they're in Romania and they're considered Romanian now. So they have anger. And the Romanians just don't seem to have any pride. They're not proud to say, 'I'm Romanian.' They're not.

Have you found friends here?

There are three girls, Székely, that I would consider really good friends. It's very strange, because I could easily be their mother. I'm double their age. Two of them I met because I worked with them on their English. The other girl was my riding student. I realised this girl is really unbelievably honest and wonderful, and I had her kind of helping me. It started out more like a daughter friendship, and then as she got older, it changed. She started talking about her boyfriends with me. Right now I know she tells me things she doesn't tell her mother. She tells me things that she doesn't tell anybody.

All the girls love their mothers. One lives in England now. She went to college in Hungary and it was difficult for her, because most of the kids go to college in Cluj or Tărgu Mureş or Bucharest, and they were so jealous of her. She went to school outside the country and she lost so many friends because of that. Again, it's jealous, jealous, jealous. They can't stand it that you get to go out of the country. Not, 'Oh, I'm happy for you.'

You know what, some of the women, you know what they're doing? They're teaching their sons differently. I met with this girl. We became friendly. About the time when her son was two years old I knew her a little better, and I would visit with her quite a bit. This girl had been to school in the United States, and she saw the difference there. 'When we eat, he has to take his plate and he has to bring it to the sink. I'll wash the dishes. He's only two, but I want him to bring it there. He has to put his dirty laundry in the bag.' These simple little things she taught her son. Her and two other girls that have little boys, they're all doing this. They want their boys to be different.

I took one girl I'm friends with, and her sister, to America. They were with me for one week and then they went to California and Miami on their own. The first couple of days, every two minutes, 'People are so friendly here, people are so friendly!' We were in New York! I was laughing. 'Wait till you get out of this, wait till you go see Georgia. You think this is friendly?' The people from this region, which is called Székelyföld, they're suspicious; this is in their blood. They just don't go and talk to people unless they know you and you've known them a long time. Then they would feed you forever. But they're just not going to let the stranger in, or the person they don't know. The girls didn't realise that they were like that until they left to go to other countries. They come back and realise, Oh my God, wow, are we different!

There's a lack of trust. This is how it is. You think that somebody is really a good colleague of yours, and you find out later on that he robbed you blind. It's very shocking, because he's eating at your house and he's supposedly your good friend, and you find out later that he's doing other things behind your back. It's very common here. They all cheat each other. Everybody pushes the other one out, somehow legally. They could be best friends, but because of business, they're arch enemies the next day.

Money's the biggest thing here. How much you make is the most important thing in Romania. It's the measure of everything. It doesn't matter if you're the most talented skier and you're competing everywhere in the world, you're nothing because you're not making millions. It's all measured by that. Talent is no measure of anything. Doesn't matter if you're a wonderful psychiatrist and you have ten degrees, because you're not wealthy, doesn't matter. I know many women here that are so successful. They're really smart and they're dentists and doctors and really should be proud of themselves. But no one gives them a hoot because they're not rolling in the dough with some kind of business.

Mike Ormsby

Bucharest

'I love the expression Ca la noi, la nimeni — *There's no place like our place. It somehow sums up the Romanian mentality. It's a delicious irony. A boast, but also a confession.'*

I came to Romania in early '94 for the first time to report for the BBC. I liked it very much. I returned in October the same year to work for their World Service. I've been here on and off ever since. It's my home and always will be, I think.

At first I was shocked, but also very inspired. Shocked by poverty and desperation, the street kids; the ordinary people with very little and no hope; the numbers of stray dogs. But impressed by the generosity too of Romanians; their good humour, their ironic sense of fatalism; their willingness to meet new people and do the best they could, and help you. I felt wary of the less-noble motives of some, but those were understandable at the time. I just fell in love with the place; it knocked me for six. I felt like the scales had fallen from my eyes. I couldn't believe that this country existed, three hours from the UK.

I was pretty much thrown in the deep end when I came to Bucharest to teach journalists, but it felt like a breath of fresh air — Romania's media was just opening up and I was where I wanted to be, with youngsters who had lots of energy and ideas. The BBC had a good name. We had good equipment, good funding. It was a real buzz. I was on a high for a long time. I didn't want to stop. I kept renewing my contract, asking my boss in Bush House, 'Can I stay another six months?'

I was running ten-week courses for the BBC school, *Şcoala* BBC. I was on the radio side and we had a TV department too. Both were run for real, with very strict deadlines. The only difference was, we did not actually broadcast. We were tough on the trainees, but anybody who studied at *Şcoala* BBC will probably say it helped them. Some will say it changed their lives. Certainly changed mine. I still see some of them now and again, we're good friends.

Daily life was not so bad: get up, go to work, go out, have a drink with your mates or the students, whatever. The shops were a bit grim and the streets could be a bit dangerous. I got jumped and chased a couple of times. I almost got stabbed; that was my fault though. But life was more interesting than dangerous. That was all part of the buzz really. You can't come to a country like Romania and not expect it to be a little bit on the edge, and I liked that; I still do. It was a fairly dismal, spooky place at times, back then. Long hard winters, hot summers. I'd never been anywhere like it. The post-communist mind-set fascinated me.

I met my wife in Bucharest. She was a journalist. We went to work in Bosnia and married two years later in Las Vegas. We still move around the world a lot. Azerbaijan is our base at the moment. I work as a media consultant, writer and editor. My short stories about this place came out in 2008; the book is still selling well in both languages. I wrote for Romania's FHM for four years, until Romania's *Playboy* asked me to join them. My first novel should be out soon, set in Congo and the UK.

How was your book[3] received?

Most readers and critics liked it. Some said, 'He's our British Caragiale,' in reference to the satirical 19th century writer. I felt deeply honoured by that. I still get nice emails, every month, from

---

[3] Mike Ormsby, *Never Mind the Balkans, Here's Romania*, Amazon.

new readers all over the world. A minority in 2008 said, 'Whoa, how dare he come and criticise Romania?'

'Well, if you can't feel the love in this book, you need to read closer,' I said.

It's a selection of anecdotes, some funny, some sad, some tragic, some inspiring, all based on experience. I'd told some of the stories to Romanian friends who said, 'Wow, you should write these down!' and eventually I did. And once I'd started, I thought, I've got a book here. It came out in two languages. My publisher and I originally planned only for a Romanian version. We knew Romanians would read it, because they're often curious to know how foreigners see their country: hence our conversation today. I must add that the country has changed a bit since my book first appeared in 2008. For example, the driving is improving. There are more parks for kids. I think street dogs get a better deal, too, through the vaccination project, certainly in Bucharest. A reader told me he used to think his wife was crazy to care for stray animals, but he read my book and changed his mind. I'm glad.

What about relationships with you as a foreigner?

Very positive. My main contact was with students at *Şcoala* BBC who were so friendly and enthusiastic. We were like family during those ten hard weeks, best of friends. The only time my dealings with Romanians soured was when I poked my nose into the affairs of a money-changer at Gara de Nord. That's not a good idea. It might be morally justifiable but it's not a very wise move. I warned an American not to change money. I got punched for that, by the Romanian. I thought he'd broken my jaw. He was a big guy, I stepped on his turf and he went nuts, pulled a knife but my friends pulled him off. I was flat out. Apparently he said to them, 'Tell your friend, next time not so lucky!' I tend not to intervene now. But they've disappeared, all those guys.

I've learned that some Romanians can be quite different to Westerners. It took me a while. I noticed it when I came back after several years away. People whom I thought I knew had changed a lot. One friend had become quite the grasping yuppie; economic progress had soured his values. We drifted apart. I'm not saying it's wrong to do well, but it's a shame when people lose sight of where they came from and start looking down on others. I have a feeling life in Romania is sometimes a bit of a rat race. People are so busy moving forward, they forget to look left, right and back. Life is getting better, definitely, but there is sometimes an element of 'me first'.

And relationships within your wife's family?

Tricky sometimes. She has three sisters, all abroad, qualified and doing well. There's often a bit of tension between the four girls and *mama* and *tata* back home. Sometimes the parents' perceived lack of ambition, or their fatalism, frustrates their offspring. The parents usually just accept whatever life throws at them in the village. The sisters will say, '*Mama, Tata,* stand up for yourself!' But their parents seem stuck in the early 70s, when they had little choice, and no voice. They've advanced in terms of material comfort I suppose, but not so much in terms of their expectations and outlook. It seems a huge generational difference.

One of the nicest things here is that most families have a strong bond with the countryside, one foot in the soil. We've lost that in the West, certainly in Britain, certainly in my family. Here it's alive and well: pickled cabbages, pickled gherkins, great wine, cheese, eggs. You get a real sense that they're still in touch with the land, and I find that quite inspiring. It's real somehow, earthy. In Britain almost all food comes from supermarkets.

They sure know how to do Easter. I'm not religious, but yes, they do get Easter. They do make a fuss, with coloured eggs, lights, singing. They seem quite religious, deep down. A young Romanian told me, 'You won't often hear us say we don't believe in God.' They have an awareness of possibilities in the great beyond. They're also quite superstitious. Everybody in the countryside makes sure their goats, horses and favourite animals have red rosettes to ward off the evil eye. It's kind of charming in a way.

My mother-in-law was walking down the path in the village the other day, turning away from me as she was talking, hiding an empty bucket behind her back. My wife explained: you're not supposed to let anybody see you carrying an empty bucket because it will mean no food on your table, bad luck. I was curious and teased my mother-in-law about that which, I suppose, you shouldn't do.

I appreciate their directness, one-to-one. They'll usually tell you straight whether they like something or not. I'm from the North of England and that's how it is up there, so I like that. I know some very bright Romanians, male and female, who have done very well, at home and abroad. You can learn stuff, if you keep your ears open. I've also met a few know-alls, full of their own importance, long speeches, been-there-done-that.

I love the expression, *Ca la noi, la nimeni* – There's no place like our place. It somehow sums up the Romanian mentality. It's a delicious irony; a boast but also a confession. They know they're cool, they know they're wonderful people, but they also know they're not quite there yet. They seem proud of the discrepancy, as well. I quite like that.

The fatalism? I wonder if it comes from the Turkish side of the Romanian genes. For example, in North Africa and in Muslim countries generally, you'll hear *In'shalah* – Whatever-God-wills. Sure, we have the phrase 'God willing' in the West, but you don't hear it on the street every day, like in those places – Oh, God willing, I'll see you at the weekend. Maybe that fatalism has filtered into the Romanian consciousness from the South?

A Romanian virtue? Extreme hospitality, on a par with northern British hospitality; the door is open, our house is your house, come in and help yourself. It's a cliché, but the people who have the least will give you the most. That's certainly true here, and I love them for that. Also, their ability with their hands, their skill in mending things. Years ago I mashed the bonnet and radiator of our big old car. Some helpful fellows in the countryside fixed it with a few tools and a lot of ingenuity – I could hardly believe my eyes. Resilience too – in Bosnia I met Romanian NATO soldiers repairing bridges and every month or so locals would blow up the bridges and the Romanians would start over, with weary smiles.

What's particularly frustrating here?

Traffic. I'm always wary walking around town. You can't relax. Bucharest is not a walking city. Constantly looking over your shoulder for the truck that's going to take your arm off, the driver who's going to mount the pavement and pin you to the wall.

And too much smoke in bars. Sure, more and more people are exercising, watching their diet. But there still seems to be an obsession with looking 'cool' and having a cigarette dangling from your fingers. That spoils socialising a lot of the time. I really don't get it. It baffles me. A Western friend told me something interesting recently. We were in Lipscani, watching lots of Romanians puffing away, and he said, 'Because of Ceaușescu, they're one generation behind. For them, this is the 1960s. Can't you feel it?' I thought, Woodstock, yes, maybe.

Still, I wouldn't say I avoid too many things here. You can't avoid Romania. If you live or spend any real time here, it's in your face 24/7. You've got to be part of it. But my health? No, I tend not to compromise on that. It's not a question of cultural snobbery if you want to preserve your lungs and avoid cancer through second-hand smoke, or if you want to preserve your neck by not walking down a busy street. That's not anti-Romanian.

Do you find any subjects that are taboo?

The problem with taboo subjects is they're the most interesting to discuss. A Jordanian friend told me he likes this place because the people are not racist. True to an extent, but there is a fairly strong strain of anti-Semitism here. In some ways, that's taboo, but it's something we should talk about, and I have, sometimes. I've fallen out with Romanians over that, been called a hypocrite, been told 'Stop spouting bullshit!' But the same people didn't like Arabs either! I was trying to explain the Islamic perspective on Iraq, and was told, 'You've spent too long in Muslim countries, they've brainwashed you, go back to Gaza!' I find that a bit weird. I wouldn't say racism is taboo, but it's a prickly issue. You do hear surprising things, and you wonder why.

I was out with friends and their daughter the other day; she'd just turned 13, and said, 'So what did they do with the president after the Revolution?'

Her mum said, 'He was shot.'

The girl gasps, 'Shot? Why?' This super-bright kid with middle-class British and Romanian parents didn't know what happened to Ceauşescu. So we discussed what should have happened and we said, 'He should have been sent to live in some dingy apartment block in the middle of nowhere, on €10 a month. See if he liked what he created.' I half-expected her to say, 'What's a dingy apartment?'

How do you like the Romanian sense of humour?

Oh, they're very funny. That's one of the first things I liked about them. Wicked, fatalistic irony. Dry, sharp, minimal wit. Cut you to the bone. They really know how to pull the rug out, with a one-liner. They crack me up. And everyone's got it. Most of them are very quick.

Do you have a feeling for who runs the country?

It seems bent as a nine-bob note to me, quite honestly. The old guard clinging to power, the dinosaurs. I met a young woman who works in parliament. She's 26, determined, keen, optimistic; swears there are good people in there, really believes that things will change. She wants to be a deputy. But I wonder, because most people I know are bemused by what they see on TV, by what passes for 'debate'. They claim it's a charade. There's a guy in Bucharest now, Nicuşor Dan, trying to be mayor. He seems a decent guy. A lot of young people like him. Ex-pats too, but most people say he hasn't got a snowball's chance in hell. We'll see.

I love this country, it gets under your skin; I miss it when I'm away. Also I feel as a foreigner, and especially as a writer, that I have a responsibility to observe, to record, to hold up a mirror and ask, 'Is this the best it can be?' Nowhere is perfect, but Transylvania is close!

Egle Chisiu

Bucharest

'It's the same in Lithuania. All the time these comparisons, before and after 1990, so I can understand them.'

I got to know Vasile when we were studying singing in Sicily in 2004. We were married in the same year. There was a discussion where we would live – in Italy, probably Romania, but never Lithuania. Since my husband was accepted at the Opera to be a singer on permanent contract, we said, 'Okay, the first job, at the National Opera in Bucharest, everybody is dreaming about it, we will stay here.'

When I was in Lithuania almost the only thing I knew about Romania was that here are the best singers in the world. Almost every theatre will have at least one singer because they have very good traditions and talent formed over the last 200 years. Not like in Lithuania, which came only at the beginning of the 20th century. The real vocal school is Italian, for very good quality singing. Long ago singers from Italy started to come to Romania to teach and I felt this difference here immediately. I was really happy that I found such good teachers.

The problem is more the economical situation. Singers can't be paid much. The best ones try to get out of the country. We sing not only to make money but because we just love it. But the small salaries make us try to sing somewhere else, for sure.

Since the first year I came I have observed this folklore singing everywhere. My husband also started with this, not with opera.

He started singing when he was four years old – all the time folklore songs. They're very popular. He's from a small village near Mediaş, 60 kilometres from Sibiu. There is also a big church tradition, to go and sing there. He was developing his natural talent without any music school, just singing from ear and developing his nice voice, and participating in many folklore singing competitions.

Vasile is also teaching at home, mostly young men who are studying theology. The Orthodox Church is very strong and many men think that the good profession is to be a priest. They all have to sing so then they develop their voices. Many singers who are now in the theatre came from there. They started studying theology then discovered their voice and moved to the theatre. I think these two, church and folklore, add very much to the quantity and quality of singers here. Almost every bigger village has its own ensemble. They try to conserve the traditions and dances and songs. Every wedding, every event is accompanied with folklore music.

I was really warmly accepted by the family of Vasile in Mediaş. Romania as a country though, it was a bit of a shock. I remember the very first time when I came here; it was a summer immediately after we finished our course in Sicily. I was travelling alone then; it was very warm and I got outside the airport, went to the tram and the smell of garbage and cars and heat – it immediately reminded me of Odessa. I thought, Oh my God, some things are so strange. Then this quarter of Crângaşi is not the most beautiful one, but then it was much more horrible, much more dirty. There was no park as there is now near the Lacul Morii, the lake. Really in these six years it's changed a lot for the positive, for me with children. I appreciate these changes, absolutely.

So first I was a bit shocked here but if you are with a person who you really love, as for me with Vasile, you can stay with him anywhere. Also in Sicily we were in a small room, half the size of this one, with only a window on the corridor. But we really felt happy. I thought I will get used to it here, we will see, maybe we will not live here all the time. We never actually thought that we will be all our lives here, but for the start, yes. Now it continues with the children and everything has settled down, I get used to it, more and more every year.

Do you feel a connection with the Slav roots here?

You know, they don't want to accept the strong Slav side to them. Mostly they don't know that 20 per cent of their words are Slav. When I was learning Romanian it was very easy for me; 80 per cent was based on Italian, 20 per cent on Russian. That's why I learnt it fast. Sometimes I was even inventing words as I talked and it was okay.

You can't live in between Bulgaria and Ukraine and not have Slav influences. Even in the folklore music there are influences. My grandmother was Ukrainian and when my mum heard some tunes or songs here, even dances, she said, 'Oh this is like Ukraine!' There are many things that are similar but sure, their language is Latin and their character is something mixed between Latin and Slav, I would say. I learnt from my husband some kind of behaviour with people, speaking more politely maybe. I'm always more direct and he's like a Romanian, with much more talking and going around and maybe less offensive sometimes.

Dealing with life here? The most unpleasant thing is this bribing everywhere, at every step, whatever you want to do. You want to put your child into the kindergarten, you have to go with some money. You want to get the parking place without giving something, you will not get it for years. When you go to the doctor... bribery.

Then many promises and not doing anything. It's like an Italian style, so that's very Latin. The bad organisation of many things, even in the theatre. If the Western theatres know their plans one year or two years ahead, here they know the performances maximum two months ahead, and maximum three or four days for rehearsals. My husband never knows what he will do next week. When I ask him, 'Could we do something next week on this day at that time?' he says, 'I don't know.' In Lithuania it never happens. I was at the theatre there and I saw in August all the rehearsals until the following June so the singers could plan. Singers do not sing at one theatre only, they have some contracts elsewhere. They can make plans and they're free to go elsewhere. But here no, they don't know anything. We can't even plan holidays. That's a frustration, yes.

Asta este! – That's the way it is! It's very easy to accept and not to change and I find it gets on my nerves. The problem of Romanians is very often to put guilt on somebody else – 'I can't do anything because such is the system, such is the politics.' But you yourself can do simple things. In the park people are eating sunflower seeds and spit them out just under their feet. Why should they do this? Every bench also has the garbage bag near so they could use this but it's just too complicated for them. Or they go and eat chocolate and throw away the paper. That's natural for them, absolutely natural. I'm teaching my kids all the time not to do this and they already know. It's just education; maybe there is a gap even at schools and kindergarten, not teaching this, not paying attention.

Also in the parks there are now exercise machines and after several months half of them are already broken. If they are there for us all to use, why should you break them? All the time this is really frustrating for me, that anything that is public is no one's and we can break this because it's public money. It's a question of responsibility. The young people are just the same. Maybe they become more European, they know more languages, but family is the basis of this kind of education.

They have very strong family networks, maybe stronger than in Lithuania. These *naşi* and *fini,* godfathers and godmothers, these are very strong relations that we don't have at all in Lithuania. There, if during the wedding you had some witnesses, maybe in several years you don't even remember any more who they were. Here, no, it is so important to choose these people and to keep in touch with them. We were choosing very attentively persons who will be the *naşi* of our marriage and we see each other very often, call each other. Also they were the godparents of our children when they were baptised. I think it's very nice; you have some friends who are really more than friends. Here family is a bit more respected, or at least this respect is more spoken about. I know that statistically there are less divorces here than in Lithuania.

I don't have so many friends here. It's different to Lithuania. Those friends that I see, that I keep in touch with more often, are Lithuanians, women who also have small kids. Maybe the situation is bringing us closer together; we go out to the park with kids, we visit each other with kids. I don't have personal Romanian friends, the woman who I could call whenever and ask advice, no. I came here not really so young, and I think real friendships are made when you are at school or your studies. You are very open, still searching for something. When you already have a family, friends are in the second place – for me at least.

Are there any subjects you would avoid with Romanians?

It depends on people maybe, but generally we can discuss everything. We have also many things in common in the past because Lithuania was under the Soviet occupation. It had the same communist regime so I understand very well what they felt under Ceauşescu. And they understand what we felt under Brezhnev and Stalin. We can speak freely about the past and the future and the changes after 1989 when the Revolution came.

There are differences but there are also many common things; like not having the possibility to get out of the country, like being controlled by somebody at your place of work all the time. You couldn't speak freely because somebody, even your friends, could go and talk to the KGB in Lithuania, or here the *Securitate*. Not having all this comfort of the Western world, having very limited access to the products, even to food. For meat we had to queue. You could get only a limited piece of meat, only once a week, in one shop. Okay, things were even worse here. Lithuanians had a bit more freedom maybe. But there are many things in common and they use the same expressions, like 'After we came into independence', or 'Look, in 20 years what we did, or what we did not do.' All the time these comparisons, before and after 1990, so I can understand them.

If I left I would definitely miss the tradition of singing Christmas carols. This is not so much felt in Bucharest but in Mediaș and in the smaller places you can't get through the Christmas without *colindăs*, these Christmas songs. Vasile and me are going every year on 24th December. In the evening we leave to visit all possible relatives and friends round Mediaș to sing these *colindăs* and people are also coming to us. This is such a nice thing to do. You can come at any hour you want during the night and they will accept you. They will be waiting for you with a table and will be very happy that you came to visit. Also on the 25th, the 26th, until New Year's Eve, you can go visiting. You just start singing at the door and it will be opened. Maybe you will go away with some *palinca*. I never felt such a thing in Lithuania – we never had this tradition of Christmas. For me this is important, this is a very special tradition.

Andrew Littauer

Bucharest

'I am happy to have been here in a sort of modern creation, to have lived the advance of a modern place.'

I was born in New York at 11.27 a.m. on 2nd September 1941. I went to Beloit College in Wisconsin, graduated in Economics and Political Science at Syracuse University in New York, was awarded a Fulbright post-graduate fellowship in the late 60s and for a decade worked with the Bank of America. Subsequently I worked for West Deutsche Landesbank, initially in New York and then in Hong Kong, as General Manager. When that assignment came to an end in 1986, I went to work for the US Treasury Department. Quite soon I had a brief to come to Romania where, as a friend of the Romanian state, the idea was to get the state banks privatised; that was in 1993. Although bank managements were mostly willing to privatise, the state was reluctant to let go. The banks were all considered to be the crown jewels of the financial services sector.

I worked closely with two or three people within the Central Bank to structure a bill that went before parliament. It seemed innocuous, the bill, stating what was required for a start-up banking operation here. It went through parliament and was passed. We then went to a variety of international banks and said, 'Why don't you set up operations in this country? It's a country with 25 million people and has a lot of potential. Why don't you get in at ground floor?' ABN Amro was interested and became the first genuinely foreign, new investment. Once it was established, ING said, 'Hey we're coming in too' and soon the floodgates opened and a growing number of legitimately arms-length lenders came in.

Then we were able to approach the state-owned banks and say, 'You know, you're in something of a quandary. You're going to have to increase your capital base in order to be able to compete effectively with the likes of ABN and ING; because if you don't, nobody will want to open up a letter of credit through you. They'll prefer to open it with one of the more solid and legitimately international banks. You're going to have to upgrade your bank substantially.'

The government then said, 'But we don't have the money to do all that.'

And I said, 'Well, in that case you're going to have to privatise, sell yourself to one of these internationally credible banks.' Anyway, we met our brief in a sort of circuitous way and all of a sudden their hands were forced and they had to privatise.

Going back to when you arrived, how did you find it?

When I landed in Otopeni it was dimly lit, rather unlike any airport I was familiar with. I checked into the Hotel Bucharest. I remember there was an elderly woman sitting on a fold-up chair, perched right in the hallway near my room, watching and making a note every time I went in and out. I assumed there was a microphone in my room and I don't think that was a strange assumption. There was a television set which was almost as big as a Volkswagen, with five or six channels, all in black and white. I remember that I wanted to read in my room and I turned on the light and it was like a 25-watt bulb – only a bit more helpful than what you have inside a refrigerator.

I didn't know where the Romanian Bank of Foreign Trade was so I took a taxi costing me the equivalent of about 10 US cents. Some people had been introduced to me before I even came – I had introductory letters. One couple were real music lovers and he and his wife took me to a concert in the Athenaeum which probably cost about 30 cents. It was very good. The only problem I had eventually, as I started going regularly to concerts, was that in the winter months they had no money for heating. We would have to sit in our chairs with our overcoats and gloves. But the music was good – a happy escape. Some performers, I recall, played with gloves, finger-tops cut off, and to our ears they were world class.

How were you accepted in the bank?

The chairman was terrific. He invited me into a Head of Departments' meeting, introduced me, said I would be there as his special advisor and that everybody should be open and helpful to me. The meeting went on for about two and a half hours. Much of it was in Romanian and I had no idea what was being said but I could watch body language and discern voice tones. At the end of the meeting he came over to me and put his arm around me and the two of us walked to his office. That wasn't lost on the other people, seeing their chairman putting his arm round me, walking shoulder to shoulder. And as soon as the door was closed in his office, he sat in his chair and looked at me genuinely and said, 'Well, how did we do?' So then I had to be the real diplomat and tell him: more decisiveness, less democracy, leadership.

When my job finished, the question was, do I try to carve out a possibility for myself here? I'm happy there was an entrepreneur in me ready to start on my own. In those days I had a capable assistant, who is now my partner, and we decided to form a small company that was in effect one of the first Public Relations companies in Romania. Eventually, as others came in who were far better known, we decided we should switch gears and become a different animal. So we went into the Human Resources field. We do everything HR now, leaders in the field.

In the beginning, in the 90s, we were on an uneven playing field. Nowhere is everything completely level, but at that time it certainly seemed that those who knew what they were doing knew how to work the system to their advantage. Others who were trying to be 100 per cent correct were being suckers and found their life didn't work very easily. One of the things that I still find a little difficult here is that I know people are getting away with all sorts of things, and I'm not. I can be proud of the fact I'm doing things correctly, but on the other hand it affects the bottom line. I'll give you an example.

We were the first company here to become a Western Union franchisee. Western Union is involved in the transfer of money. We had a group of ten or twelve business points, throughout the country, and we had to promote them. The best way, we thought – we'd seen them around – was a big banner across the street, announcing that here was a place for money transfer. Well, the next day that was torn down and we were told to go to the city hall and get permission for that. We then realised how many hurdles of bureaucracy had to be cleared. I was darn sure that other companies, small real estate companies and so forth, couldn't possibly have gone through all those things, but they got away with having a banner up there – up there till it frayed in the wind and finally broke down. In our case, within 24 hours, we, as a big bad foreign company, had to pay for all sorts.

Okay, so we switched gears and decided to put a sign over our door saying what business we were in, with our name, our logo and our colours. Well, that was another problem. There was a check list that was almost unending, of things we had to clear in order to get that sign. If it was a lighted sign we had to get permission from the power company. They had to see that our connections would not cause a fire and they could properly take a charge for the electricity we were consuming. Then we had to have the city engineer come in and make sure that the sign was affixed to the building in a secure enough way, so it wouldn't fall and hit somebody on the head. Then we had to get permission from the management of the building to put the sign on a space that we were renting. In each case we had to pay money. We had to pay for the engineer to come round, and the engineer would say he has to come back again next week, and next month, and now he's going on vacation, and it became quite clear that they needed a little bit of what they called *şpagă* – incentive.

When we finally thought we had everything done, the last one was the person who was in charge of making sure it fit within the character of that quarter of the city. Would it be the right colour to blend in with the other ones and it wouldn't make it look like an over-signed area? That was just too much for me because I could go around to other places, like Piaţa Unirii, and find 200 signs on one building. They looked horrible, all different colours and so forth, and how was it possible that ours had to blend in and had to be this shape?

Then somebody told me about a 65-year-old who had lots of good connections. Give her $200 as a retainer, we learned, and she would go in and get you all the authorisations and present you the license. So I just paid for her to be a facilitator for all the necessary authorisations that were needed. It was a lot cheaper than paying each one individually and waiting a long time. And lo-and-behold, that same week she came back with the license for all our buildings! Now we have a law firm on retainer and an accounting department with ten or twelve people in it. It's a very different situation to those days when we were real innocents.

Apart from the system then, what specifically Romanian characteristics have you found?

If you limit it to Romanians between the ages of 18 and 25, you would get one answer, not too different from characters you would find in France, Germany or England. And if you settled on a person who was, let's say, between 50 and 60, you would find a person who'd been – I was going to say 'scarred' but I'm not sure that's the right way to say it – but who'd been affected by how he grew up and had his first jobs and so forth. You have to be sympathetic with them because they grew up in a difficult and very different time. I remember there was a man at the bank I used to joke with, asking him what he did. He would always double-talk to me and never give me a clear answer. Finally the day came that he was walking back from the bathroom as I was walking towards him, in conversation with the chairman. I wasn't being very fair. I turned to the chairman and said, 'By the way, do you know so-and-so?'

And the chairman said, 'No, I haven't had the pleasure.' The guy mumbled his name very quickly. And I said, 'You should know him, he's a close member of staff.'

Well, what this guy did, he would arrive in the office at a quarter of 9 in the morning. He had an office. He would close and lock the door and he would stay there doing crossword puzzles and reading magazines, some of which I gave him because he was hungry for things to read. Except for going to the bathroom every now and then he would stay there the whole day, have his lunch there out of a brown bag, till about 5.30 when he would open the door, look left and look right, see if there was anybody around, dart out and go home. One day I said to him, 'What kind of a life is this? You're never going to get a salary increase or an advancement or anything.'

He said, 'Listen, my whole objective is to be forgotten, have nobody know I'm here and make no waves. I won't be fired, and yes, I won't be promoted, but I'll just come in and do my job and get my cost of living increases every year.' That mentality existed with a lot of older people in Romania. I don't think it's so prevalent with countries in the West, where you have personal ambition and you want to get ahead. That situation never exists over here among these older people.

Among the younger ones, yes. Some of the résumés that I read, I shake my head. There are people who are in their 20s and have had 12 jobs. And they're proud of it. And if they're people of some quality and somebody I really like, I sit them down and say, 'Do you realise what a wrong impression you are giving with a résumé like that? When I see that you've held on to your jobs on average for six months and have hop-scotched from one to the next, my instinct is, I must be wrong in thinking of hiring you because within six months of your engagement you're going to be wanting to move onto the next thing.'

However, they all seem to feel that they can best get ahead by not being loyal and hard-working and ambitious within a particular setting, but will succeed rather by jumping to somebody else. And Romanian personnel departments fall in with that and are impressed with a person having many different jobs. It wouldn't work in New York.

Do you find any cultural differences particularly intriguing?

I would put them in context and say that it's absolutely misleading to generalise. So I will be specific, but quick to suggest this does not mean that everybody's this way. There is a tendency over here to look you right in the eye and not tell you the truth. And they're good at it. So you have to be a little bit more cautious in dealing with somebody on a one-to-one basis because he or she won't feel really wrong in saying what they feel like saying, which might not be true.

I had a friend who couldn't drive. She took a taxi all the time and very often she went from her apartment to where I live and picked me up. She'll come with a taxi and I can get in and go on to the train station for a trip. And I'll be there at 9.30, let's say. At 9.30 she calls me up and says, 'We're just leaving right now, we're getting in the taxi cab and we'll be there in five minutes depending on the traffic, so go to the head of the street and wait for us!' I go to the head of the street and wait for her and 45 minutes later she shows up. Well, it's apparent that she was not hailing a cab right at that moment. She just knew that's what I would want her to say, and so she would say it. But she would come whenever she got around to it.

However, a lot of people in Romania – again, a generalisation is wrong – put this country down more severely than it deserves. I believe a significant percentage of them would actually leave if they had that opportunity. There are many who are committed to staying, but my gosh, if you told them that a) they didn't need visas; b) they could easily find a job in the next place they were going to; and c) they would be able to afford to rent an apartment and set something up after a few weeks of uncertainty, I would say that half the population would leave.

One of the things that really annoys me is whenever an article is written about Romania – 90 per cent of the time anyway – it's critical. I remember an article in the New York Times. It was a four-part article about the Gypsies in Romania, and how many of them live in sewage systems in the winter because they're warm, and they only come up for air in the night because they can then ply their trade as pickpockets. I thought to myself, and this is an article about life in Bucharest? It's so skewed. I wish I were editor of a Romanian newspaper and could send a team of crack reporters to Harlem in the United States and put them on a street that's known for its drug busts and its prostitution. I could write an article about New York which would say what a horrible city it is, with loads of prostitutes and drug dealers and murderers, and sirens going all night – and people would get that as an impression of New York.

Given that, how much longer do you think you'll be here?

You know, I honestly today would tell you that this is my last year. But I can just as clearly say that if you go by the experience I've had over here, it might not be. It'll take something happening in my life probably. I have an elderly mother. When she passes away I'll be forced to deal with the estate and various other things, and I'll probably end up spending a year in the United States doing all that, and then say, that's it. But so far I'm reluctant to let go here because to some degree I live a kind of a spoiled life. I have a woman who takes care of my apartment; she washes for me, cooks me dinner whenever I want it; she makes breakfast for me in the morning; she irons for me; she runs errands for me… and that's just one element that draws me to want to stay here and be spoiled. I go back to America and I have to go to the washing machine myself!

But also what is key to me is how in one generation, Romania has advanced from a sepia photo to a vibrant technicolour panorama. World class restaurants, French, Italian, American… outstanding music performers, both Romanian and invited musicians from all over… easily available films, terrific universities, traffic where the cars rival Paris or New York. And to a modern culture where everything seems to be at hand, add the cultural venues of Romania, the countryside, skiing and beach resorts. I am happy to have been here in a sort of modern creation, to have lived the advance of a modern place.

Franco Aloisio

Bucharest

'If I was a managing director of the biggest bank of Romania, probably I could have a different perspective on the country. But in my field, in the short term, no change.'

All over the world in various organisations they use different kinds of art to rehabilitate people living in difficult situations. Parada was set up in Romania in 1996 by a French clown who came to make performances for children living in orphanages. He had been in touch with street children living in the Gara de Nord, the central station of Bucharest, and decided to move here – to create an organisation using circus as an instrument to re-socialise children. In 2000 I came here for a period of three months to support the Parada Foundation. I've been here since, collaborating with different organisations in the humanitarian field, working with people in very disadvantaged situations – people living in the street, teenagers coming from orphanages, or Gypsy families.

Before, I was working with street children in Nepal and Somalia. All of us, as Europeans, were shocked to discover that in the heart of Europe we have street children. They used to live under the ground in the pipelines for Bucharest. All the cities of Romania are crossed by these pipelines that distribute hot water and heating, and the children lived in these. For us to see a child coming out from the ground is something strange, of course. We can imagine children living in the street, in the junkyard, in the poor areas – but we never imagine that they can live under the ground. When you do this job, at the beginning you do it for passion, for social motivation; then after 15 years you're not shocked any more, it becomes a job.

I come from Calabria which is one of the poorest regions in Italy, also one of the most beautiful. I studied tourism and then political science and in these years was also involved in political and social movements. I worked in the social field in the municipality of Milan, as a street educator. Then I started to collaborate with different international Italian NGOs and travel around the world working with street children.

So what are you doing today?

In these offices we also have the *Asociaţia* APEL, working on professional integration programmes for youth who want to enter the labour market. We collaborate also with SAMU *Social*, an organisation that works with homeless adults and elderly people living in the street. The financial crisis is hitting lots of NGOs. We are just trying to keep all the services we have – schools, housing programmes, street programmes. We work mainly in Bucharest – more or less all the street children, at a certain point, they arrive here. Because it's the capital, there's much more opportunity. It's much easier to be unknown in a big city. Here you can get lost easily.

After 17 years we got some sponsorship to open a school for social circus. Circus, the art, has a very big impact on people and can facilitate personal change. We are aiming mainly at children living in disadvantaged communities and orphanages, who don't have any chance to consume culture – they never go to see a performance. A child who grows up in a normal family has the opportunity to dance or to make theatre. A child who grows up in an orphanage, who comes from a very poor family or was living in the street, he never goes to see anything, he never participates in anything.

You can imagine the change in a child. One week before, he is underground sniffing glue. Then he finds himself on the stage making a performance for others, when he has 200 people who clap because he is good. Of course it helps you to have self-confidence. If you are participating in a performance you have not only to think about yourself, how you perform, but you have to perform in a context. You cannot do whatever you like. If your sketch is two minutes, you have to respect the two minutes, because there is another sketch coming. You have to learn how to work with a group. If you want to make a spectacle you cannot do it by yourself, you have to do it with other people. You learn. You experience personal behaviour that can help you in other situations.

We're losing a lot of things we achieved in the last ten years because of the crisis, because services are closing. The population is more and more in need but there is no finance. The people who live on the edge of society, in this period they are really paying too much. You can say the objective now is not to leave these people alone. In the past the objective was to help children not to be a marginalised adult. You have a lot of success but you also have a lot of failure. There are children we have been working with for 16 years and they are still in the street, still using drugs. There are also people who we work with a few months, and they managed not only to leave the street, but also to affirm their personality. We even have children who have now finished university! One of them started to collaborate with the Council of Europe; another is an artist in Milano.

For sure, success depends on what you do as a professional, but also on what the beneficiary, the client, likes. We are talking about people, not just a problem. You have to understand that a person can have a different dream and different wishes, a different life to the one that you as a professional would like him to have.

At the beginning we imagined that after a few years of

intervention we could have a society able to take care of the problem. After thirteen years work and five years with Romania in the European Union, we realise this is not true. The society here is still not ready, does not have the capability to face its own social problems – because of its history, the economic situation and the behaviour of the social, political and economic elite, which is not at all responsible to the country.

We've seen an increase of emigration from the social field also. First of all we weren't able to assure a certain level of wages. Also because it's frustrating to work for ten years and not see any kind of change. We have some colleagues who have worked with us since '96. Of course these people are frustrated because they realise they're still fighting with a problem no one cares about.

You're working in a society that is not really interested in social problems, so you have to be realistic. If you know Romania you know that there is still the culture of forced individualism – people who first look to themselves, and after look to others, without understanding that their life is linked with the rest of society. You cannot say, 'I'm for myself and then I will think about society,' because it doesn't work like this. You can improve yourself together with society, and society can work in order to help everybody. This is changing very slowly, but it's changing.

Where do you see the changes?

I'm talking about Bucharest which is different from the rest of the country. Bucharest is changing because of the 20 years of being open to the rest of Europe. Now you can see the next generation start to become more sensitive about social problems, to what is going on in the country, with the environment, with work. This can be a good sign because till now social intervention has been done by professionals, like me. At the beginning of 2000 the social field was a good opportunity for Romanians. But now the number of students enrolling in social studies is reduced because the social professions cannot assure a good salary, a good standard of life. Now people approach social work because they want to do it. This is the new generation. We find more and more teenagers and youth who wish to do something.

Being an Italian, how familiar do you find the Romanian environment?

For us Italians from the south of Italy, Bucharest is a very common space. We understand the dynamics because you have a certain level of informality we are very used to. Bucharest is like Napoli – you can do it, in the positive way, but also in the negative of course. If we are talking about cultural diversity, about a cultural informality, it's okay, it can be part of the wealth of the city. But when this informality means that still after 20 years there are 1000 children living on the street, it's not at all good. We're talking about the street children of Bucharest. We're not talking about a million people. We're not talking about an enormous social phenomenon – we're talking about 1000 to 1200 people, depending on the season. If you really want to solve it, you can do it. I talk about the political level. It's clear that there isn't any kind of interest in spending money, orienting policies or political agenda toward those children. When you talk about the rights of people you cannot be informal.

In the European Union there are rules, but in Romania they are still fighting their integration in the EU. In 2000 Bucharest in some areas was really a bazaar, like Istanbul. Everybody in the street, selling, doing things – you could feel the street was the place where people lived. At a certain moment in 2003 people did not have permission to sell any more, to do things there. They try to normalise the city but there is a part which is still resisting.

For Western Europeans the street is a way of communication,

to go from one place to another. For the Gypsies, the street is a part of the community – here there is the house, here there is the pavement, and here they have a table and chairs. They live outside. Unfortunately, half of the population living in the street come from Gypsy communities. A lot of the children that were abandoned in the orphanage come from these communities. One of the big mistakes in Bucharest is not to recognise the dynamics created by the Gypsies in the cities. With them, there is a higher level of mediation, certainly. Generally you have to bargain for everything. Everything is a deal. There is no culture of rights – they don't think, 'This is my right as a citizen.' 'I don't perceive myself as a citizen, I perceive myself as a member of my community, dealing with the rest of the society.' There they start the bargain. This is okay, this is the culture. Why don't we use this in a positive sense, to give diversity value?

How about legislation, is that effective in your field?

If you look at Romanian legislation in the social field it is more or less what you can find all over Europe. The child protection system here, from the legal point of view, could be the same as in Italy or France. The difference is in the implementation of the law. You have the law, the structure, but it is not put into practice. You still have to deal at the local level, and the local level doesn't care about the law. No one cares. The most clear example is the Transport Police, with a very high level of informality. If you cross a red light, you can solve it very easily; it costs you 2000 RON. You can talk about it, you can find a solution.

What is affecting me is the capacity of Romanian society not to react. I give you a small example. Three years ago, because of the financial situation, they cut the salary of the public services by 25 per cent. They also increased the VAT from 19 to 24 per cent. When you're already poor and they cut your salary 25 per cent, I expect you to react. I realise now that not all societies do. I don't accept it but I realise we have to think about a long period. I don't believe any more that in a few years the culture is going to change.

For the short period I'm quite pessimistic, mainly because when every day you concentrate on problems, generally you see everything as a problem. If you work with marginalised people, with the poorest people in the town, you have the tendency to see all the population in this situation. My opinion is that of a person who looks at the world from this perspective. If I was a managing director of the biggest bank of Romania, probably I could have a different perspective on the country. But in my field, in the short term, no change.

As a foreigner working in the country, living in the country, we don't have to integrate in this culture completely at this moment because it still needs someone who makes pressure on society. The country changed a lot before it entered into the European Union because there was pressure coming from the EU. If you look at the child protection system, all the improvement was done before entering. It's a paradox, but after entering, it deteriorated because no one was making pressure any more. You don't have a political and economic elite who is really enlightened and wants change. And the population does not have the capacity because of *Asta-i viața!* – That's life! So we should not try to integrate totally. We should try to have a critical attitude – not towards the people, but about the elite, the politics. We should try to be stronger.

Colin Shaw

Brașov County

'A very useful little phrase given to me by a Romanian friend goes – in Romania anything is possible, everything is impossible and nothing is ever as it seems.'

I needed to avoid the family Christmas and thought that a skiing holiday might be a good excuse. The only package available at a month's notice happened to be at a resort called Poiana Brașov. This was winter 1992, when Romania was still very grey, when the shops were fairly bare. I came for two weeks and I spent a day and a night in Bucharest half-way through my trip. On the way back to Brașov on the train on my own, which the tour guides had said would be dangerous, I met an elderly couple who spoke a little English. They were retired doctors and very friendly, very generous, very open, quite chatty. They shared their wine, their bread and their cheese with me and we talked a bit about the country. So yes, Romania was at the time a fairly scary, rather grey, very cold country, with apparently very warm, friendly, interesting people.

I came back in 1994 when some colleagues suggested I should join VSO – Voluntary Service Overseas. They needed a special needs teacher in Bucharest. I was not a teacher, only a social worker, but they said, 'Well, a social worker would be okay, we'd manage with that.' However, VSO and I came to the conclusion that my involvement in that project was just giving the Ministry of Health an excuse not to appoint a Romanian for the job. So after a year and a half we decided the placement should end.

I moved to the small village of Hârja in the eastern Carpathians to run a children's home for a foundation from Dorset. Hârja is quite high in the Carpathians in a wild and attractive area of mountains, with bears and wildlife around. Living in this small village, I began to realise that Romania had tremendous potential for some kind of rural tourism – or off-the-beaten-track, small group, tailor-made travel. I was the only non-Romanian in the village.

That particular job, running a children's home for a poorly funded British foundation, in a mountain village, very cold in winter, with houses that were not well heated or insulated, with 12 very young children including some babies, was tough. Certainly it was the hardest I've ever worked, extremely challenging and stressful.

I wanted to set up some sort of travel business, just for a year, to see if it was viable, if it would work. That's what I'm still doing after 14 years. I found in the first year, even though it was a very narrow niche market, that the idea of tailor-made travel, getting people to the places that mainstream tour companies were not going to, avoiding the Black Sea, avoiding Bucharest, avoiding other big cities, this was what a small but serious number of people actually wanted. Roving Romania was not set up as a means of making loads of money. My friends constantly tell me I could make far more money running a guest house or running a fleet of minibuses and doing mainstream tours.

Romania is a fascinating, beautiful country – still with a large number of country smallholders who farm for self-sufficiency, not commercially. I see them as friendly, generous, open and warm, if you get to know them. There are positive and negative aspects to Romania, and it's the positive, it's the rural and the country people and the mountains and the wildlife which I'm showing my clients. There is no typical trip. The places I tend to take people are Saxon Transylvania – this area around Braşov, Sibiu and Sighişoara –

Bucovina for the painted monasteries, Maramureş for its rural culture, and the Danube delta, a superb area for bird watching. Those four regions, plus parts of the Carpathian mountains in between.

If my clients go away feeling depressed because it's all corruption and bad news, then at the end of the day it's not helping this country and it's not helping me. I do also try to help in a very small way, to change the fairly negative imaging that Romania has in the West.

Lots has changed here but 50 per cent of the population are still smallholders farming their land to be self-sufficient, with very little or no income, able to survive providing they retain a degree of health and fitness. Romania is unusual now in Europe in that it has such a high proportion of farmers maintaining some traditional way of life in terms of music, folklore and dress.

Traditions have survived very well, partly because a lot of people in rural areas are still fairly isolated from what's going on in Bucharest and the rest of Europe. Generally they don't see their traditions and customs as being of interest to foreigners. It's their way of life. The customs are observed because that's the way people have been brought up. But a lot of the young rural people are keen to avoid a life of farming. To a certain extent the smallholders are a dying breed and in another two generations may well disappear.

What about conservation and protection? Is that a bit of an uphill struggle here?

Very much, in a country where a lot of people are still motivated by making as much money as they can, as quickly as possible – sometimes with a view that who knows whether in two years' time, we're going to get back to being an oppressed people with an autocratic government. If we have an opportunity to make money quickly, by cutting down the forest land we've inherited recently, for example, then we should do that now and bank or hide the money.

How do you feel about the religious and spiritual life here?

As an agnostic, I see Romanians, Hungarians and Saxons as being very religious. Very religious in terms of being strong believers in God and God's works – being people who observe a lot of religious traditions, even if they don't all go to church every Sunday. They find the concept of being a non-believer quite unimaginable. Doesn't mean to say that they're all totally honest, or all live to religious guidelines. In my experience far more people in Romania than in Britain have been brought up to believe that being spiritual is what life is about, and that there is no alternative to that.

Do you find yourself discussing history?

History is not a taboo subject but it can be a fairly dangerous one to get involved in. There are several different theories about the history of Romania. History is important to Romanian people, certainly. For them it's the foundation of their culture and their philosophy of life, about weathering the battles and the problems going on around them. They say their country has been the battleground of non-Romanian peoples for the last 2000 years. Their approach is to keep their heads down – don't get involved, don't protest or complain or object – and just get on with their lives in the hope that they'll weather the current problem. That unfortunately is why Romanians generally don't protest about what's happening in politics. Their view is that it's better not to get involved.

Asta-i România!

Exact! During the communist regime people felt they couldn't influence their lives, couldn't influence the way the country was run. Those who protested or complained were locked up or worse.

And people still don't feel empowered to have a role in determining their lives in Romania, because they don't have any faith in the political system. They feel they can't control the way their lives are run and their income is still very low, so the only solution is to go to the West.

What about the Hungarians? In your meetings with them, do you find a rather different history played back to you?

Yes, but I also find that the Hungarians and Székely I work with, some of whom have become close friends, tend to be more open, more aware of the different theories, and have a more sympathetic attitude. While there are a lot of Hungarians who don't believe they should be required to learn and speak Romanian, my Hungarian colleagues and friends are keen their children should be learning Romanian as well as Hungarian.

Generally, whether you're Romanian or Hungarian, things get done slowly. And through having contacts, or maybe through paying people under the table. If you insist on going about it the official way, following the procedures, the amount of bureaucracy and red tape in this ex-communist country is still phenomenal. You will never succeed because in fact people are expecting you to use your contacts and perhaps offer a bribe. You will be blocked. But for most people in Romania that's not corruption or dishonesty, that's what life is all about.

Have the security services been evident to you?

I haven't had any serious problems. I think that's partly because I'm a very small fly in the general scheme of things. I'd read a fair bit about Romania's modern history and the security services under communism which made me fairly wary in my first few years. I'm sure my telephone in Bucharest in 1994/95 was bugged. The brother-in-law of an ex-girlfriend is a senior officer in their modern service here. He said to me one day in a friendly conversation, after it was clear I was getting on fairly well with his sister-in-law, 'Of course Colin, you realise that all of you foreigners living in Romania, we monitor you all fairly constantly.' While the information itself wasn't a surprise, it was perhaps that he chose to mention this to me at that particular moment. I saw it as more of a 'make sure you look after my sister-in-law' kind of warning than anything else.

I was involved in 2000/2001 in the publishing of a couple of books relating to the experiences of people who'd been involved in the resistance against communism in the 1950s. That put me in contact with some of the organisations trying to publish and uncover information about what really happened. This was for young Romanians to read as an educational process. I became aware there were quite a lot of people who'd been involved in the regime at a fairly senior level, still active in government and business, who were keen that certain things should not be made public. My involvement in those books was on a voluntary basis and very open. I didn't have any direct threats but it became clear it was a slightly risky area. I decided after a couple of years not to pursue that.

My feeling is generally that there are now in Bucharest, and in quite a few other cities, protection schemes going on which people running big businesses, foreigners or Romanians, need to pay into for their own safety. They are certainly criminal organisations and it's now fairly common knowledge in Romania that if you're involved in running a big business you will need to pay money into these schemes.

What about the Revolution? Do you have any theories there?

Romanians now seem doubtful that it was a genuine people's

revolution. Many, probably the majority, have accepted that it was a form of coup that was sponsored, or promoted perhaps, by the CIA. I quite like the conspiracy theory that says it was the first time the CIA and the KGB had collaborated together on a joint policy. But yes, I think that's the common view, that it was not a people's revolution, that it was planned by some other organisation.

How do you see your future?

I'm hoping I can continue to live here without either being thrown out or without the economic climate requiring me to do something different. I'm a little unsure at the moment as to how that might pan out. Nobody knows what will happen to the euro and to the European Union.

For me every day is different. There's tremendous variety, there's a constant challenge, and you never know what's going to happen – it's difficult to get bored in Romania! A very useful little phrase given to me by a Romanian friend goes – in Romania anything is possible, everything is impossible, and nothing is ever as it seems.

Nancy Rice

Ilfov County

'We had this body of literature that we both had read... some of the basic principles by which we live are shared through that mechanism.'

I was working as a counsellor at San Antonio College and Eugene was taking courses to learn how to speak English. Imagine, he has a Master's Degree in Architecture here in Romania, but in America he had to see a counsellor to get approval to take courses at a community college. So I was on loan to the counselling department from Disabled Student Services where I worked. I picked up the next counselling card and said Eugene Georgescu and he came and we met. Well, two weeks later he visited me in another office, the student-employee assistance office. We sat together and he told me his story like we were old friends. This was 18th November, 1991. Twenty years ago, today. Imagine!

The next spring we went to the botanical gardens. We walked through the garden and a whole flock of cardinals followed us everywhere. Later I learned that cardinals mate for life. I considered this a very good sign. He became a United States citizen and came back to Romania. He called me and said, 'Nancy, come!' I came for a short visit. And went back, came back, went back. And in 1995 we were married, in Texas. It was thought that we would live half and half, but it didn't work out that way. We have lived mostly here, with occasional visits back. Tomorrow we go for Thanksgiving with my sons.

We lived in Bucharest, first in a small apartment. Then we

bought a house his family used to live in. His father worked for the railroad and these homes were for railroad workers. During World War II that neighbourhood was bombed. I remember this very sad story of Eugene being huddled in a house and the house next door was bombed. One of his friends was killed. But in spite of all of that Romanians loved the Americans, had an incredible love for them, which I have seen expressed in many ways, many times.

You might be interested to know how he got to the United States. Well, after we'd been here for two or three years, he showed me the house where he'd been left to die. That was because he made a lot of protests and he was demoted. He'd been a chief architect, overseeing at least 25 other architects. When we meet with his colleagues now I can see that they have a great deal of respect for him. Last month I went to a restaurant on the lake in Cişmigiu Park and joined them for lunch. There were over 50 of his colleagues that meet regularly. One of them was taking pictures. It was Andre Pandele. You can find on the Internet, Andre Pandele's Bucharest. These black and white pictures show the grim reality. There's no shortage here now. I've seen the progression. Now, instead of having a long list of things I need to bring back, I can buy almost everything here.

Eugene's colleagues were very kind and helpful. But also other people that we met were so nice. The one thing that I had to get used to was the fact that people here would ask the most personal of questions, but they wouldn't answer anything. I came to understand that much of what we said and did was observed. Our first apartment was right next to the Ministry of Industry on Calea Victoriei. When I would walk up from Piaţa Amzei, it was very interesting to note that one of the neighbours was peeping through a crack in the door to observe. Well, we were never doing anything for anyone to worry about so I didn't worry about anyone watching us.

Even now, not too long ago, one person thought we were spies. I'm sure she has changed her mind. Someone else told me. It wasn't a problem. Eugene's protests had been the reason that he was in the US but he told me that if he'd known the Revolution was going to happen, he wouldn't have left Romania. Then later, on one of the TV stations, someone was being interviewed who gave us information that there was a list of dissidents who were targeted at the time of the Revolution. So it was very possible he would have been killed. We will never know. It's one of those Robert Frost 'Road Not Taken' kind of things.

Being a retired teacher from Texas, I don't have a huge income. But with what we had, we were able to travel and Eugene and I got to see places we never dreamed we'd see. One of the trips we took was a tour of Italy. There he was able to see buildings that as an architectural student he'd never seen for real. In fact it reminds me of what he told me.

After he was left for dead, he went to the American Embassy and in two weeks they got him out of the country. This was 1989, six months before the Revolution. They took him first to Rome, to have classes to learn how to survive in America, right. Now, you take a chief architect from Romania who hasn't been able to leave the country and put him in Rome. Well, he said he didn't go to the last day of classes. He just walked around Rome. They punished him by making him stay another ten days – which I think is just wonderful. They probably weren't really punishing him but it makes a better story. And when I said I'd like to go back to Rome, he said, 'I've already seen it.' But we did see it together. And that tour was a delight.

Was it a big change in your life moving out to this village?

Actually, it was, it was. Eugene being the architect that he is, designed and oversaw the construction of this house. We moved into this house, oh my goodness, probably 2005. Once Eugene spent the night out here, he didn't want to go back into Bucharest. And before that, he didn't want to leave Bucharest. He's found that because things in Romania have become more efficient in many ways, he can do almost everything he needs to do out here. He's finding there are a lot of skilled people in this village. The loggia we just had glassed in was with the help of a young man who lives here. He provided all the windows and doors. The carpenter lives right down the street. He's skilled, does wonderful work – he helped build the guest house.

The maxi-taxi you came on, if you'd said, 'on the street where the American lives', they would have known it was this one. But it wasn't me they would be talking about, it's Eugene. We have what we need out here, what fits our lifestyle. A big garden. Eugene makes wine from the grapes. We have one neighbour who is able to come over; he works and takes care of things outside. It's likely he wouldn't be able to get a job somewhere else because of his particular situation but he does everything here and wonderfully well. While we're gone he'll take care of feeding the dogs.

We have our cultural differences, which I'll define as being things we're used to doing. I find some of the things he's used to doing here are very ecological and sound. For instance behind you is the *sobă* – stove. Out there you see stacks of wood. Well, if something happens to the gas or the electricity, we won't freeze to death. What's nice about the *sobă*, in comparison with a fireplace, you put the wood in, shut the door and the smoke goes out so I don't have to worry about breathing smoke. The house becomes very warm. Other things have to do with what they're used to. It takes a long time to introduce a new possibility. It took me about three years to get them to decide it's okay to have a strawberry pyramid. But now they like it.

The people in this village, they are like the salt of the earth. We get our milk from Mioara across the street over here. They have some cows. And Mita collects the milk, leaves it on the windowsill. Many of the ways they do things are ways they have done for generations. Those are the kinds of things that make you know you can survive. I watch as our neighbour goes around. They visit with each other. The neighbours often sit out there in the sunshine and they visit. So instead of visiting in the home, they visit sitting outdoors, when it's comfortable. And they don't forget easily. Two neighbours, two generations ago, had a disagreement, and the families still don't speak with each other. Which is a shame.

I understand that under surveillance and the terrible times that people endured here, the truth could get you put in prison, or worse, killed. But now, and I don't think this is particular to this country from what I've been observing, telling the truth seems to be a big problem, a big problem. Variants of that you don't want me to try to go into. What I've said to one of our neighbours is that it's very important we are truthful with each other – 'You have to be truthful with me!'

And one of the neighbours was told, 'Don't steal! We will give you more than you can steal.' Tools. I don't know how many times we bought tools when this house was being built. All I know is that the total price for building this house was probably okay. Here you don't know that something has been taken until you reach for it, and it's gone. But now nothing vanishes. Hardly anything at all.

Our grandnieces come out occasionally. The youngest one has to finish her master's degree this year. They lived out here with their grandfather. Their mother was buried over here in the cemetery, close to her father's grave. Those two girls were never going to leave this village and now you should see them. They're beautiful young women. They see possibilities they never dreamed of. They were very poor. But they finished high school. They're very independent and they have their own apartment. One of them works for a company in Bucharest. She has a master's in business. The other is working on a master's in psychology.

Young people here are protesting at the poor education. Many of the women that I spoke to, who had children in the Romanian system, were very upset. The picture I got was that in order for a student to learn anything they had to have private tutoring from the teacher. That had to be paid for. There's another thing too. As an educator I know that there are more levels to learning than memory. The system here was very good about that aspect of learning and was probably excellent for many students. But I also worked in disabled student services where I had a lot of students with learning disabilities of various kinds. I know that doesn't fit everybody. If you have people with a reading disability, you're going to have a lot of people who are excluded from education.

Romanians read. They have very good libraries. Eugene's two brothers were very well educated. One was a retired colonel in the military, whose retirement payment was a pittance. The brother who lived out here was a teacher. They encouraged him to read a lot. I had read a lot of the same things so we had this body of literature that we both had read, which I think pointed to shared values. Some of the basic principles by which we live are shared through that mechanism. The younger generations may not read that much because they have access to television and movies.

This is home. This is where I'll be. Eugene had purchased a cemetery plot in Bucharest. We built the thing around it with our initials on it. But we didn't die, so we sold it. And now, we have another plot out here. Life goes on, you never know what's going to happen next.

Judy and Spike Faint

Bucharest

SPIKE   I went to an agricultural college. Judy was domestic bursar there – that's where we met. Before coming I was managing a farm on a large country estate in Herefordshire. I was the farm manager and we lived at Eastnor Castle, the Malvern side of Ledbury, in a big farmhouse on its own. It's stunning. God's country.

JUDY   It was a bit of a shock coming to live in a communist flat in the middle of Bucharest after the Malverns.

SPIKE   I had problems with certain aspects of what we were doing. It was time to move on. Romania was the opportunity. It chose me. I was introduced to somebody already farming here. He was looking for someone to manage his business. I arrived on 31st October 1999. Judy came eight months later.

JUDY   We'd never been to Eastern Europe and we did come for a look, didn't we? You came twice. I came and stayed with you and had a wander round. Yes, I did find it quite shocking – the buildings, the horses and carts in the street at that stage, the stray dogs which of course are still with us and just the hustle and the bustle.

SPIKE   It was not so much Eastern Europe but also the city. We'd been used to living in the middle of nowhere with no neighbours and suddenly we were living in a flat in the middle of Bucharest. The office was based in Bucharest. We had guys doing the practical farming. I was doing the business management in an office full of women.

JUDY   You'd never had anybody but a gnarly tractor-driver before. Then suddenly, all the paperwork and the bureaucracy.

SPIKE   It was a British owned business. The guy was farming 14,000 hectares up on the Danube delta. He got concessions from the government… fantastic opportunity for him but he ran out of money. Arable farming, growing wheat, sunflowers and maize. I'd been managing quite a large farm in the UK growing crops. The scale of it was all very different. I worked for that guy for one year and then I was headhunted by an American agricultural company and ended up managing land in southern Romania. Living in Bucharest, I travelled to work every day, only 45 minutes down the road to Giurgiu.

Judy, what had you been doing in the UK when Spike was busy farming?

JUDY   After I'd had children I decided I was going back to work doing something I actually enjoyed. I retrained and became a fitness instructor. I was working in the gym in Gloucester and I'd been working there for seven years. I stayed behind for nine months while Joe, our son, finished his GCSEs. In the meantime Spike had become quite friendly with a few ex-pats here, one of whom was the manager in the Hilton. He was into fitness and heard about me. I'd been out here to visit a few times and he said, 'Oh, you've got all the qualifications.' Whilst Spike was out here I'd also been down to London to do my personal trainer's qualifications. Paul said, 'Why don't you come and be the in-house trainer at the Hilton?' And that's what I've been doing for nearly 12 years now. I also go to people's houses and train them at home or out in the park.

SPIKE   Over the years you've had hundreds of different clients coming and going. There've been all sorts.

JUDY   They span a complete variety really. Most of them are expats that live here but also people that just stay in a hotel can ring up and ask if a personal trainer is available. I've got Romanians who are members of the gym… several ambassadors, haven't I? Maybe somebody will just want two or three sessions with me just to get a feel for the equipment and for me to write them a programme. Or I keep seeing them for years on end because they wouldn't be motivated enough to come on their own.

I did come here with a bit of a mission. I realised that women of a certain age didn't do any fitness training. Middle-aged Romanian women here just seemed to disappear. The headscarf falls on and they don't seem to have anything for themselves. I would say once they start looking after the grandchildren for everybody, they never leave the house. They don't have a role model like me, like a 50-year-old woman doing these things…

Who runs marathons.

JUDY   Yes, indeed, but I'm a fairly normal…
SPIKE   Oh God, normal!
JUDY   You know what I mean. I like life, I like eating, I like enjoying myself, I'm not a complete fitness freak. You have to have a balance; enjoy your life but you can still incorporate exercise and fitness.

Are there Romanian personal trainers who do fitness training?

JUDY   Yes there are, but they tend to be male and of the old school variety – no pain, no gain – and there are still people coming into the gym in the old-fashioned sweatsuits, sweating their way in cling film and plastic and silver suits. So it's a little bit of a different attitude.

So are you responsible for any change there?

JUDY   Among the people I've worked with – definitely. All of it is word of mouth. People see me in the gym, working out, and like my approach. You see a great difference in Romania. When I first came out to visit and Spike was living in Dorobanți, on his own, I was running a couple of marathons a year. I brought my stuff with me and Dorobanți is, as you know, one of the wealthier areas. I put on my stuff to go out for a run and I literally stopped the traffic. I was quite shocked. I only went for about 15 minutes and there were hundreds of people staring at me – at bus-stops, cars stopped, dogs appeared from everywhere. Things have changed dramatically in 12 years.

SPIKE   Now you go to Herăstrău Park on a Sunday morning and you can't get round the lake for people running, and cycling. There are so many people. Cycling is now a middle class hobby whereas it used to be the way poor people got around Bucharest.

JUDY   It has changed beyond recognition from that perspective. Seeing the gymnasts at the Olympics, the tennis stars, the football team, I came with the impression that Romania would be fitness crazy, not realising the communist way with sports; that you were spotted at the age of five or six, with potential, and that was it – you were channelled to do well.

People used to say to me, 'You do all this running, but do you ever win anything?'

'No, I don't do it for that reason, it's because I feel better, and I'm healthier, mentally and physically.' They'd be shocked.

Do you see any kind of effect beyond the physical?

JUDY   Yes, definitely – the old mores that their life is over and they don't need to go out and they just stay hidden away…

SPIKE   But they're not the people you're training, are they? The people you're training are more and more the burgeoning middle class…

JUDY   I'd be interested to see Spike's workforce who are half female and mostly in their thirties aren't they, all with young children. What are they going to be like when they're at their mothers' age? What will their attitudes be?

SPIKE   They will not be looking after their grandchildren. My staff have all got little kids, most of whom are looked after by their grandparents, and not necessarily in Bucharest. These kids are scattered round the country. The parents probably get to see them at weekends. They can't afford to put the kids into nursery. They've got no choice about it, if they've got a well-paid job.

Spike, what are you doing now?

SPIKE   I went from working for the British guy farming to the American farming corporation. Then I set up a business for a British animal feed company and now I run a French-based animal health company. We are the fifth largest in the world and I run the business here. I have 17 staff here and business is good. We're selling complete portfolio products from dog and cat wormers to high-tech cultural vaccines. All over the country. I've got staff based in all the cities and the office is in Bucharest. We've got a warehouse outside Bucharest and we distribute from our warehouse. I travel round a lot to meet up with all the major clients.

What about the challenges?

SPIKE Bureaucracy is a challenge you live with. Our company is operating in countries where bureaucracy is a much bigger problem than it is in Romania. As long as you follow the rules here – and we always follow the rules – we can do business.

On the personal side, we're very fortunate in that we've got some very good people who are friends who look after us so we never have to worry about the little things – that gets solved for us. We never pay any bills. It's a lot easier now because you can do stuff online – but any bureaucracy with the car, that gets sorted out. And legal issues, that gets sorted out.

JUDY We actually moved into a more corporate world since we came farming. We bought our own house here, seven or eight years ago now, and that makes it home, when it's your own place. Romania is home. I make the odd slip-up and say, 'I'm going home to UK.' You miss this place. I don't think we'll ever go back on a permanent basis. Well, you can never say never because you just don't know what's round the corner, but I don't envisage us going back.

Bizarre as it sounds, what makes my life nicer here on a day-to-day basis is climate; I much prefer the climate. I'm an outdoor sun-worshipping type of person and I just love the fact that a lot of the time we have a blue sky here.

SPIKE And there's the nanny state in the UK; it's when you're going through lovely villages and there are signs flashing at you telling you to slow down – road graffiti, I think that's the correct term. Signs everywhere.

JUDY   Yes, it's the edge here isn't it? Perhaps there isn't as much as there was but I always felt that every day was an adventure. Nothing was going to be boring and samey – you never knew what was going to happen every day.

SPIKE   Also the openness. It's changed a little bit but I used to be able to knock on a minister's door and get to see a minister. I can go and see a secretary of state now. In the UK it's something you wouldn't even dream of doing. You feel like you're doing something, that you can actually get somebody to listen – whereas you can write to David Cameron and it's just thrown away.

JUDY   It does sound like being a big fish in a small pond.

SPIKE   It is big fish in a small pond – that's what I like.

JUDY   It makes life challenging and interesting. I used to have a to-do list every day when we first moved here and everything was more challenging. If I tried to pay the phone bill or tried to go to the post office to pick up a parcel, something would go wrong. Something would be more challenging than I thought. So if I had a list of five things to do and I achieved three of them it would be – yeah, result! I've had a good Romania day!

In terms of relationships with Romanians, Spike, how is it dealing with the people you work with?

SPIKE   I've got 13 qualified vets working with me – I've been working with them now for four years and they have responded to my management style, I think. I treat them as I would treat anybody else. I expect them to deliver the same as anybody else and they've responded very well. They're great people, fantastic people. They're bright, they're funny, they all speak very good English, they get jokes, they get sarcasm, and they are very hard working. The oldest is 41. They've grown up together, they've all been in the company a long time. In the four years I've had two people change jobs. They motivate me.

JUDY   They're a great bunch. You take the company on holiday with their wives, partners, children – we've just been to Antalya – and it is just fantastic how well everybody gets on. There isn't any of them that I wouldn't want to spend some time with. They're all lovely interesting people, aren't they?

Judy, thanks. Are you off to take a class?

JUDY   No, I'm actually having some treatment on my knee – got a marathon in three weeks and my knee's been bad so I'm having some physio on it.

Spike – let's talk about Romanian characteristics.

SPIKE   One Romanian characteristic is never admitting they're at fault. If they make a mistake, they will try all sorts of ways to cover it up or to blame somebody else. They'll never put their hands up and say that was me. It's because in the good old days, if you made a mistake it was a big problem, you were disciplined. Even in big Romanian companies now, if someone makes a mistake, they penalise their salary.
With my staff I've now made a rule – we're not allowed to say problem in the office, we say we've got an issue or a situation. The only time they can say problem is when it's solved. If they come in and say to me, 'Oh, we've solved this problem', they explain how it's been solved, that's fine. They've got to take responsibility for it.

You've cracked this business of responsibility?

SPIKE   Absolutely. It's delegating enough, giving people enough power, empowering them to make decisions and when you get to that stage they'll take the responsibility. I've seen massive changes in my staff, absolutely huge changes. In their delegated powers they've got the responsibility to make decisions.

I like doing business here. I'm given autonomy which perhaps I wouldn't get working in another country. I like getting to meet decision-makers. My counterpart who runs our business in the UK wouldn't be going right to the top to meet the decision-maker and negotiate contracts.

We know bureaucracy is very bad so we find ways of dealing with it. We employ enough staff, we employ lots of people to help and make sure we deal with the issues. In fact bureaucracy can be a little bit more flexible than in the UK where you've got people whose job is to stop you doing work, whereas here at least you can get round things. I'm not talking about a Romanian way of getting round things. I'm talking about negotiating, so if you have a fiscal inspection which finds a problem you can say, 'I'm aware we've got this problem but this is how we're going to solve it', whereas in the UK it would be, 'This is a problem.' There's more flexibility in the bureaucracy, without *șpagă*. We don't pay any *șpagă* at all, it's company policy.

We make friends with people. For example we've just moved our warehouse and we've moved from Ilfov into Giurgiu County. Before the move, almost while the warehouse was still being built, we invited the inspectors from Giurgiu to come and see our warehouse. We got them involved in the way we set the warehouse up and so when the authorisations came they just put a stamp on it because they'd been involved in the process.

What about the potential of Romania's agriculture?

SPIKE   There is a huge shortage of livestock in Romania and irrigation is a big problem but the agriculture of the country is a sleeping giant. The potential is absolutely massive, not been tapped at all. I reckon, driving around, there's still 30 to 40 per cent of the land not farmed. The arable land is not farmed, just left because of the restitution problems and the lack of capital for farming. But everybody's recognising it. The big multinational traders are now here; they're giving money to Romanian agricultural businesses so they can carry on and do business.

The problem is that everything is so political, the positions are politicised. You know the minute we have an election everybody changes. Every community has an agricultural engineer who is a civil servant. That is a politicised position, so if the mayor changes the agricultural engineer disappears as well. Giurgiu County; if in the local elections a new party gets into power, everybody in the Agricultural Department gets kicked out. Ruins any kind of continuity, not just policy. Where do you get the experts from? These people should be experts in their field; they're not.

At every level it's the same. The Veterinary Association and the State Registration Association, again it's politicised, so after the election all the ministry vets can be changed. I mentioned this inspector we have for our new warehouse; if the political parties change in Giurgiu, she'll disappear.

Changing the subject, are there any you can't talk about? Do you talk about the pre-1989 period?

SPIKE I never talk about politics… I mean politics is a mystery to me here. I'm fascinated with how people lived pre-89 and talk to people about it, people who went through national service. I've got no problem talking to anyone about that. Their memory is dimming a bit now. Most people still think they are being spied upon, most people think phone calls are being tapped… I'm sure that my phone is being tapped, but I don't care.

When I was working with the Americans we had one room which was swept for bugs and we used to have meetings out in the middle of fields. We would all have to go out there and lean against the trucks, and we could be two hours. It was bizarre.

A particularly American business approach?

SPIKE He was an American Israeli.

Sonja van Zee

Bucharest

'I have learned that hospitality is a great thing. I don't know whether that makes me more Romanian than Dutch, but something changes inside you.'

After I finished my schooling I went to Finland for about five months as an exchange student. That was my first way of meeting a different culture, living in a different environment, which at the beginning was a real challenge. But by the end I started to like it and in many ways that helped me to leave.

I had a good friend of mine who was making trips to Romania quite often, working for a Dutch Christian foundation. At a certain moment I thought okay, maybe it is an idea to go with him and see what this Romania is like. That first visit was short but it meant a lot for me. Of course, I didn't have it in mind that I would stay here as long as I have done, but I did have the idea I would like to go back, and I did.

In August 1999 I moved to Timișoara and worked for the local team, which consisted of some Romanians, me and this friend of mine. The foundation was having all kinds of projects in the fields of education and working with companies as a consultancy. The main goal was certainly not to proselytise but to share what we have already learned, with people who were somehow more at the beginning, after the Revolution.

I found it really interesting. Romania is so different from Western Europe. If you go on holiday you see some things, but if you live in a country for a longer time you get much more of an idea of what's really happening. Maybe in the end you will never understand it completely, but you get a better idea of it at least.

In many ways Timişoara is quite a small place in which you were meeting people you knew all the time. Looking back now, things have changed very much since then. There were no supermarkets at all – there were only the very small shops. You had to go to the shop and before you learnt Romanian you had to point, 'Okay, I want this. No, no! I want that one, that one.' It also helped me to learn the language because there were few people who spoke any English or German.

Language is very important to them. Let's say you have one word in Dutch, they can have about five words in Romanian, and each a little bit different in exact meaning – like the Inuit have so many words for snow. In some ways their language is much more developed than Dutch. It's also, for Romanians at least, very important to have exactly the right word, which of course for a foreigner is something wild because we're already happy if we know one word!

I remember I made a visit to what was then still a state-owned company and that was something of a culture shock. There were all kinds of people there. They were in their working place but they didn't really seem to do too much, with people going outside to have a break and coming back one hour later. People were eating in the time they were there. Me, coming from a Calvinist background, when you're at your work place, you actually should be able to see people working. So that was a bit of an interesting experience, I must say.

I was the contact between the Dutch and the Romanian side mainly. I was involved in projects like the education week and the summer camp, which were with the local university, so that meant contact with professors, teachers and students. There was also some consultancy to very small, young companies, and that meant things like 'How do I Write a Business Plan?' or 'Is it Important to Have a Budget?' Very basic ideas which at that time at least were not yet very much known in Romania, because during communism everything was told to them from above. People didn't really have to think about those things.

Of course it's a bit of a challenge to leave your own country, to leave your family behind, and just live on your own. Then I'm a rather shy person; that also doesn't help. Dealing with people is different. Romanians are very hospitable, so they will quite easily invite you to come to their house and even to have a meal, which doesn't really happen in Holland at all. You can also just visit them and not let them know about this beforehand, which from my point of view was always a bit tricky. They are much more spontaneous, at least than I am, and quite possibly the Dutch.

It's an interesting idea that you can just visit people; if you go there you get offered a meal, you can stay maybe as long as you want to. It's warmer than what I am used to and it has a beautiful part to it, being able to share what you have with others, spending time with people. But if someone knocks on the door and I'm not ready for it, I don't like it. It's probably very visible. But I do find it inspiring and it makes you think somehow. In Holland people come for a cup of coffee, a cup of tea; maybe they get a cookie, but for sure not a meal. If you're invited for dinner, it's a different matter. But if you just visit somebody then, why not the meal also? It's not necessarily so incredibly strange.

Some people are just more sociable than others. I'm always somehow thinking about all the things that I still have to do or I'd like to be doing at that moment. The planning side for Romanians is a bit less important. For them it is very important to spend time with somebody and it's okay if it takes a long time. If they have something to do, they can always do it tomorrow. But for me, if I want to do something, I actually want to do it today. That was a bit of a challenge. Life is less organised. You're not always sure what's going to happen. It has a nice part to it, but everything to a certain extent has its limits.

And you've crossed the cultural divide by marrying into Romania!

I met Marian in 2002. We got married in 2006 and just celebrated our fifth anniversary. In many ways we think the same about things we find important in life, decisions that we make. I find it striking that in many ways we're not so different. Marian has been abroad quite often, even when he was quite young, which makes a difference. He was also raised by a mother who was not a traditional Romanian. Let's say that I think it would not be very easy, if not impossible, for me to have married a very traditional type – traditional as in, 'I am the man, you are the woman, you do all the things in the house, and you raise the kids. Even when you work, you still do all the things. I, as the man, take the decisions.' It still happens. Especially when you look at people over 40, 50. You see it more there. Of course with the younger generation, and especially in Bucharest, things have moved on a lot. In Holland, and also in Britain, the status of the man and the woman is quite equal.

Romania is still traditional in many ways. When you look at the position of elderly people, for example. It's very different to Holland. Very often it is seen that if you are over 60, you are old; you're not supposed to do too much anymore, you're supposed to stay home. People also feel it that way. Well, of course it depends. If you have physical problems, it's hard to leave the house. I can understand that. But you also have people who are actually still quite able and somehow the idea is they are old and they're not really contributing too much to society anymore.

Marian and I hardly talk about the age we have. Marian is younger than I am, and by their standards the difference is big. We don't really discuss that, not with our friends. For us it's not really anything at all but they understand it as a problem, that the woman is older than the man. I'm not exactly sure why.

Apart from traditions, what other aspects of life strike you here?

Food is very important. I suppose it has to do with the communist period in which a lot of time there was not enough food. People had to stand in line to get it. It's important that there is a lot, especially when you talk about the holidays, especially for Christmas, Easter. It's usually prepared in the home. That is still done, even in Bucharest as far as I can see. Although maybe less by young people, but the mothers and the aunts, they still spend days, maybe even weeks, before Christmas preparing for the main meals – thinking of the things to make, buying everything and making it from the very beginning. Not how it often happens in Holland, when you just buy something which is already partly prepared. Meat is very important. I've heard things like 'If I don't have meat in the day, I haven't eaten.'

For me it's not easy to understand what the communist period really was, what it meant for people, what it did to them. For some people here it's still hard to take initiative. Probably because they are somehow afraid that if they do, then something bad will happen afterwards. Something like the Big Brother is watching you if you're too visible. You also still hear, 'They pretend that they pay us, and we pretend that we work' or once in a while, 'It is so good to have a job in which you have nothing to do.' Which for me is horror all over the place, because that's more tiring for me than having a lot to do.

They are still as creative as they always were. I'm thinking of the need to arrange something, or if you need a document. In many ways the systems didn't change so much. In Western Europe you know if you need something you go to the website, or you know exactly what you need and you go and get it. Here sometimes it's hard to find exactly what you need. You have to go two or three times maybe, you have to know somebody. In many ways it's still like that as far as I can see, being able to resolve something on the spot. They won't necessarily need to think about it for a long time and they wouldn't even think of doing it any other way, because it's not going to work. And for many Romanians it's difficult when they go abroad and they see that things obviously don't work like that. They cannot come with their own solution, they have to go with what has already been arranged.

Orthodoxy I don't find easy to grasp, especially coming from a Protestant, Calvinist background. It's all the traditions in the church, all the things that happen in the service which I cannot understand, although apparently even most Romanians don't understand most of it, which is a bit of a pity I suppose. What I have seen is that most of them believe there is a God, and they're quite sure about that. But this doesn't necessarily mean something personal for them. God is there, he's far away, he's deciding certain things for my life and they are happening. I have no control over them. I'm not saying they all have it, but it's quite common in Orthodoxy, this idea. It's very different from the view of God which I'm used to, which maybe is a bit too much that you have control over your own life. But this idea of a God, who is far away and you cannot have any relationship with him, is not for me.

You could say it's a kind of fatalism. What does Asta-i România *mean to you?*

Well, I must say I sometimes use it, although I don't like it very much – it gives you the idea that there is something which is not exactly the way it's supposed to be, and it cannot be changed. So you don't have to do anything about it. Personally I always have the idea – and it's probably more a Western European idea – that to a certain extent you can create your own life and enjoy your own life. But I also know that certain things in Romania do not really change, you do not have any grip on it. When I go to the doctor I can decide not to give money, but it doesn't mean that is not done. If you've been here longer you start to understand *Asta-i România* more and more but I still don't like it.

Do you have strong relationships with Romanians?

Well, they are probably different, in the way that in Holland it's possible to have a good friendship and not see each other very often. Romanians need much more to meet somebody, to talk to somebody, to touch somebody. With people of my age, I think they find foreigners interesting. They also find it very interesting that I've been living here for such a long time. 'Why in the world do you want to live in Romania, why don't you just go and live in Holland? It's a lot easier and a lot nicer.'

In the beginning Romanians were looking up to me, as somebody coming from the West. Lately I see that a lot less. That might also have something to do with the embassy where I now work. Some of them have already worked there for many years, so they're very used to us. But indeed, in the beginning I found that made me uncomfortable. They were somehow looking up to me. I was thinking, yes okay, but why should I, because I come from Holland, be so much better than you are?

I've heard it from many people – and they consider that as a compliment – that I have been romanianised. I suppose in some ways I've changed. Probably time got a little bit less important to me. I'm still the person who likes to be on time but I've also learned that some things take longer than they should and to a certain extent I can live with that. I've learned that hospitality is a great thing. I don't know whether that makes me more Romanian than Dutch, but something changes inside you. Of course I speak Romanian now, which gives you a much better possibility of understanding people and culture, and seeing how you could fit in.

Rupert Wolfe-Murray

Bucharest

'All that old dinosaur stuff is constantly being worn down.'

It was December 1989 and I was in Edinburgh. I'd just written about Romania for the Scotland on Sunday paper, and then when the Revolution happened they said, 'Can you cover the story?' That was my first break with a newspaper – I did a serious story and suddenly it was front page news. I wanted to come out immediately, but they wouldn't send me because they were tight. I got here in January 1990 with the London Observer, and was a reporter for a few months.

By the middle of 1990 the papers weren't interested in Romania anymore, and I got involved in helping the orphanages. My brother had come out with me just after the Revolution, and had gone back to Scotland, raised £10,000 and came with a little convoy and some people. Basically we moved into a kids' home for three years – one of the really bad ones which hadn't got any heating or windows or water or food or anything. A hundred and twenty kids packed into this house, and we worked there trying to turn the place round. We were renovating a building and training staff. Loads of people came to us and it became a centre for all kinds of activities.

It was in Botoşani, in an old chateau on a hill in the middle of nowhere, a place called Ionăşeni. We started delivering aid to them. They said thanks, and we stayed around in the area and kept going back. We realised that the aid was having no impact at all. It would just get stolen, or even if it was being used, it wouldn't actually change anything. We felt this aid-delivery business wasn't going to have any impact beyond first aid, so we spoke to the local authorities and went to the local press and said, 'This place is totally scandalous. You guys in the town don't even know about it. People in there are dying of starvation and malnutrition!' We asked the local authorities if we could work and live there, just me and my brother.

'Sure, yeah. Go ahead,' they said.

We had some resources and we started fixing up the windows and doors and water supply, and phoning people to bring more supplies in. Then more and more people kept joining us; all these volunteers started showing up. Half of them were pretty useless, so we ended up managing them. Managing volunteers and dealing with local authorities became the main job.

A lot of the kids knew Romanian but weren't speaking. They were so traumatised and brutalised they hardly spoke. We introduced a bit more care into the atmosphere, and they started talking to us. So we started learning the language with these kids, aged from three to twenty-three. They had every kind of disability you can imagine. Also there were some perfectly normal ones; they were just naughty and had been chucked in with the others because they were a pain in the neck. The place was a kind of dumping house for handicapped kids that the communist system didn't want to know about. They sent them to remote country houses to disappear. It was an embarrassing problem that no one knew how to deal with.

We were dealing with the local mayor, the secretary of the town hall, the prefect of the county and representatives from ministries. Every ministry has an office in each county, and we would end up seeing these people. The secret police used to get sent to us all the time… the police and the tax office being told we were a gang of crooks. We reported the director of the institution for stealing and she would report us as the thieves. All the different authorities would come and visit us and find we were doing a good job, and we'd work out how they operate, how they function. We'd get on with them. This kind of conflict went on for a few months and then they got rid of the director.

On a human level, the local authorities were all really friendly, and quite curious to meet foreigners too. We were a pair of scruffy Scottish brothers who weren't the kind of typical consultant-businessman type in a suit. They liked us, we liked them, and there was a certain humour there. They really wanted to help, wanted things to change, but the system in this period of transition… ! Nobody seemed to be in control. Nobody was very secure then, in the sense that no one had any experience in the new post-communist system. Everybody was finding their feet, and I felt very much on an equal footing with them. That really helped the communication, and there was mutual respect. The Romanians have got a great sense of humour, if you know how to see it behind this very gruff facade. A bit like the Scots, I suppose.

I came back here in 1999 as a consultant, running a project called The Improvement of the Roma Situation in Romania, working with the government office for the Roma. There was this huge expectation on the part of the Roma people, thinking we were going to perform miracles. It was a bit like being Jesus in a way, in the sense that they expected us to turn water into wine. They were disappointed when it didn't all happen like that. Our job was to talk to them and the ministries, to come up with a strategy and a law to help the Roma integrate into society.

One of the things I'm most proud of is that I got some parts of the more liberal media involved in looking at the Roma issue. With them there's obviously a huge amount of poverty and a little bit of wealth, and everybody looks at the wealth and the crime and draws wrong conclusions. The big thing for the Roma now is that they can travel to Western Europe. People always complain about the fact that some of them go and beg in the big cities in the West, which is true, but that's just a very small minority. Most of them go and work and bring back money. The fact that they can travel and work means that there's money coming into their system. Some Romanians say the Roma can all go to school if they want to, but they don't want to go. Anyone who knows the situation is aware they *do* want their kids to go to school, but as soon as they do, they get discriminated against. The thing that annoys Romanians most is that they assume everybody in the West thinks they're all Gypsies in Romania. They think that all the Roma going to the West ruin their reputation. At the same time, they're not willing to look at what they're not doing to help integrate the Roma locally.

Going back to the post-communist system, as you put it, how is this changing?

I worked once for the Mayor of Avrig, a small town in Sibiu County – an ethnic German mayor who was modern-minded. He'd been educated in Germany, spoke fluent German, English and French, and really wanted to make this town into a centre for renewable energy. I did his communication policy. I said to him, 'I see that you sign all the papers that need to be signed by the town hall. Why is that?' All the mayors and ministers end up signing off on everything, taking up all their time and energy. Grossly inefficient, because if they're signing off on everything, they can't possibly take in all the detail. Which means that all the bureaucrats underneath don't have any responsibility. The result is a lot of Romanians are unable or unwilling to take responsibility for their decisions. There's plenty of old dinosaur companies still staggering along, being subsidised by the state, doing it the old way in the old industries. But you now have the advertising agencies, TV stations, mobile phone companies – modern companies operating in a modern way. There was nothing there before, which means that these were able to set up a modern structure with no dinosaurs.

But the attitude in the public sector hasn't really changed. It's still the same as it was under communism. They need to have a sense of control over things, and there's an inability to be open and cooperative with other people who want to do something. The system isn't really geared up to working in partnership in a transparent way, because it's Balkan, more family-clan based. When it comes to public tenders, they prefer to do it with people they know, like friends and family; not only for corrupt reasons, but also because they trust them more, feel they can control the contract.

You see it very much in the school system. Being a teacher is an unrewarding and underpaid job, and the whole system is very stiff and old-fashioned – very much rote learning, top down. The Ministry of Education can't deal with all these old teachers who've learned to force feed the kids nationalistic history and super-complicated mathematics and science at a very young age. I hear amazing stories all the time.

Recently the Ministry of Education gave schools a free week in April, calling it School Another Way. They could do what they wanted. I was approached by some teachers who are very friendly, nice ladies. 'Can you come and help us? We've got this challenge to do something for the kids this week because for 50 years we've been told exactly what to do and, quite frankly, we don't know what to do now. The curriculum and our activities are prescribed at ministry level. Now we've got to think up something ourselves.' They've got no operational freedom at all. They can't even kick a kid out of the classroom.

Romanian kids are just amazing. The real hope comes from the younger generation. I give talks in schools and colleges, and whenever I go in, the teacher will say, 'This guy's from Britain, he wants to talk to you. He speaks Romanian.'

And all the kids clamour, 'Speak in English, speak in English!' The younger generation are totally modern, and they're coming up with no regard for the old rules at all. They're doing it their way and they're going to change the country. These kids who've been born in the last 20 years haven't grown up under communism. People forget that schools and public institutions and most things in the country are run by people who were formed under communism. How can you expect them to behave like capitalists?

There's a clash of cultures within politics. On the one side a very traditional pattern is being sustained, and on the other there's modern initiatives. The Americans would call it culture wars. For example, there's Roşia Montană, one of the biggest investments in Romania, if it goes ahead. The proposal is to build a 3000 hectare open cast mine, destroy four mountains and three villages, and build this massive reservoir that will be filled up with billions of tons of cyanide waste. They claim it will make €19–30 billion from gold. They demolish the mountains, wash it in cyanide, sell the gold.

A local NGO which is opposing this project had success in the local county court. Planning permission for the mine was rejected, and without that they can't get any of the permits needed to do the job. The whole thing's been stopped, but the mining company obviously claims it's still carrying on and will re-apply. The PR machine is carrying on. It's the third biggest advertising budget in the country, and the Romanian media won't publish a word against this project. They get these huge ads from the company saying what a wonderful project it's going to be and how everybody's going to be given a job. This huge conflict has been going on for 17 years, but now Romanian civil society has come of age and has really proven itself – stopping a $2.5 billion corporation on cultural and environmental grounds. If the legal system works, even though the president's fighting on behalf of the miners, that's impressive.

On a personal level, how have you found establishing relationships here?

I always feel very welcome here and at home. Even in the early 90s I felt very accepted here. I got on with them easily, and close personal relationships were kind of normal, in the sense that they would be back home. Obviously, the big difference is this whole family thing here. The family never really let go of their kids here. I went to a state school in Scotland, and when a kid there left school at 16 and got a job, he'd have to start paying rent at home. By 18 he's married and off. Here the parents never let go of the kids, never stop considering them as kids. I was married here, divorced last year. My in-laws used to refer to me and my wife as the children. We were in our forties! That was all kind of amusing at first, but I've seen the other side of the coin. They don't allow the kid to experience much. They don't know how to catch a ball; they don't know how to ride a bike or swim or climb a tree; stuff that I'm always pushing my kids to do. For instance, climbing trees, which every kid wants to do – I've seen so many parents grabbing the kid and saying, 'Don't you dare climb that tree, you'll fall off and kill yourself!' They're very averse to any small risk.

Blaming other people for things; that's another major issue here. I've seen it from the kindergarten level up to the top of government, the tendency to blame other people for everything, not to take responsibility. My son says, 'You know, Daddy, I notice that the other kids, when they do something stupid, they blame everybody else.' This culture of blame is completely widespread, as is complaining. As with anything negative or anything prevalent, you get people fighting against it, so there's a new generation of people who reject that, do take responsibility, and do change things. I remember a Hungarian TV producer who said, 'It's great working in Romania compared to Hungary, which seems like a much richer country. The people are stubborn and rigid there, whereas Romanians are very flexible.' And that's coming from a Hungarian!

How do Romanians get on with each other? Well, there's a traditional answer and a modern answer. The traditional one is they don't get on, and one of the prevailing factors which remains from communism is this tremendous sense of suspicion of anybody introduced to them – new partners, new contractors or new hires. It's very easy to come to the conclusion that the country's dysfunctional, because they don't get on with anybody they don't know or they're not related to. But it doesn't really apply across the board. It's fragmented by the modern approach; you see it in business. There's a lot of openness among the smaller sectors where there's new companies with a modern approach – which is to give everybody an equal chance and trust people till they blow it. I've seen that.

There's so much travel and integration into Europe now. So many Romanians are coming and going abroad. That's another major factor. People come back from the West with modern ideas and experiences, and that's also fragmenting the system; they're gradually breaking it up. Even in the public sector, new people who've been abroad are being hired. All that old dinosaur stuff is constantly being worn down.

Ricardo Alcaine

Bucharest

'The sense of loyalty. When a Romanian can have confidence in you, he will give it back three times.'

I'm married to a girl from Bilbao, my home town. At the time she was working in Brazil I asked her to come to Romania. She did, and four years later we got married, in 2005. She's a person who travelled around quite a lot, she's very used to living abroad and she has adjusted to being here. She's a businesswoman and runs the company with me.

In 2001 I moved here and established a company called GIS Group. At the beginning it was mainly directed at the private sector because it's difficult to work with the public sector. I was selling my services to big companies trying to get financing from the EU. Our main activity is consultancy. Later we started to do implementation issues for foreign companies; looking for land, contracting, tendering, establishing companies, a bit of accounting. Overall we have around 30 people working for us, including my brother. A very solid team, we are four foreigners and the rest are Romanian. Fifty per cent of them are Spanish speakers. They are very good at languages as you probably noticed. I think the generation from 20 to 35 years old here are extremely well prepared, very focused on their career development, very responsible. We're very happy with our team here.

Professionally we're coming from the EU funding sector. At some point it was very difficult to work here. It was a little bit of a disappointment for us. We were bringing projects but the evaluation of those were based on issues that were… I really don't want to go very much into this.

The competition was always winning?

Yes. There are ways to do things here that sometimes put the business in jeopardy. It's not our style. There are issues with the system that are sometimes difficult to cope with. At some point it was too much, the pressure was too much. But in general we are very happy with the way things developed for us in Romania. I'm confident in the professional class that are now 25 to 35 years of age. They are sceptical about the system, they don't like it. They don't like the way the country is developing. On the other hand they are the ones that are better prepared, they are the ones that are more in touch with the international reality, the way of making business. I see a big change in that. Whereas five, six, seven years ago there was no hope for change, I really believe in Romania now, the sense of responsible leadership and government is starting to be more important for them.

In the workplace women here are very strong and 80 per cent of our staff are women. They have more sense of responsibility, they have a greater loyalty to the company. Men seem more worried about career development, making money. Women are more solid. For us there's no doubt. It's not something that we do intentionally but at the end of the day, when you go out in the market and you start hiring, the women in Romania are more reliable.

We have people working for us from the beginning. We used to have a payroll system in which you had 14 payments a year, plus participation in the benefits. With the start of the crisis, they came to us and said, 'Okay, we want 12 monthly payments, we will renounce two. Let's go ahead through these hard times.' Now, I'm thinking about a country like Spain, that sense of loyalty would be very difficult to find. When a Romanian can have confidence in you, he will give it back three times. In principal, when they meet somebody, at first they do not have confidence, but once the barrier is passed they are very solid people, very loyal.

They – the 25- to 35-year-olds – are staying in the private sector but they are demanding more and they will be a growing force in the country. We have some people in this company who have been with us for ten years. The salaries they are receiving now are basically eight to ten times bigger than they used to be. They have time to travel, they have means to travel. They like to get around, to see other things. When we came here, that was impossible for this growing class. It will have an impact.

In Western Europe we were too optimistic about the time period necessary to change the system, to oblige people to think and do things in a free market democratic system. It's not 20 years – a country needs a lot more than that. We were too naive. It's probably a matter of two, three, four generations before the new approach is completely established.

People came here with investment expectations. I'm thinking about the real estate boom here, when a lot of people thought the middle class in Romania will be able to spend €200,000 and will be willing to do it. It wasn't the case. Romanians like to feel secure before they make any moves. Whereas in Western Europe, we were coming from a time when money was flowing, investment decisions weren't very well thought out. We came here and said they will do the same but Romanians are conservative. They aren't in debt, which is a sign of the way they think.

Eight years ago people thought the system was unchangeable. Now I believe the urban, professional, younger generation think of Romania in a different way. They are more conscious of what they want and what they think they will need. The political options here aren't very different between one party and the other but there's room for somebody to appear. I always thought a left, social democratic party with young people, with good people, will have a chance here. But it's a matter of leadership.

So things are changing?

They are prouder of themselves now than ten years ago. The sense of country, identity – it's stronger now. Little by little the country is again having a greater national identity. In the social and economic aspect, urban classes really developed quite a bit. In 2002 the monthly salary in the public sector was €200, the salary in the private sector was €300 to €400. Those salaries multiplied four or five times. But there is a lot of social inequality here, there are a lot of issues and one of the big tragedies is that the government or the society isn't taking care of them. In general terms changes were quite significant, but maybe less than we expected.

I'm very happy and people are open enough. But in our particular social segment it's difficult to make friends because people who are in our position, financially speaking, have maybe other ways of thinking. I sometimes feel it's difficult for us to interact with people at our social or economic levels. I don't know why, but that's the reality. There's some kind of barrier. On the other hand, and I'm very grateful for this, my younger brother got married to Ana, a Romanian girl, which really opened a door for us. You see another reality in that generation of young professionals.

Maybe at some point there was too much of a focus on money, on wealth, on image issues. What car you drive – it's an important thing. But it's very easy to criticise. We have to remember this country is coming from 40 years of limitations, of not being able to own things, so it's a normal reaction.

Foreigners here tend to complain. I've also lived in the United States, Brazil, and Belgium. This is the first time where I really feel at home. Whereas from the outside, it's probably the most aggressive country and the most difficult country to live in, the reality is that it really worked out for us. And I'm not the only case. A lot of people came here in the early 2000s. Difficult situation, difficult business environment. But most of the people I met at that time are still here. Whereas in other countries a lot of the people that we met have already gone somewhere else. Maybe it's business opportunities, maybe it's the sense of growth and development that the country has. I don't know what it is, but this is home for us.

I'm more optimistic than I used to be regarding a Romanian business class. Obviously there are a lot of crooks around. Maybe that's not the right word, but more and more we see very professional business people with clear objectives and good management decisions. We used to be more focused on foreign clients but in the last two, three years our client base is more and more Romanian. They trust us and it's a good feeling.

After living in Romania you will be prepared to go anywhere because it's not an easy country. Me and my wife, we would live comfortably in Spain I'm sure, have a very good standard of living. But the intense experience of day to day life would be different. In that sense it's changed me. When you come here you are exposed to a really intense country, professionally and socially. It's challenging and yes, sometimes a bit stressful.

Do you need to get away occasionally?

Yes. We either go to the Basque country or travel somewhere else. Every one and a half, two months, we like to take a few days off. It really works for us. But Christmas time we go home for three weeks and at the end of Christmas, we really want to come back. This is home but every so often you need to breathe.

It's the little problems here that really consume you because to solve them you really have to dig deep. We represent a lot of companies, take care of their administrative issues and so on, every day, every week. Sometimes you have the feeling like, please, I had enough! Don't come to me with more problems! It's also the nature of our field of activity. People come to us in order to solve their issues. You need energy but on the other hand it keeps you alive. It's a challenge. But sometimes, if you spend three, four months without leaving the country for a week, you feel like... aaaah, I cannot deal with this anymore!

Our son is three years old and it is true that sometimes we think, when he is 12, 13, 14, we would like him to go back home and have this feeling of being from the Basque country, developing relationships there. Why? Because at the end of the day I've been away from Spain for 22 years, but my real friends are still there and I do have this feeling of belonging to the place. This is the only issue that sometimes make us think about going back – that we'd like my son to have this sense of belonging, not being the son of ex-patriates. We will see what we can do.

Peter Hurley – The Long Road to the Merry Cemetery

November 2011

The Long Road to the Merry Cemetery, this festival in Maramureș, where did it come from?

I first visited Maramureș in August 2003. That was one of those moments that I've had in Romania when I really thought to myself, there's something incredible here. It had a profound impact on me. When you come over the top of a hill at one point from Dealu Ştefăniţei in the south, there's a big sign saying: Welcome to Maramureș. You stop the car. It was early morning and we looked across hill after hill of hand-tended fields. It was so clear that this was something that had been tended by hand, a patchwork of small fields. This reminded me very much of what you see in the stone fields of Ireland, the skeletons or fossils of a long lost tradition that could have looked as rich as this.

I went to a religious festival because it was the feast of *Sfânta Maria*, on the 15th August 2003, and the family we were staying with were participating. They and their neighbours were all dressing up in their best clothes and going off to the monastery of Moisei so we went with them. Again that was another outstanding moment, where there were thousands upon thousands of people of all ages, throughout the grounds and on the hillsides around the monastery. They'd been there, most of them, keeping the vigil all the night. People had brought their blankets and had slept on them. There were many priests; they were doing confessions. There was a calmness and a beautiful peacefulness about the place but at the same time the intense energy of young people, something very special that you certainly wouldn't see anywhere else I've been. Many of them had walked there because the old tradition was to walk across the hills, the 20, 30 or 40 kilometres, as part of your pilgrimage. They stop at all the *troiţe* and all the crosses on the way and get down on their knees and say a prayer, celebrating this great feast day. So very special, to hear people singing as they walk. It's something completely unmodern. It's very natural, very pure, quite outstanding.

A few years passed. I met Nicu Covaci, the founder and lead singer of Phoenix, established in 1962, which basically invented Ethno Rock in Romania, or 'traditional meets the modern world.' Nicu has been famous for his exploration of Romanian traditional values through rock music and they had a huge success. A friend of his had been saying that he wanted to explore the Dacian – Celtic connection in music and his idea was to have a rock concert to do that. I met him because I was Irish and he feels a very strong connection with what we would call Celtic music. Indeed, when I first heard them at a party in 1997 I was sure the music was Irish. For a couple of years we bounced ideas around but we never really got beyond the pub-talk stage, let's say. Then in 2008 something else happened from a different direction.

That was a phone call from a friend of mine, John Fairleigh. He's been visiting Romania since the 70s, working mostly in the area of theatre. He called me and asked if I'd ever heard of the composer Shaun Davey. I'd heard of him of course, because he created that 1980 work *The Brendan Voyage* which is a household term in Ireland now. John had persuaded Shaun to come and see Romania. He was going to spend a few days in the country to see what he thought. And my job was to introduce him to anybody that would be interesting from the music world or from traditional music. I spent a couple of days with Shaun. A few months later he gave me a call and said, 'Come to Sibiu! We're having a concert. I've created something and I'd like you to hear it.' I went and that's where, in June 2009, I heard for the first time what Shaun had created for Romania: *Voices from the Merry Cemetery*.

John Fairleigh had arranged for him to go to Sibiu to see Silviu Purcărete's production of Faust. Shaun was fascinated by the idea – here I am for the first time in an Orthodox country. He went to the cathedral in Sibiu on the Sunday morning, stayed for the mass and heard the wonderful choir. At the end of the mass he went to the director of the choir and said, 'You don't know me, I'm an Irish composer. I'd like to write something for your choir and you'll be hearing from me.' About four months later he sent a letter with some music to the same man saying, 'I'm coming in three weeks. We're going to have a concert. Can you see if your team can learn this.'

After Sibiu he gave me a recording. I felt a very strong empathy for the people that were in the songs. Those epitaphs, which were part of this Merry Cemetery story, had suddenly come to life through Shaun's work. When I looked into the words of each song and started to really understand what these stories were about, I realised that they weren't just happy, superficial, jokey epitaphs. No, they were much more than that. Shaun sensed this and he created *Voices from the Merry Cemetery*, this suite of 13 melodies, each melody being an epitaph, each epitaph a life.

I started to investigate a financing line to bring it to another level. I wasn't really sure what that would be. It became clear it would have to be in Maramureş and I suppose that's when the accumulation of different ideas, discussions and thoughts began to coagulate and I started to think about a project which would see Shaun Davey's creation come to Săpânţa. I wrote this application for a grant but it became clear there was no way we were going to make the deadline to stage this in 2010, on the 14/15th August, the date we had set upon. But something inside told me that we should really go for it, on that day in 2010. The concert would be a Saturday night, the Feast of the Assumption of the Virgin Mary. This is a solemn moment in the Orthodox calendar.

When all the refusals came back and it was clear that we weren't going to have funding for it, I decided we would have to do it this year and I was going to put the money up myself. It's very difficult to get people like Rita Connolly, Liam O'Flynn, Noel Eccles and David Brophy to say that they're available for a date, any date. The moment was right. Who knows what's going to happen in a year? It would take all my savings. It took more than all my savings.

I had enough money to do what I thought was necessary which was €100,000. It actually cost €143,000 for various reasons. But I didn't look back once. I had persuaded my wife, God bless her, because obviously this was a huge undertaking, financial and human. Probably she understood more than I did at that time how difficult it could be, but she agreed and we set off on the Long Road to the Merry Cemetery.

It was a beautiful experience to go through, fantastically charging on many levels. It proved to me so many things about Romania, on the good side. There are bad sides to everything – you can't do something like that and not have problems, but there were moments that proved that if you really have to do something, all the other people will pull with you and things will come together. And they did. I don't think you could do in any other country the things you can do here. People are willing to see a spark and to pick it up and to go with it. It's had so much tragedy, it's an incredibly complicated country with a huge baggage and a drama. So many contrasts and so many interests seem to mix here. And that creates a spirit in the people that they're also willing to do things because they'll help each other out.

Really, nobody said no to anything we wanted to do. It was a huge chronometric challenge because we only had enough money to bring all the musicians together for three days. We had to record an album; we had to do a concert in the open air of this orchestral creation with 80 musicians, on a wooden stage in the Merry Cemetery itself, at night time; and we decided we would have a festive day, because *Sfânta Maria* is a feast day. These three things had to happen in very quick succession.

The priest who had the keys to the cathedral in Sighetu Marmaţiei, where we wanted to record the work, was away on holiday in Italy. He didn't know that we were going to use his cathedral as a recording studio, that we would have to cover all of his pews with plastic sheeting to protect them; build a wooden stage over all of his church, all of the pews; change it into a recording studio on Friday and have everything taken out and cleaned in time for his four o'clock Saturday service. I knocked on his door when he came back – on the Wednesday – and told him what we wanted to do, starting that day. He said, 'Please, I'm going to get hung if anything happens to this place' – and he let us do it. That's a great example of the things that people helped with.

Everybody came away from Săpânţa with a huge positive energy. But we didn't hear anything and we had no progress on getting that application approved to fund the second year. I became resigned to the idea that probably if we were to do anything again it would be on a much smaller scale. I had no financial resources to consider funding anything further.

But during this first *Drumul Lung* we built a strong connection with Grigore Leşe. He came from a very small village, in the south of Maramureş, from the Lăpuş country. I describe him as the shepherd who did the music conservatory. He inherited his singing voice from his mother. They sing a very archaic double inflexion guttural trick. He would say you can only achieve it if you've actually grown up learning this from your mother. I felt that I could call him up and ask him if he'd be interested in being a joint creative artistic director together with Shaun Davey.

He readily agreed. Grigore is very much what you could call a link man to this ancient lamentation singing. His songs are about loneliness and pain, and one of his mantras – I don't know if I can say that – is that traditional music has never been fully recognised for its huge therapeutic role, played over countless generations. Especially in the 20th century, it has become mish-mashed with music of divertissement or entertainment. But at its roots the music is connected to the community in a therapeutic or even ritualistic way.

He was the person that told me it was shepherds who first played on a pipe and they didn't play to people, they played to their sheep. They play the music to the sheep to soothe the sheep and keep them near on the dark nights. They play on the pipes to the sheep so they give better milk. You go to Maramureş today and you can still spend time with shepherds who are playing on the pipes to their sheep while the other shepherds milk them. It's purely functional.

Can you still hear the same songs being sung in the Lăpuş country?

Absolutely, and this is what we did in the second *Drumul Lung*. In 2008 I had visited the founder of the Willie Clancy Summer School in Ireland. His name was Muiris O'Rócháin. He died earlier this year. Myself and my wife, we went and visited him and he told us how for 40 years they had really been part of this regeneration of interest in Irish traditional music and how, when they had their first summer school in 1973, there was a handful of pipers left in Ireland. Now there are hundreds. There are even Irish pipers in other countries of the world. It has grown to the point where there are now over 1000 students who come to Miltown Malbay village for a week every summer, the first week in July. There's no written music. People are divided into their different classes of ten or twenty people. You can be in a beginner, medium, advanced or master class. In a master class you could find yourself sitting in the room with one of the greats of Irish traditional music, who gives his time freely for the week to teach other people the songs. It's a mixture of storytelling and songs and it gives the human touch behind the music.

I found this a fascinating model, something we had to bring into the project somehow, and I started to talk to Grigore. He liked the idea very much and to cut a long story short, if I could arrange it, we would go together to Ireland to spend a week at the school, for him to meet them, to see what was going on there. We would then bring the lessons back and try to incorporate them in the second edition of the Long Road.

Those things more or less happened. We went; we had a great trip to Ireland, a complete eye-opener for Grigore. He discovered that here on the other end of the earth there's another group of people who sing the same way he does, that sing these lamentations. In every traditional music scene there's music for lamentation, there's music for weddings, there's music for lullabies; these are the three main categories. You can find them in Romania and you find them in Ireland. It wasn't all about the sad songs, but I think in the sad songs you can understand a lot more about a country.

On the night of Saint Maria Grigore delivered a concert which was called Where the Day meets the Night. The concert was absolutely stunning, this time from the wooden church on the top of the hill in the middle of Stoiceni, the village where he was born. 400 or 500 people had gathered in the cemetery around the tiny church on the hill. Grigore sang from beside the church. It was an hour and a half and was transmitted live on Radio Romania on the Sunday evening. They said up to a million people were listening. As the sun went down there was this amazing concert of haunting music, which thankfully exists as a very good recording now. At the moment of silence you could hear the crickets, like a natural hum, and a full moon came up. It was really a very special moment. Quite a place to be.

The days after that Sunday night Grigore led people on a guided tour. Anybody that wanted could come on a tour with him to visit those people who he personally knew from his years as a music teacher and his years growing up in the Lăpuş country. He basically did a series of walks, nature walks, visiting the old shepherds, visiting the people, visiting the singers, visiting the households. If you want to discover these traditions you have to get off the beaten track, you have to go and start searching. The feedback from the musicians afterwards... they'd never believed that anything like this existed. One of the Irish musicians said this was the closest thing to time travel he'd ever seen. It has made them re-evaluate their role as traditional musicians.

Would you see non-musicians coming to future events?

Yes, I see ethnographers, musicologists, people who are interested in tradition coming, but there is a very delicate balance here because those kinds of people are not interested in tourism. They're interested in seeing places that have not been touched. We're really talking about a very delicate balance. That would be the challenge. I have ideas but I want to be very careful in taking them forward. I do believe you should have a big opening event and a big closing event and then something in between that should be as personal, individual and as uncommercial as possible.

Going back to the festival, what's the aim of it all?

There are some things about Romania that are truly unique, things still living here that we don't have anywhere else in Europe. They're probably not going to be here for much longer if we don't take care of them. On that list I would name the virgin forests, a habitat for people but also especially the large carnivores. There's a beautiful eco-system, if I can use that word, that exists in major parts of the country, examples of an incredible harmony between man and nature. There are wilderness areas where nature still exists, as you would have found it in other parts of Europe long ago. There is also man as a kind of timekeeper, a *ceasornicar,* who, in following this natural clock of the passing of the seasons, has carved his life and his livelihood and his community in harmony with this nature. Here you can still see people living their lives this way.

The more I've got into that the more I'm impressed by how complicated it is, how deep it goes, how interconnected all these things in the village life are – how village life as it is in Romania has a hugely complex set of rules and customs and ways of doing things that in our consumer world, in our urban world, we don't have any more. I suppose when I started out I thought it was a music mission, let's say, to start something where young people especially would be able to access a type of music other than what they're exposed to in the regular MTV, nightclub scene. Those things have their place but there's an awful lot of baggage that goes with them. People need a holiday from that. The more I got into it the more I realised that there was a lot more to this than just music.

The village person is a creative person in his moments of work. There's an artistic approach that village life has, a very sensitive approach to work and the way they do things. It's almost like a spell, where everybody plays their part in weaving the spell and if everybody plays their part then the spell is good. There's a word in Romanian called *har*, which means grace, and there is a kind of *har* about the village life that the villager can have. You can see this when you visit somebody's house as I did this year. He was a man who was in his late eighties and living in a very isolated place with his wife. You could see that their homestead was a reflection of who they are. A good person has a good farm, maybe not such a good person doesn't have such a good looking farm… it all comes through in your creation.

A Romanian said to me, 'I'm embarrassed that we aren't doing what you seem to be doing for Romania.'

I said, 'Well, it's a bit like when you have your grandfather and he's still alive; even if he's a sick old man or whatever. If he's still alive, he's your grandfather and he's there with you. Your living peasants' tradition is grandfather. In our tradition, in the Western world, our grandfather has died. We don't have him anymore. We don't have the stories, we don't have his presence, and we don't have his grace to charge our lives anymore.'

Peter Hurley

Bucharest

'I know what he feels like. I see that myself, continually trying to machete your way through work to try to get to the tree that you know needs to be hugged.'

It's a huge story, this country. It never ceases to amaze me. The people that are here. Maybe I was too young when I left Ireland; that could be it as well. As you go through life, you just discover more and more but I do find Romania continuously revealing itself. The longer I stay here the more I realise how little I know. It's almost impossible not to meet somebody really interesting at every turn – especially if you take the train to Sighetu Marmaţiei in Maramureş – and that can take you into all sorts of different directions. And has done.

Friends? It's hard for me to say, you know. I have a huge respect for a lot of people and I think that out of the mutual respect we have, we have a friendship. Certainly I asked those people to help me in things that only a friend would do, and they've helped. Can I explain it that way? When I first came here I probably did spend a lot of time in bars and pubs and I suppose I made a lot of friends. But then that's not so difficult to do in the pub scene, especially when there are two pubs in town and 20 ex-pats and we were three Irish guys. We were already a walking party, three single Irish guys in Bucharest.

Do people see you as Romanian in any way now?

I don't see myself as a Romanian. Ah no, not at all. The more I'm here, the more I realise how big the difference is. I feel very much at home, I feel very comfortable with the people. I feel that somehow I'm sharing in the same kind of drama of what it means to be living here – it is a drama to be living in Romania to some extent. It is difficult to get through the day. I walked up here today and it's like an obstacle course trying to negotiate the pavements. This can really get on top of you at some point. Between the dirt, the parked cars, the holes – you really wonder how it all sticks together sometimes and it really is a challenge. And then I say, I'm really lucky. I am really lucky…

We built our business on Romanians, on young Romanians, who were fresh out of college, fresh people who wanted to grow. We had much more loyalty, dedication, hard work, creativity, communication and honest-to-goodness results than you could ever have in Ireland. I like this positive, youthful energy that the young people still have. I know you can get people going here, they like to do things. Yes, hardworking if they're behind it. If they're not behind it, forget it. I think they'll dig the same hole and fill it in so long as they're getting paid to do it. They're peace-loving, Christian, communicative people. Many of them are really straight, honest to themselves, not polluted in some ways.

I've managed to get through some sticky bureaucratic mix-ups or difficult situations with benevolence from the bureaucrat with whom I'm involved. I've been in situations where I could have been burned if somebody really wanted to stick with the book. They probably were able to make a judgement call that everything was okay. I never got really caught badly as a result of that; I've always had things signed off when I needed them.

Have you been affected by the şpagă?

I've been here almost 18 years and I've never paid *şpagă* for anything. For 15 years we built a company from zero. One of the companies in 2009, when I left advertising, had 160 employees full time, with five offices around the country, almost €20 million turnover. That was all done straight, that was straight business. Now most of it was with private companies, not with the state, but we did a lot of European projects and I know in all those European projects no *șpagă* went on. It was straight, everything was really clear. So I know it can be done, or I believe it can be done.

I don't know what's going to happen next. There was definitely this generation – my wife's part of that generation – now maybe in their thirties, that were 15 when the Revolution came. They had enough of an upbringing in a place where there was no television, where there was a library in every house, where there were lots of books, where there was a kind of a naivety. That generation have a huge role to play as Romania moves forward. I don't think it's ever going to be an easy country to run. I wouldn't like to be the government of Romania. Things are so complicated for them. They've made it complicated for themselves. It just seems to be so difficult to get anything to move sometimes.

You have to adapt and you can be in tears and you can be laughing at the things you see. I find the elderly poor very disturbing. How can this be going on? I'm sure I only see the tip of the iceberg when it comes to poverty here and I don't know what to do about that. I don't know what Romania can do about it. I don't know how easy it is to solve some of these issues.

In 2004 and 2005 I travelled around the country to 80 different projects that had used European Union funds, selected ten of them and made a movie about each. That was one of those other watershed moments for me in Romania. It gave me an opportunity to travel, to meet people, to really get into their stories and to understand how they got to be doing this thing with European money. That was a lift for me, one of the greatest lifts I've had in this country, because it really refreshed me. I had an experience this summer. I was in Maramureș in the county council. The story came up about these ten films. I told the lady working in the department of foreign investment that this was a project I'd been involved in.

She said, 'Wow, you know the people in those films became models for me. I can tell you that as a result of understanding these people existed I went and did a refurbishment of a historical landmark in Baia Mare, with a Norwegian grant. I wanted to do that, even though it was going to create a lot of personal drama and hassle in my life, to push this project through. I wanted to join that club of people who are doing that.'

To some extent I had probably forgotten the reasons why I came in 1994. Then bang, there I was, face to face with that Romania, those people that had the hope of the country in their hands. It really boosted me and became one of the things that pushed me towards thinking that I should do The Long Road. I knew I was part of a group then. I felt there are people who feel this way. We know that there are. I do think it's important for people to understand that it's okay to do those things and when you do, when you take responsibility, other good things happen. This is probably a major message to try and somehow propagate. It's not a message from outside, it's their message.

You talked about har *or grace earlier. Do you feel that spirituality has a particular importance here?*

It's hard to generalise of course and it's hard to put a quantity on something like spirituality but the short answer would be yes, yes I do. More so in rural areas and more so in the older people. When we were starting the business I had a much closer relationship with a lot of the young people and it was surprising how many of them were keeping the Lenten fast. 20-year-olds in a major European capital and they're keeping the Lenten fast, most of them, and this was something very normal. And when we came back to work after Easter, to hear them all greeting each other, and me, with their *Hristos a înviat!* and this on the telephone for 40 days afterwards – to anybody. The first time you contact somebody after Easter, your first words to them are *Hristos a înviat!*

Christ has risen.

Christ has risen. And they respond, 'Indeed he has risen'. And Orthodoxy is a great mystery as well. It's almost a dirty word in Ireland to mention religious belief because the church has taken such a hammering over the last few years. The church had a very strong controlling influence in Ireland and this management, almost clerical management of the country, you could have said, creates a distrust at some point. It's very far removed from the messages of Christ, it's kind of the opposite message actually. You have the same problems in Romania. There's a structure and any structure tends to have inefficiencies, dare I say it even corruption, going on in there.

If you can separate out the discussion about the institutions and focus on the purely spiritual side of it, there is a deep spirituality here and I do think it has a very close connection to Orthodoxy. Monasticism is a really interesting area which has a role in this modern day. It has a very important role as we get more and more modern. Orthodoxy does too and I don't think it gets the kind of respect that it should.

One Year Later in October 2012

[Peter is now Head of Promotions for the Support Unit for the National Rural Development Network].

You find this living rural civilisation everywhere to a greater or lesser extent. More in the mountains. If you were to make a map it's the Carpathians mountain chain that was not collectivised and this is 40 per cent of the country. Four million people live in the mountain areas of Romania and so this alone is a country almost. There's a great man, Professor Radu Rey, who is the grandfather of this whole movement to have the mountain area here recognised as a real civilisation, to have a big investment plan to promote it and to give it value. For 20 years they haven't really had any investment – not since the first 30 years of the 20th century when Romania was a great cooperative producer. Then there was a lot of investment in agriculture but in this last 70 years this mountain area hasn't received any.

You have very old farming methods going on there. I was in Vatra Dornei two weeks ago with Professor Radu Rey and he showed me some of the pasture lands, where the cows are up the hill, so it's easier for the farmers to shovel the waste downhill, and natural alkali produced by the fertiliser over hundreds of years has created a certain system. If it's not tended by the same methods, in eight years it goes. The wildflowers there create a polifloral diet for the animals that then feed off it, leading to this wonderfully natural import into a very beautiful food chain. The Carpathian mountain area creates food in an artisan production way; that's really what's going on up there. Despite the best efforts of our institutions, it's surviving. Surviving is the word, I think. I don't know how much longer it's going to survive.

This represents a huge food value-added opportunity for the economy. People are becoming more and more sensitive to what they eat, and how they eat, and where it comes from. The idea of being able to eat food that comes from an unspoiled food chain in the Carpathian mountains, produced by food artisans who represent an unbroken chain of creators of natural products for thousands of years, surely there's a story in there. You can create many brands around that. Those brands can then become gateways to tourism, and tourism can become a gateway for the villagers living there to re-evaluate the culture they live in.

You know the people that destroy the wooden houses in Maramureş County are the Maramureşan. It's not people coming in and buying up houses at ridiculous prices. No, no, it's houses being flogged, taken away. They don't want it anymore; it's old. 'We had enough of that'; I understand where they're coming from, when I see really old pictures when these houses were the norm. It was really close on poverty in some ways. I'm sure it was very difficult at the time so maybe there's not a lot of love lost between the owner and his wooden house, but maybe that will come back in a generation, that appreciation. But it can only be done with a rural economy that has found its niche.

The traditional life here – if it does survive, it's going to be despite the efforts of the public institutions, which are heading in the other direction. Two weeks ago I went to Constanţa County, to a village harvest festival. I wasn't in an official capacity – just wanted to hang out there for the day. After that I wrote a letter to the lady responsible for that department in the Ministry of Tourism, to share my observations. In this particular case all of the music in this village festival was pre-recorded on a CD. You had fake professional artists lip-syncing traditional music. The only reason they are doing it is because somebody's filming it for a cheap television station. They're going to get on television, get more business for weddings and funerals or whatever they do. It's like a promotion for them; it's not real.

Searching through the place, at the other end of the field, I found an authentic brass band fanfare, eight or nine piece, with dancers from Moldova – the only true musicians who'd come. I had my own recorder with me and I had a great little interview with the mayor from this village which I then transcribed into the letter. They'd been the only people who could really play and when they got onto the stage there were no microphones for them. They needed about ten microphones to hook up but there were only two. The tragedy was that all the pre-recorded music sounded much better than the authentic.

This is happening all the time. This was an event that was supported with Ministry of Tourism money. Hence my letter. Here is a classic example of how the lunatics have taken over the asylum. The lunatics aren't in the Ministry of Tourism, the lunatics are in the town halls. There is this crazy kitsch industry that somehow has taken over tradition, has hijacked it and is promoting it. The sad thing is that most Romanians are actually starting to believe that this is their traditional music. Romania is doing nothing short of committing cultural suicide and the institutions of the state are assisting. It wouldn't be the first country to do it.

You talked about being a voice in the wilderness. Do you feel you're on your own?

I don't think I'm alone, but that's the interesting thing now… hard to know. It's hard to know. Yes, there are people that feel the same way. I don't know how many there are and they don't seem to operate together. But it's bad what's happening in the villages. The information I get, the things that I see, what the people from the villages tell me, the cultural people…

There is a cultural death going on?

Yes. Unfortunately everything in Romania at the top level is all about political survival and it always has been, since I got here anyway. Political survival, that's what's dictating six months, six days, six hours, today. I've been in meetings with the Secretary of State for Agriculture who says, 'I want you to think about the village.' So they want to, but it's hard for them to get to it. I know what he feels like. I see that myself, continually trying to machete your way through work to try to get to the tree that you know needs to be hugged.

December 2013

On 26th November 2012, Peter Hurley started a journey of 650 kilometres, on foot, having as his only source of survival the kindness and hospitality of the people he would meet. He walked covering 30 kilometres each day and arrived at the National Museum of the Peasant 26 days later.

He describes this in his book, The Way of the Crosses[4]*, a journey of initiation to the Romanian spirit through the eyes of an Irishman. Starting from the belief that Romania is the last 'Western' European country that still keeps alive an unadulterated authentic rural civilisation, as much as it can, he tries to encourage the Romanians to discover this priceless treasure and assume the responsibility for taking care of it.*

To quote Peter: 'Ireland is an ancient country, but we live with the remnants of our peasant civilization, through a cultural revival. In Romania, the same traditions can be still found but in their living form, with flesh and blood, people that have directly inherited their peasant knowledge from previous generations. This is the defining aspect of Romania's positioning in Europe.'

---

[4] Peter Hurley, *The Way of the Crosses*, (Kindle Edition).

Count Tibor Kalnoky

Miklosvar

'When we came back people didn't really know how to deal any more with this part of society which had been annihilated.'

The Iron Guard, the Romanian fascists, knocked on his door here on Christmas Eve of 1938 and took him straight to the border. My grandfather was anti-fascist, and anti-communist of course. We are an old aristocratic family. He was basically thrown out of the country by the fascists. I was born in Munich and raised in France. Then I rediscovered the roots of the family. Because I grew up so restless, staying in different countries, four or five years then always moving again, perhaps that's a reason why I now try to settle where we came from originally.

I came back first when it was under Ceauşescu, to have a look at the old stones, the family heritage. We came every year until the Revolution and then I decided to direct my life so that I could live here. I was sent by a large company to Bucharest to build up a pharmaceutical subsidiary. In 2001 I left that company and settled here in Transylvania, in the old property of the family.

Today we are making a living practically exclusively through the guest houses. There are two manor houses but I am not a rich man. I did not have the financial background to start to renovate large houses, so we started with smaller ones in the village, to do them in a traditional way and rent them out to guests, and to take care of the guests with guides. Now we also do horse treks. Basically it's a tourism company that allows foreigners to experience the true face of rural Romania. The clients come mainly from the English speaking world. In the globalised world of today they look for a place which has its own identity and where they know they're in an authentic place.

Heritage? It has values that have been passed down from generation to generation. It's like antiques; they have survived so long it means they have a certain value, and I want to continue to save these values for the future. But if we speak of the place where we are, perhaps more important than the family background, is the lifestyle the local population still has. This is also what attracts the guests, much more than anything else – this authentic, pristine way of life, of subsistence agriculture – people making a living from their own hands. This is also something that in the rest of Europe is barely to be found, and it means also that the landscape has remained as in medieval times. You have these hills with pastures, meadows, forests; there is no fence, there's no wall, there are no roads – perhaps it's also something like a travel in time for our guests, back 100 or 200 years.

How does that square with the modernisation of agriculture in the country – is there a clash there?

There certainly is a clash. But we are not in the lowlands, we are not in countryside that is suitable for industrial agriculture, where you can just go through with huge machines and do thousands of hectares in one go. Here we have hills that can get rather steep; forests also. It is a landscape which is suitable for subsistence agriculture. If you have a look at the structure of the villages, you have the village itself; then around the villages, the closest are the arable fields, which are more labour intensive; then come the meadows, which need to be worked on twice a year; then the pastures and the forest, the least work-intensive, further away. This creates a landscape which is not wilderness, it's man-made, but it is very appealing to the human soul. It has something soothing, where you relax, where you can get back to yourself. This is really what makes the charm – it's the balance, it's the harmony between man and nature.

We also try to offer work to the villagers. The problem up to now was they had to leave their subsistence farm alone if they got a job. Until 2008, until the recession, you could see more and more farms being abandoned because people had to go the city to get a job. But as the recession came there were fewer of them. Also they became aware that if they live in the town they have to pay for absolutely everything – the rent, the gas, the electricity, the water, the eggs – and the salary of a hard day's work does not necessarily cover much more than their needs. They realised that in the village it wasn't so bad after all – true they don't have so much cash, but they can create for themselves everything they need. We also had this in mind from the very beginning, so people who work with us do that on a part-time basis. The kitchen staff, for example, work for one day and the next day they're off, so they can also take care of their farm.

You're trying to maintain this ancient rural agriculture by supporting it in a small way.

Exactly, and these villages are in danger of depopulation. There's one thing that made it possible to survive up till now. If you look back at how the West started with industrialisation, they needed labour for the factories in England and France, so they started taxing the land. If land is taxed you must actually generate income so you can pay. That is not possible in small scale farming as you have it here. In the West these small farms had to sell their land and the people left the villages and moved into the cities where they started to work in the factories. This never happened here – land is not taxed here – well, it is taxed, but ridiculously low. If some politician in Romania would have the idea of increasing the tax on land then the whole social structure of this country would be changed. Up to now no one has dared to do so but there is the idea of starting to tax land – and this would mean that village life will collapse or dramatically change.

What sort of reaction have you had from those who perhaps knew your family?

I came back in '97 – so it's 60 years, two good generations, and don't forget that we went through communism, which means that all the families like ours were bad-mouthed, their identity totally distorted. When we came back people didn't really know how to deal any more with this part of society which had been annihilated. On the one side people here were proud and happy; they felt that it's part of their identity that they got back. I certainly found my identity here. At the same time they had these reflexes, of what was told them by the communists, that the titled families were just holding slaves.

They didn't understand why someone like me, who has been everywhere in the West, would choose to come to such a place – not just to Romania, but to the last little dirty rural village of Romania. They started to say, what does he look for? There was some jealousy and misunderstanding. Does he have a hidden agenda? Most of the people here wanted to get out to the West and this man came back – what for? For ruins, because the houses that we took over – also the houses that we restored in the village – were totally, totally wrecked. Slowly I tried to make people understand that I came back, basically, because of our place here. There's not more to it really.

They started to understand and then they noticed that through our guests people were coming to these villages, people who perhaps even had some influence in the West and certainly contributed to making the image of Romania abroad a bit better. I will always be some sort of foreign body within this post-communist-Hungarian-Romanian society but I feel that I'm very well accepted now and there is actual pride.

I always kept a very polite distance from administration, from officials. I didn't really need them because I just did my own thing and that went rather well. I knew that cooperation would be very difficult and in Romania it's easy to become rather cynical when you speak of officials and the whole political and administrative system. It's true that I have diplomatic immunity which made them take a bit more care of how they were dealing with me. I'm sure that helped. Now they see the benefits that this little venture has for the whole region. And public opinion in Romania, if they know anything about me, I think it is in a positive way. It could be much worse. Sometimes we heard in the last ten years that we're against progress and things like that, which is not the case.

By promoting tradition, do you mean?

Exactly. It's difficult for them to understand renovating a house with old techniques when you have polystyrene and stainless steel and concrete, materials which are much better quality, according to their point of view. It's easy to be misunderstood, in what I'm doing and with my background, as someone who is nostalgic for the past and not at all motivated by the future. Now I think people understand. It's also become a trend, to take care of the environment. Globally, mankind has become aware that something has to be done.

What about the government approach to tourism?

The problem with the ministry is they can only think en masse. The brand for Romanian tourism – Explore the Carpathian

Gardens – was much more honest than anything else that had been done till then, like Dracula Park and planting palm trees on the Black Sea, which were either lies or just aiming at mass consumers and low-level tourism. Now at least, with this brand, I think they got closer to the real values of Romania seen by a foreigner. The uniqueness of Romania lies in its landscape and its rural life. I think they went in the right direction for the first time in 20 years.

People became aware that to open a *pension* can be profitable, can be worthwhile. There was great support for these local *pension,* and one reason why so many opened, there was European money for it. The downside of that was that it was mostly given to those who built new places, mostly horrid. The way they built them, the way they decorated them is certainly not in keeping with the local.

No harmony at all.

Yes, they wanted to be flashy, they wanted to be modern in order to attract local tourists. Our type of guests, foreigners, would never go to such a place. They would actually rather have much less comfort but be in a place that is more authentic than go to such a flashy place in the middle of a charming village. In this case European money did not really help to preserve the aspect of the villages.

What we're doing grew out of our family venture. It's certainly there to make money but it was not an investment, with a budget and a calculated return on investment, and it will never be. This generates money that we use to restore the manor and further houses. It's a constant reinvestment. In this whole story it's not the money which is the most important thing – there is the aspect of contributing to the upkeep of the village, of offering jobs, of using the produce of the village.

Are there particular challenges being Hungarian, coming from Covasna, this county in the middle of Romania?

Hungarians certainly have a different mentality to Romanians. I'm a Hungarian myself although my mother and grandmothers have all been German for the last generations. I was not raised here and didn't even speak the language. Hungarians are more serious people; by serious, I mean also that they might be a bit more introverted, more difficult to get along with, sometimes more prone to depression even. They are more reflective, meaning also that if you can count on them, you can really count on them. We are in the middle of Romania and the influences have been very strong for many generations and all this is now becoming more and more mixed up.

Actually we're Székely. The Széklers have always been renowned as the most noble Hungarians because they were a warrior people, who were all personally free. They didn't have to pay taxes and they had their own property, even in medieval times. I would say the Széklers are a very proud people, with a strong personal and communal identity – if they get something into their head they will try everything to go through with it and do it. But they are bad in working together, in doing something as a community. It is very difficult to get teams together; at least that's how I felt in the last 15 years. Yet they put their soul into what they're doing, they're not at all superficial. They do not seek the easiest way. I suppose the reason for this is also that they have been challenged so often, being isolated out here in the Carpathians, and the only way to stay and to persist was through this character – to be a bit more stubborn.

So a very strong sense of identity?

Certainly.

Which makes ethnic Romanians very much outsiders in this part of the world.

That's true, that's true. Now let's not misunderstand things – they're certainly not xenophobic. On the contrary, one of the great features of Transylvania is that everyone is very hospitable and welcoming to foreigners – I'm sure you noticed that when you came here. There is a historical background to this because Transylvania was practically left alone by the Turks – all they had to do was to pay very little tax to the Turks and they left them to do more or less what they wanted.

They were detached from Hungary then and from the Habsburgs. Transylvania was a state and an entity of its own, and they decided as early as 1568 to guarantee religious freedom by law – they were the first in the world to do so. For the last 450 years there was no religious problem in Transylvania, meaning also that they welcomed other populations who were persecuted in other parts of Europe. Communities came and settled here. So you have this basic aspect of hospitality belonging to the whole of Transylvania.

Does the Romanian-Hungarian relationship here make everyone political?

If you speak about the big picture, everyone is political of course, but if it goes down to people's own lives, then they would just get on with it and with each other. As I said, the local Széklers are not xenophobic. They live until now in a very homogenous society where there are literally just Széklers around. There are no Romanians practically. However they are certainly aware they are living in the centre of Romania and someone will not be rejected because he's Romanian, so Széklers will have Romanian friends.

There is this great cultural difference of course, and they feel that they want to have their own freedom of identity. Here is a point where they are political, because they feel that this might be challenged and jeopardised from time to time, and you know very well that since Machiavelli it has become a political tool – if you have internal problems, use an external enemy to divert the attention from your internal problems. It's always very welcome for the Romanians to use the Hungarian problem as a political tool – for every election you will see rhetoric against Hungarians and so on, but after the elections this goes away and life comes back to normal. From a political point of view I think that it's getting better and better.

Are you trying to get Romanians to visit?

Yes, and they are now, and I'm very glad because in the first ten years very few Romanians came at all. Now there is a segment of Romanian society, especially in Bucharest, of intellectually active people who also have a certain amount of financial power, who start realising the value of rural Romania and places like these.

That's heartening presumably. But talking with some Romanian colleagues, I got the feeling they didn't know anything about this area, and some didn't appear to want to know.

I lived in Bucharest and for the weekend we brought up here people who were helping at home. They were afraid of coming because they had heard all these fairy tales that would circulate in Romanian society, about the bad Hungarians. They felt very insecure here, until they became aware that it was all just lies. The problem with Romanian communism was that it was a nationalistic communism. They did a lot to fight against the Hungarian identity. They tried very much to push it back and they used all sorts of propaganda against the Hungarians. That stuck with many people and it still sticks with many. If only Romanians from Bucharest and other parts of the country could come here to see, not just how beautiful this place is, but also how welcoming the people are.

Leslie Hawke

Bucharest

'I'd miss having a sense of mission. That's what I'd miss.'

I'm an American who worked in New York publishing for about 25 years. In 2000, at the age of 48, I decided to go into the Peace Corps, the US organisation that sends American volunteers to less developed countries for two-year stints. I wanted to go to Ecuador but they sent me to Romania.

I was with the Peace Corps for three and a half years. I was working for an NGO in Bacau and I got very interested in all the little kids who were on the street begging, and obviously not attending school. I applied for a USAID grant to help them get into, or back into, school. In 2003 when I left the Peace Corps, I started an NGO – *Asociaţia OvidiuRo* – with an experienced Romanian teacher, Maria Gheorghiu.

In the beginning our challenge was to get USAID to fund a programme for Roma kids and to get the local authorities to take it seriously. To me the kids just looked like any other impoverished, downtrodden kids, but the locals considered them Gypsies and were convinced they begged because that was their culture and there really wasn't anything you could do about it. Even USAID wasn't keen to fund programmes for Roma. The Roma weren't on many people's radar screen until Romania joined the EU in 2007.

The local authorities were never against our helping Gypsies; they just thought it was a waste of time and money. But it wasn't their time or their money, it was US dollars. Today of course the situation has changed dramatically. Most local authorities recognise that this is an issue they ought to be addressing, although few have any strategy for doing so. And that's where we come in – helping the local communities get their impoverished children into early education programmes so they have a chance of succeeding in primary school. It's not a Roma programme per se, it's an anti-poverty programme.

I don't think the situation of the poorest people in this country is any better than it was when I arrived in 2000. It's worse in the sense that there are more people now living at the bottom of the socio-economic-education ladder.

People in the countryside can live for less because in many places it's still largely a barter economy, but some things you just have to purchase, and goods and services are a great deal more expensive than ten years ago. Half this country is rural, which is something that people in the cities forget when they think about progress. There's a huge chasm between the quality and style of life in the two places. The rural people are still living very much the way they lived 50 years ago. Many of them still don't have cars and most of their purchases are in the local market once a week. And the rural schools are not preparing the youth for 21st century jobs.

I feel especially good about being here when I talk to young people, people 30 and under; they seem to have a really different mind-set – except when it comes to politics. Most of them don't want anything to do with politics, and they often don't vote. There's this sense that politics doesn't have anything to do with their lives.

When it comes to their own individual lives, and prospects, there's a lot of optimism. They feel like they can change things there. A lot of college-educated young people think their life is going to be substantially better than their parents' lives have been, and that in ten or twenty years they're going to be better off than they are right now. They don't see government as having anything to do with their personal happiness. But it does you know. This whole issue of who's going to pay the pensions in 30, 40 years is a very serious demographic issue. Of course when you're 25 you don't think about that.

Something typically Romanian that I'm not too fond of is the sense of fatalism, the sense that fate will have its way and there's not a whole lot you can do to change it. I guess it's the *asta este* attitude – this is just the way it is. In America, we sort of have the opposite attitude, that we can do anything – which is not true either. I grew up in Texas. Romania and Texas are complete opposites in the sense that Texans have an inflated sense of Texas, and of themselves – they're so proud. They genuinely think Texas is the best place in the world to live. Romanians' feelings about their own country are just the opposite. It's a lack of cultural self-esteem, which well may be a Balkan thing, not just a Romanian thing.

There's still a general respect for the Orthodox Church but the church is not really integrated into the lives of most young adults. They may observe the customs, say, cross themselves when they see a church, but I don't think it influences their life choices very much. And I don't know anyone who doesn't think the church has gone overboard in building more and more churches, ignoring social problems.

What I find really strange is that Romanians are nicer to foreigners than they are to each other in a lot of social situations. I find they tend to have a rather old fashioned approach to social intercourse. People on the street rarely make eye contact, and never smile at strangers, but if a friend introduces you to one of these same people, all of a sudden they'll go far out of their way to be helpful to you. Much further than most Americans.

Their friends, their family, those are the people that count and in that context, they're very warm and generous. But the sense of civic duty is completely missing, and civil society is still largely absent. That's changing a bit with younger people. We get a lot of young people who want to volunteer, want to do good; they want to help people they don't necessarily know. I see that growing.

Today there are a lot of multi-national companies led by Romanians, and Corporate Social Responsibility or CSR is part of their company culture. We get great support from companies, or at least we did until the crisis continued for so long. The interesting thing is that we get very few individual donations from Romanians. We get them from foreigners and not just Americans. The Germans, Dutch, English – they contribute from their pockets, but I can count on two hands the number of Romanians who donate out of their own pocket. People constantly tell us how good it is what we're doing, how they support our mission, but it just doesn't occur to them to make a personal contribution.

One of the things a lot of us foreigners like about being in Romania is that it's never boring – partly because getting things done is not easy, but it is possible. So it makes the process more interesting. I meet so many people who like it here, who don't want to leave, people from different walks of life – ambassadors, corporate executives, do-gooders. I've heard it called 'Europe with an edge', which is apt.

By 2020 we want the government to be using our methods to get impoverished kids into early education programs. We give food coupons to families that live under the poverty line, if their kids attend pre-school from the age of three. They desperately need that educational foundation to succeed in the world today. When we first started we helped kids of any age. But the results were so much better with the children who started early – so that's all we do now.

I'm pretty optimistic about our chances of getting the government to use our methods. Western Europe's concern about the migration of unskilled workers and criminal elements is driving the process. It's going to force the government to show that they're doing something. And *OvidiuRo* has a track record. What we are doing really works at getting these children into the education system early. It's simple, it's not as expensive as most poverty programmes, and it's implemented by the local community.

Another thing that attracts Westerners to this place is that they have the power to contribute. It's not easy to work here but it's rewarding, it's much more rewarding. If I were doing this kind of work in the US I'd be taking somebody else's place. Here I – and Maria, without whom I wouldn't be here – both know that if we weren't doing this, nobody would be doing it. In a lot of ways our staff feel the same sense of purpose. We know what we're doing is important. If I left, I'd miss having a sense of mission. That's what I'd miss.

Andrew Begg

Bucharest

'The people I met and the things that I saw – it's just an unforgettable experience.'

This is my eighteenth year here. My first year was spent living in a little village called Sebeş, 15 kilometres from Făgăraş, between Braşov and Sibiu, in Transylvania. I dressed like a villager which they all thought was rather funny. I had a kind of a sheepskin jacket and leather boots, breeches, hat, things like that, and a dog I'd rescued. I went native for a while. They thought I was eccentric.

When I was 29 I left Australia for London and now I'm 50. I was working in the City in London, working in a rather obscure area of banking, trading derivatives. I didn't really want to do that anymore but didn't feel like I wanted to go back to Australia at that time. I had a friend here. I formed a company in England and our idea was that we'd buy antique furniture in Romania and sell it into British antique markets.

We'd hire a truck and go from village to village, park the truck and people would come and say, 'We've got a bench. Would you like to buy it?' or 'We've got a chest of drawers, do you want it?' Sometimes we'd find ourselves having to unearth these pieces of furniture from places like pigpens. It was all great fun. There were villages where there were probably more horses and carts than there were cars. There was one fixed telephone in the village where I lived and people would queue up to use it. You had to book a time.

The house we took over was interesting. The previous occupant had died and it hadn't been opened since several years earlier. He had been a kind of a wizard in the village and pregnant women came to him to predict the gender of their unborn child, which he did with unerring accuracy apparently. The first thing we did was take down all the crucifixes – the walls were covered with them. My friend, on at least two occasions, had the most horrifying nightmares, as if there were a kind of a presence in the house. I never saw anything.

I didn't know any Romanian at the time. As you know many Romanians speak English quite well so I got by. They were open. They saw I was a fish out of water and they helped me. I was invited over to people's houses and found it easy to make friends. It was a very happy time. We'd travel around the countryside in a beaten up old Dacia, and the people I met and the things that I saw – it's just an unforgettable experience. I met a girl who was visiting her grandparents who lived in the village. We fell in love and about a year later got married. We were married for nearly ten years and though divorced are still in touch and get on well.

And you're in Bucharest now, and not in the same business?

Yes, we discovered that an antique in England isn't an antique unless it's 300 years old. This furniture was 100 years old, or less, so that didn't last very long. I came here and after resurrecting my banking career began an English language magazine, *Vivid*. The magazine, although on hold at the moment, tries to make sense of Romania. The motive behind starting it is that I always thought Romania is rather poorly explained, and what is known doesn't put the country in a positive light. So I set out with the intention of addressing that. In the early days I would see very few portrayals in the international media, but what did appear would invariably involve negative stories of abandoned children, or street dogs, or neglect and poverty. There is neglect and poverty here, I'm not suggesting for a moment that there isn't, but the magazine tried to promote the positive aspects of the country. That's not to say that it wasn't critical, but the criticism tried to be positive. Over time the magazine attracted some good writers who mostly lived here. It was a happy blend of Romanian writers and local ex-pat writers who'd been here long enough to know the territory. They were generally owners of their own companies so they couldn't be fired for not toeing the multinational line in their article. It had a good reputation and it had integrity.

I always liked to stand up for minorities. I remember a particular episode when *Playboy Romania* ran an article and the title of it was 'How to Beat up Your Wife without Leaving any Bruises.' I thought if I say nothing about this it's silently condoning this silly article. I researched the incidence of domestic abuse here, the highest in this part of the world, and wrote quite a strong article opposing it. After a while I got a call from our largest advertiser who'd recently signed a contract worth $20,000 with my magazine. She said, 'You shouldn't have brought this up, you shouldn't be meddling in our local politics or our local life. If you hadn't said anything no one would have noticed, the foreigners wouldn't have noticed and it would have all blown over and everything would have been fine. So we're going to cancel our contract.' I just couldn't believe it. She was a woman, she was mid-thirties, I'm sure she'd been around a bit. I went to plead my case with the company, sat around a circular table, with her and about four or five other women, and they were all of the same opinion.

I went over her head, to her bosses who were foreigners and their attitude was, 'Yes, we understand the situation, we believe you, we're behind you but we are trying to give her decision-making responsibility. So I'm sorry, we just have to go with what she says, we want to nurture her.'

Apart from losing income, did you have any problems taking this kind of stand?

I had a series of nasty letters at one stage, targeting me and also mentioning people writing for the magazine. The letters became increasingly more threatening, over a period of about three months, to the point where the penultimate one said 'Don't publish any more!' But I did and the next one said, 'You did what we didn't want you to do. Your time is up. Prepare to meet your maker!'

At that point I got scared and showed some security people at the British Embassy – at that time there was no Australian government representative here. The British Embassy's attitude was it's probably someone you inadvertently wronged in the magazine, or someone who's been fired from a job, fired from a multinational and has a chip on his shoulder about foreigners, something like that. I think the Romanian secret police just covered me for a while and nothing happened.

But I think people largely liked *Vivid* and the mix of writers. There were Romanians who'd been abroad and had a taste of what it was like to live in another country; also ex-pats and foreigners whose first language was English. Quite often I'd be stopped in the street or called up, or emailed, people saying that was a really nice article, we liked that or we didn't like this, or you should have said this. Generally speaking the response was pretty good and it was well liked by Romanians, I think because they realised we didn't have any kind of hidden agenda. They knew I was as independent as you could possibly be here. All in all it was a magazine that managed to maintain its integrity over a decade and I think it still has a pretty good reputation, which is what encourages me to get it going again. I talk about it a lot – it's about time I did something!

Something I am proud of is that after reading *Eternal Treblinka* by Charles Patterson, a Holocaust scholar – a study of how the Nazis focused on early mechanisation in slaughterhouses to industrialise the killing of Jews – I wanted to know more, so I started reading. Then I started reading about it in a Romanian context. I researched and researched. After a while I realised it was an issue that was bigger than *Vivid* and deserved a wider audience. Not only a readership but an audience. I went to PRO TV, and ended up making *The Forgotten Holocaust* in 2005.

I found that the Holocaust was not discussed, not taught in schools. I know people who went to schools in the area near where atrocities and pogroms occurred. They still deny that anything like that ever happened. They look at themselves and think we Romanians are a god-fearing and peace-loving people and we would never do something like that. After consistent government-level denial that a Holocaust took place here during the Second World War, the government bowed to pressure and financed something called the Wiesel Commission, chaired by Elie Wiesel, which has since found that a Holocaust did indeed occur here. So the historical record has been set straight.

I was in a school recently and saw some Holocaust teaching on the walls so I'm sure it is taught now. I know the documentary I made was distributed among schools and I hope it's being shown. It's quite a succinct version of what happened here. There are three or four other documentaries as well which have focused on different aspects of the Romanian Holocaust. It's no longer hidden away.

Have I found any kind of prejudice? No, I haven't to be honest. I always feel really accepted. If my girlfriend has to go to a doctor or to a hospital, or if she is trying on a dress, she always says, 'Can you come with me because people are much more polite if you're there?' For some reason, and I've never really understood why, foreigners are well treated here, probably because we're so few and far between, probably because we are still something of a novelty.

Or perhaps because they see a certain civility in us that they don't see amongst themselves. I don't really like thinking that but that's the only thing I can come up with.

One could translate that into an inferiority complex. Do you feel that's too strong?

It's a bit strong, yes, but Romanians are always polite to me. They speak in an abrupt manner with each other. I see it with the children as well that I teach. You begin at a young age and it goes on throughout life. It may just be a Latin thing, or maybe a communist legacy. It is here, yes, and I've just accepted it. If we weren't Anglo-Saxon, maybe we wouldn't even notice.

I feel safe here. That's an aspect that's easily overlooked. There are areas in Bucharest which you wouldn't want to walk around at night, but generally speaking it's safe. I've heard of very few instances where people have had any kind of issues; I'm talking about ex-pats now. A couple of female friends of mine said they've been a little bit harassed from time to time, but that's over the space of almost 20 years. In that time I would have seen and perhaps experienced a lot worse in Sydney, Melbourne or London. They might be scallywags but Romanians are not aggressive. There is a level of violence in most cities that doesn't exist here, which I appreciate.

I don't see people rolling around drunk either, like you certainly do in Australia and in England too. You don't see drunken gangs walking around at night, you don't see women drinking like you do in the West, there isn't the pub culture. You don't see people getting terribly drunk at parties but I do see women sometimes with awful black eyes, so I can't believe that domestic violence is something that doesn't go on here. I can't believe either that alcohol isn't a leading factor in that. But I don't see it talked about.

I'm interested in animal rights and have visited the Mayor of

Bucharest and talked about the street dog situation, trying to get him into the idea of spaying dogs and neutering them, rather than killing them. I'm convinced that killing them doesn't work. It might have some temporary effect, but in time the numbers are always back to the pre-kill levels. The street dogs suffer terribly. It began as a small issue 20 years ago and now it's a big problem. The response was 'Yes, we'll do something about it,' but it was probably passed on down the line and that was that. It requires a long-term solution. Spaying and neutering dogs will not fix the solution overnight, but killing them will never work.

What about politics generally?

I would really like Romania to have a politician who is selfless, has a vision for the future and is a real leader. I'm talking about somebody like a Kennedy or a Clinton perhaps, someone who made a great difference for the country. Romania deserves someone like that. It must be galling for Romanians to see business and politics so enmeshed, so in bed with each other, businessmen milking the public purse the way they do. It frustrates and confuses me. You just feel helpless. I think Romanians can feel betrayed. There was a great sense of hope in the early 1990s because it was chaotic and the dust had not settled. Government after government since then has just failed the people.

How about you? Has living in Romania changed you at all?

I'm not as trusting a person as I was. Romanians looking for a sucker probably found one in me. I remember finding a place to rent, very early on. A small apartment with a window that I thought opened on to a view. I couldn't speak Romanian and it was dark. I paid three month's rent and said, 'I'll take it.' When morning came I found the window opened on to a brick wall. I could almost stick my arm out of the window and touch it. I went back to find the guy who rented me the place and said, 'I'm terribly sorry, I think I've made a mistake with this, perhaps I could give you a few days or a week's rent and you give me the rest of my money back.'

'Are you kidding me?' he said, 'You've already paid three months' rent and I'm not going to give you three months' rent back.' Even today I'll park my car and I'll give 50 RON and they'll say, 'I've just got to go and find some change.' By the time 20 minutes has lapsed I think why do I fall for this? That's what I mean by calling Romanians scallywags. I'd far prefer that to be the extent of their criminality, because I'm sure other people are far worse. It's a criminality I can live with. I think we all can. I'm on my guard much more. It's probably a good thing not to be innocent and as trusting of complete strangers as one was in the beginning. At the age of 29.

You hear people don't want to begin lawsuits because it's fairly common knowledge that judges can be got at. That's really something at the very cornerstone of society. If a judge can influence the outcome of the case, then what hope is there? Integrity is important and it seems to be something that is lacking. In the first 15 years of the post-Revolution experience Romanians grabbed at everything Western without really questioning whether they really needed it or wanted it. Now they are starting to be a little bit more discerning. There are characteristics, human qualities that people are starting to look for again, so that's something that makes me stay here. I do criticise Romania but the fact is I want it to be a better place and that's one of the reasons I stay.

Do you see your long-term future here?

I feel like I have got two homes but the longer I stay here the more I'm feeling this is home. But for some reason I don't feel I want to accept that yet. I don't feel I could ever be Romanian. Australia now is a different country; it's a great place to grow up in, and it's probably a great place to retire to, but between the age of about 20 and say 70… the wheel is turning, I can feel myself being attracted to it, but I'm not ready to go back any time yet.

Rob Rosinga

Bucharest

'Elderly people... have got another education, the education of the older times, before communism... and they've got a quality which nowadays you don't meet.'

I am a tall, grey-haired, 53-year-old Dutchman, who lost his job two days ago. I fell in love with the gymnast Nadia Comăneci, when she won the Olympic gold in Montréal back in 1976, and since then I started to take an interest in Romania. I was more aware than other kids of my age about the country. After my fascination with Nadia faded, I had some occasions when I actually met Romanian women. Once, a political refugee who was my colleague when I was a law student in Rotterdam. Then later, when I was in a conference in Denmark, again I fell in love with a Romanian woman. We spent a week at this conference and at the end of the week she said, 'I'm sorry, I'm married, but never mind, come to Romania next year. Take your summer holidays there and you will be convinced that Romanian women are much more beautiful than Danish women.'

So next year I went to have my holidays in Bucharest. It was the very hot summer in '92. On the second day I noticed a very charming lady in the street, but as I had to find a hotel I put her out of my mind. Then I saw her some 20 minutes later. I was walking around with a suitcase and a backpack and there she was again. She came down the staircase of the Ministry of Labour, and I thought, well, let me slow down a little bit, I hope she will come by and then I will address her. We met exactly in front of the famous balcony where Ceauşescu, back in '68, strongly denounced the Soviet intervention in Prague. It's the same balcony where in '89 he tried to prevent his downfall.

I told her I was looking for a hotel and she was asking me, 'Oh very nice, what are you doing here in Romania?' I told her about the libertarian conference I had just attended in Slovakia and that I had come to Bucharest, having some invitations. Being an economist, the subject of politics had her interest. I liked Mihaela from the beginning. I asked for her telephone number and a couple of days later I called. She took me on a trip through Bucharest and showed me around. I spent two weeks there, almost all of my time together with her, seeing things and talking. We went to her place and I met her mother. One day we went to the seaside. In those days I was a convinced libertarian and quite involved politically, and we discussed cultural life, history, politics and economics.

When did you get married?

Well, this is a delicate matter. We will get married, probably by the end of this year. We've known each other 20 years and I've been in Bucharest 15. After five years coming here in holiday seasons I decided to come and live here. We've been together a really long time and it's due to external circumstances we never managed to get married. We have quite a difficult life in Bucharest. Always things to be resolved, people to take care of. In the beginning her mother helped us a lot, but when she fell ill we had to take care of her. This took six or seven years, and when her mother died we were involved in helping an aunt of hers, so from this perspective we've had some hardship.

Tell me about the job?

I will give it one more try, to see if the owners of the company will change their minds. It's a company offering space and all kinds of archiving services, indexing, making hard copies available digitally. Basically this company comes from one I established together with a friend in the archiving business 11 years ago. I worked very hard to make this one a success as well. Now they've laid me off, without any severance pay. Frankly I consider they're making a big mistake. They are two Dutch people. We've got 50 employees, all of them Romanians. Most of them have got a reduced level of schooling, and the majority of them didn't have any contact with foreigners previously. In the past five years I was a kind of cultural interface, sometimes explaining to the employers how their behaviour was not well understood. And the other way around, to make the Dutchmen understand something about Romanian society, how people here respond and react to certain things, to avoid cultural misunderstandings.

In my free time, together with Mihaela, I am working as a city guide in Bucharest. I love history and I think Romanian history is extraordinary. There is so much to tell – it's very interesting and complex, they are a friendly and creative people, well capable of making improvisations. They're very sociable, vocal and talk in a vivid way, with gestures. I feel a kind of pride, and I want to represent Romania in all these fields. Also Bucharest is a city where you need a guide, either a well-written guide or a guy like me. It has been hurt so much in its history that no area is completely intact. Modern, ugly buildings made since the Revolution intrude on authentic downtown neighbourhoods, with their beautiful ancient mansions.

And I love classical music. I'm an admirer of George Enescu. Unfortunately he is quite unknown in the West because he didn't catch the real development of audio technology. He was an outstanding violinist, one of the best of the first half of the 20th century, perhaps one of its most influential classical musicians, as teacher of some of the best violinists including Yehudi Menuhin. He knew his value, but he wasn't an arrogant person and was very approachable.

He must have been a great personality with a quality you rarely meet, with extraordinary integrity, not only in the field of music. He had an amazing memory for music. There is the story of how he went to meet his friend Béla Bartók in Cluj. On the way back in the train to Bucharest, Bartók showed him a manuscript of a new orchestral work. Enescu was to perform the premiere in the Athenaeum. He went through the handwritten manuscript just twice during the trip back, and the next day he conducted this piece from memory. A genius.

I think the local authorities, since the Revolution, did a very bad job. On the national level, but also at the city level. People who have been responsible since the Revolution in Bucharest have not been able to figure out a concept for the future of the city. On a national level the same is true with the government. It didn't develop any medium-term and long-term perspectives for Romania. It should be one of the wealthiest countries of Europe and it's due to an amazing lack of perspective that Romania is in this precarious economic state. I must say that from this point of view, Ceauşescu was 100 per cent better than the modern politicians, because at least he had a view of the future, he had a vision. These guys now lack a vision completely.

I consider that Romanians have a lot of solidarity among each other. Not only in the family but also in the blocks; people helping each other out. Bucharest has got two million inhabitants and the vast majority of people live in blocks. You wouldn't expect that people would show so much solidarity – more than in Holland in the big cities. Also in the area where we live, in houses, people are communicating with each other and you will find people who take care of elderly people.

We both of us appreciate the values of the old, and we have a lot of sympathy for elderly people. We spend a lot of time with them because we love them. They've got another education, the education of the older times before communism, and that's wonderful. They've got a quality which nowadays you don't meet. Middle-aged people had their education in the communist period and you feel the different attitude, different responses immediately, unless their parents had a good background in the older times, like my wife's family, who had a very good education during the time of the king. You can clearly feel this positive influence in their upbringing which we appreciate very much. This is why we like to spend time with them. We also help them a lot whenever we can. On the one hand it is something which inspires us very much, but on the other hand it's also a big personal burden for us. Mihaela frequently does the shopping for them. We've got another couple of elderly people who we really try to take care of, taking them to the doctor or out for a little stroll in the park.

Something striking about Romanians is that when you spend time with them, sooner or later they will start talking about food, about recipes, about restaurants, about where you can buy good food. They are very preoccupied with eating well, though I consider their recipes are not very sophisticated. The Romanian kitchen is something between Turkish and German or Austrian. It's a mixture. It's not very special, but I appreciate their preoccupation with food. There is also a preoccupation with what is written on the label. They are quite aware of the menace of genetically modified products and the use of herbicides, more so than in Holland.

This may well have to do with the fact that even those living in the cities have got strong family bonds to the countryside. Until 1950 Bucharest had only one million inhabitants. Due to the industrialisation programmes of Gheorghiu-Dej and Ceaușescu, within a period of 40 years the city population increased to about two million. They were taken from the countryside and that had several effects. One is that the cosmopolitan atmosphere in Bucharest was quickly changed. Quite a loss for Bucharest.

If you have travelled in the countryside here, you may have observed that many good things come from there. I'm talking about values – respect, politeness, social coherence. Many values we used to have in the West you can still find in Romania. Young people in Bucharest are much more polite than in Western European cities, in terms of being respectful towards other people. We have got no fear whatsoever to roam through Bucharest, even in the middle of the night. I've been living in the small university city of Utrecht with 400,000 inhabitants, but every evening in the downtown centre things happen; ugly things, nasty things. I find that life in the Western world has deteriorated, suffered a lot, due to two causes – the dominance of socialism and the dominance of youth culture, both leading to the breaking down of older values.

People from the parents' generation have a difficulty in adapting to this youth culture which is now starting to emerge here. I'm not talking about that small group which has a lot of money, but the average Romanian. In the parents' generation they're burdened, trying to make a living, to make ends meet. And they take care of their children, sometimes their grandchildren, and their parents. As the medical facilities giving support to elderly people are almost non-existent, mainly just depending on some private initiatives, this generation is burdened. This gives the youth a lot of freedom. They really escape. Until let's say seven years ago you didn't see any graffiti in Bucharest, nothing at all. Now if you walk around, it's as bad as in the West.

In what way did I change? I resigned from this very rigid way of being that is quite usual in Western societies. I accept we change our programme or that things are not always like they should be; more than the Dutch living in Holland. You can adapt, you can improvise. Due to living together with Romanians I also became more attentive to what I eat. I really lack any feeling of homesickness. I haven't got it at all.

Romanians are very much alive. Here it's very vivid. All the time funny things happen, and people respond. When something is happening, people are interacting – in the bus, in the street. I feel attached to what is happening here, socially and politically. I discuss a lot with my colleagues, with friends, with Mihaela. Until now we had those who were in power fill their pockets. They fragmented, they cut into pieces all of the work of Ceauşescu. All factories were torn down, segmented, sold as old iron; this to an Italian, that to an Arab. All of the strategies that Gheorghiu-Dej, and especially Ceauşescu, had for this country, the long term strategies, have completely disintegrated. Those who came to power after the Revolution destroyed much of his work. And now Romania is suffering a lot. The lack of supervision, the withdrawal of power in the countryside, led to the dismantlement of Ceauşescu's irrigation programme. Whole complexes of factories, logically grouped together, all these industrial areas have been erased from the face of the Earth. I really hope that the new government will start to make a change, an absolutely necessary change. It's vital.

Anne Arthur

Arad

'I'm very superstitious anyway so I was comfortable when I came here. Particularly in Bucharest.'

A friend of mine who had done some work for the World Bank rang and asked if I would be interested in working for them in Romania. I had decided to leave the Civil Service and thought, well, I haven't got anything else to do and literally that was it. She got in touch with the World Bank, they got in touch with me, I sent my CV and left on 30th October. I was in Bucharest on 7th November 1992.

When I got to Otopeni airport, you've never seen anything like it. There was hardly any light, you were falling over your feet in holes in the floor, there was no carousel for the luggage, it was just all piled up. Somebody had ripped the label off mine. Nobody had said to me, 'Don't put the hotel name on your label', which I had, and this taxi driver said he'd take me to the hotel. They'd warned me to be careful, to make sure the meter worked, and that it should cost no more than $15. Anyway he said his meter worked but it didn't. When you don't speak a language it's quite difficult. He wanted $40 when we got there, so I rushed into the hotel to get the doorman and of course nobody was interested. The Bank refunded it but I was livid. My first introduction to Romania was being ripped off big time.

I came to work with one of the ministries. This was a little bit unusual at that time, a foreigner working with them full time.

They were very friendly and helpful but, I think, very suspicious because sharing information was difficult. Everything was fine – but sometimes, if you wanted information, you wouldn't get it. It took me quite a long time to work that out. I never really had any problems, it was just that I couldn't always tell whether they were in agreement. In time I understood that when people said, 'Yes', it wasn't always yes. Something to do with not offending you; anyway, once I realised this it was a bit easier. They were very friendly and when they got to trust me – it took over a year – they were much more open, to the extent that once when I suggested something one of them said to me, 'That's absurd.' I said, 'Well, think about it!' In the end we came to a compromise, but they would never have said that in the first year. They would have just said, 'Oh yes.'

How were office politics?

There's a very simple answer to that which is *nu este vina mea* – it's not my fault. It's a huge blaming culture and it's not just in offices. If anything goes wrong you find the one that is guilty and punish them. I think this came from communism, I really do. The secretary used to lock her typewriter in the cupboard every night. It was a big heavy thing. I asked, 'Why do you do that?' and she said, 'If anybody typed something on it and it's wrong, I will be the one to be punished.' Apparently before '89 typewriters were allocated to individuals, and if anything subversive was typed on it that individual probably got hauled in for questioning.

While it comes from communism, it's also from birth I think. I don't know how many times you've been out for a meal with Romanians, but they sometimes find it quite hard to decide what to eat from the menu. They certainly don't like telling you what's good because if it's not, they'll be blamed. In the early days, when we foreigners could pay for everybody, if I went out with

Romanian friends and said to one of them, 'What would you like?' they would say, 'I'll have what you're having. You can choose.' Some of my Romanian friends really don't want to take responsibility for very much. I'm talking about personal things in their own lives. They're waiting for some magic to change things.

Is there a greater belief in the supernatural world here?

You are talking to the converted. I think there are some magical properties… some say there's a special magnetic centre somewhere in the centre of Romania. I'm very superstitious anyway, so I was very comfortable when I came here. Particularly in Bucharest. I always refer to it as my spiritual home. Whether I lived here in another life I don't know. I don't feel the same about Arad, a city I love, but I feel immensely spiritually comfortable in Bucharest, which I've never felt anywhere else. I've always felt that. When I came in '93 there weren't streetlamps, and you couldn't see your hand in front of your face outside the Athénée Palace. No lights in the shops, no lights on the streets, not much heating in the flat, sometimes no electricity, occasionally no hot water. Filled the bath with cold water every morning because you never knew if you were going to have water when you came home. You had three or four saucepans in the kitchen for cooking and the bath full. Life was hard in that sense, but for me there was something magical about Bucharest. I would wander the streets just very happy. Can't explain any more on that.

How were you accepted generally when you first came?

People here were innately suspicious of foreigners then. Before '89 they were not allowed to speak to them. In '93 I had this big flat and Romanian friends would drop in whenever they felt like it. They had more time then. They'd come round and sit and talk, but there was a level of suspicion which I found very strange, very strange. Another friend of theirs would ring and they'd all make a sign that I wasn't to say they were there. Why, I've never understood. Because they have no explanation for it. 'Why did you want me to say that?' I would say. 'Well, that's how it is, you know,' or the Romanian shrug of the shoulders, without saying a word.

I remember travelling by train from Deva… two Americans and me and in the corner was this army officer. A little mouse ran out from under the seat and we all laughed and started to talk. He was on his way to Bucharest for a training course. All of a sudden he threw his hands in the air, laughed and said, 'This is the first time in my life that I've ever spoken to foreigners, because we were not allowed to.' He was just so happy. I've never forgotten that.

I was asked when I arrived, by the people that I worked with, what qualifications I had. They are a bit diploma bound here. They weren't interested in what you can do or what you are like, just what piece of paper you have. Maybe that's changed but I doubt it. If you don't have the qualifications on paper you're not really worth a lot. In the ministry in the early days – it may be the same now – if you didn't have a degree you could never be more than a *referent*, the bottom grade. It didn't matter how good a job you did, that was it, you were a *referent* for the rest of your life. I had a friend who didn't have a degree at the time of getting married. But the man did, and his parents came to speak to her parents – to explain they wouldn't be able to sit and talk to her after dinner, because clearly she didn't have the proper educational qualifications. I'm not joking… this is true. She was so upset. I told her not to worry about it. She got her degree and now has a good job.

It's a very tolerant society in some ways, not in others. Many of my friends have got what we would call quite high moral values. Some of them would be horrified at anyone having an affair, but many of them would see it as perfectly normal for the man to have illicit one-night-stands. They would see a difference between the long-term relationship and men using prostitutes or finding other women. The men think it's perfectly alright and they talk amongst each other, not just with me, with other women, thinking it's very funny and perfectly normal.

When I came boys were brought up differently from girls. The girls were there to serve the men and do what they were told. The men were treated like little gods in the house, and expected to behave like little gods for the rest of their lives. I've actually seen it in the treatment they got from the maid. You'd sit down to dinner and the men were always served first; as soon as they put their spoon or knife and fork down their plate was whisked away and the next course served, because they're men. I tried to explain to the maid, 'I'm the hostess; you wait till I'm finished.' She found this very odd. Friends explained to me that's how they were brought up. I've certainly seen enough of it to show that many women do as they are told.

Some Romanian friends of mine say it's normal for a man to beat his wife and his dog – ha! ha! ha! They are being serious but they are laughing. A very good friend of mine, a wonderful young man and his wife, they cared about each other deeply. His father beat his mother every day of his life and before he was born probably. He hated his father who once said to him, 'Why don't you beat A, just to make sure she behaves.' His mother died at a fairly early age; probably from the beatings was his view. He was so upset about it; he loved his mother. And she stayed, she didn't leave. She didn't have a well-paid job, and with a shortage of housing it was probably difficult to do so.

In '93 this American sociologist and I visited the provinces, and he asked about domestic violence and child abuse. As to the domestic violence – yes, it happens everywhere. Child abuse? In Romania? They were horrified. They did not accept that there was any possibility of sexual violence towards children. It was the same in the UK years and years ago. It is only when you open the box you realise how big a problem it is. There are now NGOs providing support, and there is an acceptance that there is an issue.

A friend of mine in '93 said Orthodoxy is a religion of the gut rather than anything else. There's a lot of ritual and I suppose that's what I like about the Orthodox Church, the ritual. But it has a big influence, particularly in the country. They could do more to help the poor. Having said that, they used to have a social canteen at the Patriarchy. I don't know if it's still there. A friend, a priest as well as a social worker, helped set it up. They invited me for lunch once. I was impressed; there were really poor people chosen by the local priests that came for lunch. There was a homeless man that day; he'd been living in the sewers in Bucharest, and they'd bought him a suit because he'd got a job. Everybody clapped and he almost cried. It's a long time since I've been as moved as I was on that day. I hope it's still there.

I really don't know how some people manage today; the prices here are huge. For basic foodstuffs I pay more here in the supermarket than I do in England. Their salaries are less, they have very small pensions. My neighbour has 300 RON a month. I have no idea how she manages. A lot of friends of mine have family in the country where they have pigs and vegetables, so they manage better; they kill a pig once every six weeks and share meat between everybody. Every time they go there they come back with fresh eggs, a couple of chickens, vegetables. For them there is a cushion, but without that it must be very hard.

Some of the medical care here is very good, but it's often a question of money again. There are some extremely good doctors and I had expert care when I was first diabetic. The specialist was brilliant, very approachable, helpful and I can go and see her any time. My friend, the doctor who referred me, said, 'She won't want any money, but put some in an envelope because their salaries are so small.' I've had other excellent doctors here too. I had problems with my back and my knee and I had an MRI here and got good diagnosis. Physiotherapy – *kineto* as they call it – and other allied services are brilliant, used much more than ours are in England.

What's going on? When something goes wrong some of my Romanian friends will say, 'What's going on? What's going on?' They're always looking for the hidden agenda. I'm sure there's a lack of transparency at many levels. Some of the talk shows are doing quite a good job at the moment but my first thought is, what's in it for them? What's their agenda? But some of the talk shows are 'what you see is what you get'. They're asking open questions and actually wanting answers – some of them, some of the time.

Ian Tilling

Bucharest

'I've no idea who adopted who, whether it was me that adopted Romania or the other way around.'

I was asked by the Mayor of Bucharest to open a night shelter for older homeless men. We had no experience of homelessness whatsoever so we approached Médecins Sans Frontières and they introduced us to some homeless people. We managed to get 20 of them together to meet regularly twice a week. We discussed what a night shelter was, what it should be equipped with and what the regime there should be, including the rules.

Remus and Gabi were the first two supervisors. They were elected by the others in the group, which was quite surprising as these two guys were clearly in their twenties. They had great personalities. The first two rules they insisted on were no smoking and no drinking. I laughed and said, 'Yes, they'll be broken the first night.' It was explained to me that if they were allowed to be drunk inside, it wouldn't be very secure for them. Secondly, if they were allowed to smoke, they would all smoke in bed and create a fire hazard. They were very keen to protect their safety and keep a calm atmosphere in there.

We made the difficult decision to say that outside normal office hours there'd be no member of staff there. It really was their responsibility to manage the place, keep it clean and tidy, look after it and make sure all the equipment was working properly. It was amazingly successful. I say amazingly, because although I wasn't amazed at the time, everyone else seemed to be, including the mayor.

As the demography of homelessness changed we responded as well. About four years ago we decided to concentrate on families and single vulnerable women. We were quite often taking in single parent mothers who were looking after children and living in parks for three or four months before coming to us. We had a 60-year-old who'd been living in the waiting room of Gara de Nord for the past four years – she'd been put out by her family. They were extremely vulnerable. The emphasis is on getting them back on their feet, the kids back into school, parents back into work and eventually into their own accommodation. All in all there's about 40 or 50 people living in the shelter in Olteniței, and there'll probably be round about 30 in Bucureștii Noi.

On average they stay between six and eight months. Most people are then back into work, with enough money saved to move on. Some take the full year, whilst our older residents, they're with us for life. Nobody else is going to accept them. In the last five years we've probably had six or seven families come back, so everything indicates that they move on and that they're successful in that. Poverty levels in Bucharest are the highest I have ever seen them. At the end of last year we had 380 families waiting for a place in Casa Ioana – the first shelter here in Bucharest – which is just extraordinary.

One thing that worried me a little bit was that very rarely did we have beneficiaries actually coming back to say, 'Hi guys, this is what we're now doing, this is how we've moved on.' Then I met a family who'd been with us for quite a while. It was such a success story for her, she'd really moved on and was back on her feet and the kids were wonderful. I said, 'Well, why've you not told us this or given us a phone call?' She explained it was actually the worst period of her life, this period of being homeless and living in a shelter. She just didn't want to go back there again, she did not want to revisit those times. It made me happy really, because there was I worrying why these people weren't coming back, and here was an obvious answer.

Can we go back to what you were doing before you came to Romania?

My former life, as I call it, was in the British police. I started off working with the Metropolitan Police, moved to Kent County Constabulary in 1972 and retired in early 1992, which is when I came over here on a permanent basis. Between '90 and '92 I was here probably every other month, while still with the police.

I had a charity called the Kent Children's Cross Holiday. We took eight terminally ill children away each year. We used to go to Lourdes, so there was that religious element to it, but it was very much a fun-packed holiday as well. One August I had just come back from one and my wife said to me, 'Have you seen these pictures coming out of Romania?' The news channels were absolutely full of film of children living in these so-called orphanages. She turned round and said, 'Look, at the moment you are dealing with quite privileged children. What about these children? Can you not do anything for them?' Little did we know, but that challenge was to change both of our lives forever.

[In 1990, having raised some funds, Ian went to Bucharest with the head nurse of his charity. They worked for a month at one of the orphanages, the Cămin Spital in the village of Plătărești, before returning to England. The following year, having raised some half a million pounds through another campaign with the local newspaper, he went back with 100 lorries and 300 people. He developed a link with the Ministry of the Interior to start a project in Zăbrăuți in Bucharest, with local NGOs. This led later to the establishment of Casa Ioana in 1995, a charity which runs the Homeless Shelter project today.]

So Ian, what were the biggest challenges?

Corruption, *şpagă*. We were faced with it all the time. For instance we needed a signature from a Mr T for a project we were submitting. It was well supported by the Ministry of the Interior, but every time we went round checking on our file, to see its progress, we were told that it was still at the bottom of the pile.

Cristina, my assistant, was quite clear the guy wanted paying, and then our file would move to the top. I kept refusing, 'No, it's a good project, it should go through on its own merits.' Eventually we went there one day and they'd lost it. Then we put in another file and they lost that one. We put in another and they lost that one. This went on five times. In the end I demanded to see Mr T. Eventually we got a meeting with him and one of the first things he said was, 'You have to take me to England for two weeks so that I can see your organisation back in the UK.'

I said 'We haven't got an organisation in the UK, it's all here. Come and see the project, we'd be delighted to show you.'

'No, I have to go to the UK.' That would be fully expenses paid and everything else. What really frustrated me was the fact that there were quite a lot of fairly large international NGOs here and he was getting all these photographs of him in these various places, having been entertained in all these different countries. Eventually he just simply asked for €2000 for the signature, having said that his job wasn't very well paid. I told him very undiplomatically where he could go with that. I actually went round to the Minister of the Interior and complained and he said, 'The guy will be out of a job in two weeks.' Two years later he was still there.

Things moved on. You can get by. We never paid anything in *şpagă*. But what it does do, it robs you of time. The expression here is *cercul vicios* – everything is this vicious circle. If you can succeed without paying it, you don't get asked any more. People have stopped asking now, they just comply. If we satisfy the legislation or the regulations, then we're entitled to it.

Do you see things getting any better?

No I don't, not really. People don't pay taxes. I've actually asked lots of people why, and if you talk to the middle class, they will turn round and say, 'What do I get for my money? Why should I pay taxes, because I'm not going to see anything from them?' From the poor it's 'I would love to pay taxes if I could find an employer who was willing to pay me legally, with a workbook. Then I'd be happy to pay the taxes.' So you're getting less money going into the government coffers, and even less money coming out. It's a dire situation and I don't see that changing in the short term. As an employer I run an NGO dependent on private funding, so you can imagine our income is quite small and the salaries will reflect that. What I pay my staff in hand, I pay again to the government in taxes and social taxes.

You mentioned Cristina. You're now married?

I had taken Cristina on as a kind of interpreter/translator. She generally looked after me and got meetings arranged and so on. To cut a long story short, we'd had a disastrous meeting with the Ministry of Interior, realised then that the project was lost, and were having a cup of coffee in Piața Amzei. After a little while Cristina said, 'Look, I'm getting married in September, would you like to come to the wedding?' Well, this is in June. I knew Adi her boyfriend very well. They were both hippies at that time. Of course I said 'Yes,' and went back to Casa Ioana on my own.

I realised I had some feelings for Cristina. I was a lot older than she was, and I had nothing in the bank. I'd lost everything myself anyway, lost my house. I was going through a divorce as well so everything was upside down. In the end I convinced myself that at least I should tell her how I felt, if nothing else. I borrowed some money and took her for a meal. During the meal, in typical

English style, I said, 'Cristina, I have to tell you something. I think I might be in love with you.'

Her jaw kind of dropped; it was totally out of the blue. After what seemed like an eternity she just turned round and said, 'Well, I guess you've got three months in which to prove it.'

So I wooed very hard and won. Amazing!

That's a story! What about other relationships here?

All my friends really are Romanians, and we go out and we share times with them. It's not that I don't get on with ex-pats, it's that I'm localised. I enjoy their company because it's much more down to earth, it's much more grounded. These are generally young people who want to see changes, see themselves being part of the change, but are very frustrated at the same time in not being able to really kick in and get it going. They're less inhibited, they're much more sincere in general, and they're very open and transparent. I can talk with them on a whole host of subjects, personal and otherwise, and the conversation flows.

Cristina is 18 years younger than I am, and I got to know my Romanian friends very much through her. That was when I started socialising with Romanian people. I was absolutely amazed at their acceptance of me being with Cristina, because of the obvious differences. It wasn't just age, it was culture and everything else to go with it. It was as if Cristina and I had been together all our lives.

I've never ever had problems making friends with Romanians, be they older or younger. They just have this thirst for seeing things from other peoples' perspectives. Still top of their list is the chance to travel. They are hungry for anything outside Romania and have a fascinating curiosity for life and other cultures and other traditions. I found it very easy to settle in. Maybe that's because I've always felt at home here, I've always seen it as a place where I wanted to spend a long time.

Originally I came over on the two year project. When I was in the middle of that I knew I was going to be staying longer. I used to say at the beginning, when I stepped on the plane at Otopeni airport to go back, that I put my English head on. And when I was on the TAROM flight back to Romania I put my Romanian head on. So there was a difference, there was a different way of thinking, a different mentality if you like. Now I just have one head.

So you've become a bit of a Romanian?

It's become my home, there's no doubt about that. I certainly feel I belong here and I feel that Romania has accepted me. I've no idea who adopted who, whether it was me that adopted Romania or the other way around. It doesn't really matter.

When I first came they were quick to point out that they were very hospitable people. Very caring, very family orientated. And I think maybe that was right at the beginning. I used to be fascinated by train journeys, because come lunchtime or an evening mealtime, people would open their food boxes and share the food among all the other passengers in that carriage. You were expected to do the same. I'd never come across this sort of thing before. It all depends of course where you come from as well, because rural people are so very different to urban Romanians. A lot has not changed too much. They're still generally poor. Most Romanians would find it impossible to save any money for a rainy day. They live virtually from day to day, or week to week, month to month maybe, so they don't have those long term visions that I certainly have.

Living as I do in the project, I've seen a lot of selfishness amongst families. Maybe because of the job that I do. Most of the people we've got are here as a result of family breakdowns, and family dysfunction, family abuse. But it does appear to me that outside the immediate family not much else really matters.

I suppose like many other nationalities, they hate foreigners criticising their own country. I've got a very hard, thick skin, so if something is wrong then I point it out and they are used to me now. I'm happy to criticise my country as well where it needs criticising. They are very nationalistic. There's another Romanian trait. If you believe them they are responsible for stopping the Ottoman Empire spreading further westwards. They are absolutely adamant that if it wasn't for them, we would all be living as Turks.

Yes, they've had a chequered past. I've been travelling quite a lot in the north of the country on a refugee project, with a research assistant, who was absolutely gobsmacked that they talked Hungarian in Timişoara, and not Romanian. 'But this is Romania, they should be speaking Romanian!'

'Right, okay – why?' History is a number one criterion on citizenship. You have to have a very good knowledge of Romanian history in order to get through this citizenship exam. I was reminded of one of my favourite quotes – 'If you want to really learn about English history, read French history!'

When I was first over here, I was well aware that my phone was being listened to. Still is no doubt, because I've been here a long time. I was quite good friends with a Swiss banker who was arrested for an alleged fraud here, for which he was never charged in the end. He was under arrest but on bail, so he couldn't leave the country. Every time we met, the security services were quite open, taking photographs of us. He was covered everywhere he went. We just got used to it.

Did that make you feel uncomfortable?

No. I've been involved in security before in my police life. At the end of the day, if they want to see you as a possible threat, then that's fine. There's the old adage that if you're not doing anything wrong, what's there to worry about? So it doesn't worry me in the least. I know others who are less laid back about it than I am, and they've gone. So what!

What hasn't changed is the political will to change the country for the good. I still feel that politicians are there for their own self-interest and not necessarily for those that elected them. The general population have grown so weary of politicians. It appears to me – nobody has convinced me otherwise – that those who had the political power also have the economic power. The two have gone hand in hand, whether that be directly or through relatives or bogus companies or whatever. Very soon the political class will change here, but they will still hold on to the economic wealth. So pessimistically Romania's got at least another 20 years before real democracy starts settling in. I wonder sometimes whether the younger generation are becoming more and more despondent and more and more compliant.

An exodus out of the country? Yes, we're already seeing one, but what's largely put a stop to that is the financial crisis. From Romanians I've spoken to, they all aspire to working abroad. I haven't met one who's said, 'I'd prefer to be in Romania', except for the older ones.

You were talking earlier about this nationalism. Does that fit with wanting to leave?

You can still leave a country and carry your nationalism with you. I can remember travelling to Dubai for the first time to meet a friend there. I got picked up at the airport and he said, 'We're going straight to a party,' and we went to this hotel. There must have been about 80 Romanians having a party. Half the waiters and waitresses were Romanian. My God, I've just travelled 5000 odd miles, spent a fortune to come over here, and I'm back in Romania again.

Liria Themo

Bucharest

'Being a small woman on a construction site, what is that?'

My dad comes from a well-known Constanţa family, wealthy doctors. Doctors lived well during the communist regime because people would always come with cheese or chicken, whatever. He worked in a hospital and he was also allowed to consult at home. He was an ophthalmologist, as his father had been. They were Muslim – my great-grandfather had been exiled from Turkey. My dad grew up with this very privileged background.

My mum was from Braşov and they got married around '68, and he leaves legally on a trip. He's with a friend and goes to Paris and doesn't come back. That places a burden on the family that remains behind. The police would come and take you in for questioning, but that died down after a while, although you were considered to be a danger to the Party after that.

The legend version is that when he got to Paris he bought a Citroen DS, did something to the gas tank, made it smaller, got a tan, let his hair grow – this was the late 60s in Paris – and borrowed an Algerian passport. He spoke French fluently. With the tan and a beard he looked like the guy – he had the Algerian look. He came back for my mother, got a message to her and smuggled her out of the country in that little compartment in the car. They got back to France, then went to the States. I was born probably nine months later, my sister came after. They applied for political asylum. They got their American citizenship, at which point they renounced their Romanian one. My sister and I were born American citizens.

My dad was an engineer by education and my mum was smuggled out of the country in her fourth year of medical school, so she didn't have a diploma. When she went to a university in New York they said, 'Listen, you have two choices. First choice is to start all over again. But we recommend the second; you go back, finish your diploma, return with a nice neat piece of paper that says that you're a dentist, and we will give you an equivalency.' And in time that's what they did.

So my dad comes back an American, no longer a Romanian citizen. He is the director of a rep office for a ball-bearings company. He set everything up and we came here as children. While he was working, my mum went back to medical school to become a dentist. She had to re-do her fourth year, do her fifth year and then left with a diploma. We went back to the States, and then in another two years she was a practising dentist.

We were placed in schools for those two years here. We spoke the language but it was kitchen-Romanian. We were the only two children that weren't allowed to wear the red scarf because we were Americans. We weren't allowed to participate in the extra curriculars or get academic prizes. We were somewhat ostracised. My sister had a very nice teacher, I had a very mean teacher. She probably had issues with my way of being because in the States, starting from kindergarten, you are asked to think – whereas here, you were not. You had to stand up, stand straight, salute, sing the anthem; so I had a little bit of a tougher time.

When did you come back here?

Years later, in '95, we were all living in New York and my dad had to settle an inheritance in Romania. I'd just finished college and was looking for a job. He took three weeks off and we returned together. During the three weeks he was here we got things ready for the court case, but it was put back to September, and then to January. So my dad went back. I'd met Liviu – now my husband of 15 years – and by the second case in January we'd already been living together for a while. I told my parents I'm not coming back. They weren't very happy. I stayed and we got married three years later. I've been here since.

When I came in '95 there were definitely things that would take you back. The regime had changed but Romania was behind. I went to Constanța, where my dad was from, also my husband. Everywhere I'd go, I'd have a fit. I would teach waiters how they should be serving things, telling them they shouldn't take an ashtray without covering it, because the ashes fly everywhere. We were at the Casino Restaurant in the old port, a beautiful art deco building. The waiter brought me a schnitzel, one without the breadcrumbs. It's a schnitzel, which takes very little time, but it took him two hours. He brings it and I said, 'But I specified I wanted a schnitzel with breadcrumbs.'

He said, 'Don't worry about it, I like this one better.'

I joined my cousin who ran a small advertising company, working for her. She would send faxes without a cover letter. I said, 'How can you send a fax without a cover letter?'

'What do you mean?' she asked.

'Well, you have to tell them how many pages are coming, you introduce what you send.'

I was constantly criticising her, and this is how I met my husband. She said there are two brothers here, they have a company, and you'll see they're very professional. She was my guide and was always trying to show me the bright side. She'd take me to restaurants, to clubs, showing me how great and wonderful it can be and that it's not all bad. I was 25 at the time. The two brothers that did things properly were in the computer business, so they had more of an opening towards the West.

Once married, how did you fill your time?

In 1989, before the communist regime fell, the house of my in-laws had been demolished. The land was needed for a project of the city. They offered them two choices – either a new apartment in a communist type apartment building or one in an *interbelic* villa. They chose the villa. But in '98 the old owners got their property back. My mother-in-law, for the second time in her life, was being thrown out of her home. So my husband and his brother decided they would build her a house. This would be hers and no one would kick her out of that. Who can do that? Well, we'll give it to Liria.

So I built my first house. I met with architects. I didn't have the background. At college I'd majored in human communication. But I'm organised, and being from the States I had more of a professional outlook on things than many Romanians at that time. People were not used to having to think, to solution-based thinking. There was always, 'Tell me what to do!' I probably would have had an easier time if I just gave an order. But I would want some sort of consultation. I would want to find the best solution with the resources we had. It was a different way of thinking.

I started to write things down. I had chalk with me so I'd write on the wall, 'This is crooked,' 'Take it down!' 'Fix it!' At the beginning, everywhere I went there was always a problem, there was always something wrong. They weren't doing it properly, they weren't saying the right things, and they weren't writing the right things. I started giving orders. I was quite young to be on a worksite. I don't have experience. Plus I'm a girl, I'm physically small. They were older men who'd been all around the world working on construction sites. Being a small woman on a construction site, what is that?

The head of the site would split his people at my worksite. At that time it was his largest project and he would do that at 6.30 in the morning. He started to give me workers that I wasn't happy with. I should have had qualified people. Telling him the day before, he'd go, 'Yeah, yeah, yeah!' and the next day I'd get the same guys. I started to get there at 6 a.m. in winter time; it would be dark, and very windy in Constanţa and I would sit in my car and wait for them. Then at 6.30 they would arrive, they would look at me, not understanding, and I would say, 'No, starting today you are giving me the people that I choose!' I began to put up the project schedule all over the house. When they were late I would use red markers so that even the workers would see that they were late.

Honestly, I liked doing it. Was it frustrating? Sometimes, sure, and then with time you start to adjust and maybe you don't have the same expectations. Maybe you drop your expectations. Or rather, you start to adapt to a more local attitude because that eventually is what integration means.

For the past six years I've been taking care of the children. I gave birth to them here in a private hospital. When I first came back I had vertigo. I went to the hospital. I remember taking a towel with me to cover my mouth because I thought I don't want to get sick in the hospital. The hospitals were just beyond belief. They were dirty, they smelt, they didn't have the disinfectant.

They wouldn't explain anything to you. The doctor looking at me for the vertigo didn't say, 'This is maybe from your internal ear that could be inflamed, we just want to make sure.' They just said, 'Take her to neurology!'

I looked around and thought, what do you mean, neurology? Because neurology sounds bad when you're 25, but no one would explain. They wouldn't sit down to talk to you about a treatment plan and the medicine. If you asked questions they would look at you like, why do you need to know? You're not a doctor. That would be the attitude – take an order, why do you need an interpreter, why do you need to understand it, why do you need to be consulted? You are my patient. This is what you need to take, and that's it.

When my sister-in-law gave birth, I remember looking for her in the same hospital. I gave the mother's name. Above some double doors there's a sign: Keep Out – Medical Staff Only Allowed Beyond this Point. I'm standing at the double doors and someone keeps crossing the large hallway on the other side. I'm trying to make signs and waving. She's waving to me, like – come here, why are you trying to talk to me? She's about five doors down. I point to the sign. 'I can't get beyond this sign, this point.'

She's looking at me like there's something wrong with me. 'Just come here, I waved you to come over.' I go to her and said I'm looking for so-and-so's baby and she says, 'Follow me!'

We're going from room to room because the mothers wouldn't stay with the babies in the room. She was in an incubator. You know in American diners you have those glass lids that stay over cupcakes and cookies? That's what the incubator looked like. The babies were swaddled exactly like mummies. She lifts up this diner glass and she takes out the two babies in the same incubator. She's picking them up like hotdogs and is trying to figure out which one's which. She thinks this one's okay, let's go find the mother. I'm in awe at everything.

Now if I go into a hospital I'm probably seeing the same things I saw back then, maybe with some improvements, but I'm not as sensitive to it all any more. I'm no longer the person I was. I've probably become bossier. I've become accustomed to the way things are. My perception is no longer the same. It's not as hard. People also changed here. Today I would say things move much more fluidly. There's a more Western way of doing business. They have more experience, plus you have all the materials in the construction field. The Internet has evolved and has become such a large part in my life with getting information.

Life in general has changed so much since '95. Romania had to develop quickly. People were very receptive to the West coming in. Anything that was American was special and so from this angle

I did have an edge. If I would go into a shop in jeans and sneakers with a ponytail, no make-up, and if it's an expensive shop on Calea Victoriei, if I spoke in Romanian to the women selling, they would barely look at me. No 'Good day', no 'Goodbye', nothing. I would remember because that annoyed me. If I'd return to the shop two months later dressed exactly the same, go in and speak English with a very nice American accent, the difference in the way the same salesgirl would treat me would be from here to the sky. It was such a different attitude. They were very pro-West.

I remember the day I met Liviu when my cousin introduced us. We went to his parents who had a tiny bungalow on a lake in Constanța. They were having a barbecue. I'm 25, American and meeting 20, 30 people probably in their late fifties. It's a family gathering on a Sunday. Lots of food – that's very Romanian. 'What are you doing here? Who are you? Why did you come here? What do you think of our Romania? What do you think Romania's future is going to be like?'

I remember sitting there, the centre of attention at this barbecue and they're asking my opinion. I said, 'You know what, honestly I think it's going to take three generations.' Big words.

My husband in the early 90s was driving an elderly Italian businessman from Bucharest around the country. He turned to Liviu and said, 'You know, you have a very beautiful country.'

'Yes, thank you' replied Liviu.

And the Italian continued, 'It's a rich country but the people are very poor. That must mean there's a lot of stealing going on.'

Every time I think about it, I think wise words. It's true; everyone steals. That's another thing I just couldn't understand when I came. You would hear people talking about the cleaning woman stealing. 'Yes, but I'm not going to change her.'

'What do you mean, you're not going to change her? You caught her stealing detergents!'

'Whatever, yeah, but she'd didn't steal a lot.'

'The whole idea about stealing is that you have values. Don't you find that's a problem, to have that person in your home working in your home with your things? You can't trust that person. How can you continue?'

'She doesn't steal a lot.' I think the idea 'doesn't steal a lot' can still be found today. Probably everywhere in the world there's a problem with office supplies being taken home. But here, because it was okay to steal during the communist regime, you were stealing from the state, you were not stealing from someone. You're not really taking it away from Melissa or Bobbie or Sue.

The black market in Romania was alive and kicking during communism. You could get gas that way, you could get clothing that way, and you could exchange currency. The black market was a normal part of everyday life. It's a way of thinking, that you do things under the table. In the States you don't feel that. I'm sure it's done at very high levels, bids for highways, oil companies; from time to time you get something on the news, but it's organised crime at a much higher level, it's further away from you under normal circumstances. In Romania it was everywhere. I would go to the post office and I would leave a little tip so that the notices for packages would get to me. Friends would send cookies over and I wouldn't get them. So I'd have to go give little tips and presents.

Liviu and I had an infertility issue. I'm not getting pregnant. The doctors are in a system that perpetuates bribes or paybacks. If you're giving the bribe afterwards, it's not really a bribe. But it's expected that you pay for the service, somehow. I became a master at slipping envelopes to doctors because they all say, 'No, no, please don't, there's no need.' But their pockets are already worn by envelopes. Am I generalising? Yes, but believe me, it's so much the way things are done here in hospitals.

The bribe infiltrates schools as well. It can be direct or indirect. Direct can be – you pay for your diploma. You have that real, open version. Then you can have a sicker version where the teacher will give poor grades to the child. I had a very close friend of mine whose daughter switched schools, about the eighth grade. She was very good, an A student in physics at the former school. She gets to the new school and she's getting sixes, fives, maybe even fours out of ten. The mother went to see the teacher, who told her that maybe she needs tutoring, private tutoring.

Is it understandable? Can you say it's justifiable? The teacher is only making €250 a month. It's unacceptable that teachers are making so little money. It's unacceptable that doctors are making so little money, by legal standards anyway. Illegally or off the books, what are they doing? I know doctors that are driving cars you would rarely see on New York streets. Babies are a good spot to make money because people are willing to make sure that everything goes well. Stakes are high. They'll make €1000 or €1500 a pop. If you have three deliveries in one morning, all of a sudden you have almost €5000 a day, and it's tax-free, it's cash.

So how do you identify yourself?

If I'm here I'm American and if I'm there I'm Romanian. I'm somewhere in between. Each place has its downs. If you go walking round in Walmart, I'm definitely not from that America. There's waste, and now the poverty level in the States is growing so it's definitely not the same America I left in '95.

Where do you feel most at home?

Where my children are, probably. For me, children tend to be an anchor. So wherever you are with them.

What about their future?

Tough to say. It has to do with education and the way they think.

My children are probably raised a lot more American than they are Romanian. They definitely have an opinion and they are told to go do things on their own. They're more independent and they're used to having things explained to them.

My daughter just started school. The American school here is very expensive. I placed her in a Romanian school and there are 41 kids in the class. There's only one teacher, no teacher's assistant. But this is her reality, this is where she is. If they are in Romania I don't need to make a bubble for them.

You can live in a bubble; you have the nice neighbourhood where there are ex-pats, you take them to the nice American school, you hire a driver and then they're not actually living in Romania. But will they be mentally healthier for it? Probably not. It's artificial. I sent them to the Romanian school because I want them to get a feel for this. They play with Romanian kids. I want them to see Romanian households. They're here and this is their reality.

We do plan on leaving. To go where, I don't know. Something similar to this place. It would either be in America or in a country developing the way it was here in '95. I would prefer to go back to the States with the children. I would like them to see a school where people ask your opinion, where they want you to analyse what your choices are, and where responsibility is accepted and embraced.

Here, even the young, they're not responsible for themselves because their parents take care of everything. Everything! The kids don't know how to cook, they don't how to get dressed, and they're not partaking in anything like doing the dishes, cleaning rooms. In the upper-middle-class here you can get cheap labour, so everyone has a cleaning woman. I didn't grow up with a cleaning woman. I remember ironing my mother's lab coats. You were part of the whole household experience.

Scott Eastman

Sibiu

'Don't get right in his face!'

I first came here to photograph the country, to give a perception to the world of what Romania is like from an outsider's view. I was taking pictures of daily life; like birth, baptisms, weddings, funerals, and people working in common jobs, in factories, in the fields, trying to get a big range. A little bit more of a rural view than city life.

I shoot for a local magazine called *Sibiu Business*. That's the business section of my photography. I also photograph cultural and religious projects and I do a lot of work with the Orthodox Church. One of the challenges is the way that photography is viewed here compared to the States. It's not a valued profession. People wouldn't see why I should be paid very much. I can't even sell a photograph for a high price in Luxembourg and then for 20 times less here. For example, a photo of an old woman opening up her windows – seeing reflections of her face in both windows, incredible face – in Luxembourg I was selling this for €400. Here at €50 maybe I won't sell it.

This was a really unusual country for me, where people are so pro-American it was surprising. Bags in grocery stores had an American flag on them. People were positive. Actually they would almost defer to my view as opposed to accepting their own. They would tend to value our judgements and opinions above their own. That was unusual to me. There's a lack of confidence but I think it's changing over time. I hope so.

I've talked to a lot of business people, including those in German companies, and asked them why they decided to locate here. They've said that the local government is somebody that they can work with, that they are not having a lot of roadblocks put in the way of building factories, getting permits and all that process.

Mayor Klaus Iohannis is a Saxon. Something really fascinating about this – he's running for mayor right now. He will get probably somewhere between 70 to 80 per cent of the votes. He has incredible popular appeal. One time when he was not running, our nanny said she was voting for him. 'But he's not even running!' I said to her. 'But I want to vote for him.'

I may have the numbers wrong, but on the town or county council something like eight or nine out of twelve positions are held by Saxons. The Saxon population is about two per cent of the city or the county. The vast majority are Romanian, and they consistently vote for Saxons. They say they're better administrators. They have more faith in them to be effective bureaucrats than they have in themselves.

Asta este! Saxons might say that, if they're speaking about trying to get things done through the Romanian bureaucracy. They acknowledge the power structure that exists. If you want to get something done you can't just ignore it – you have to navigate it. In business often people don't want to make a transaction before having several conversations, having a coffee, having face-to-face conversations. In a way I find this very friendly, very comfortable, but it's not quick. Basically I want to say, 'Here's the proposal, you tell me exactly what you need, let's cut to the solution, and then we can have a chat.' That's what I'm comfortable with. Traditionally in Romania time is running a different schedule. I've slowed down some in terms of doing business, of making more personal contacts.

Many things get done through personal relations. If something's going to happen, it often happens incredibly fast. You know one person who knows another, a couple of phone calls are made, and if everybody knows the right people then an approval is given. Often there's no contract, no formal document – maybe one halfway through the project, when it's almost done. When I went to somebody's secretary I thought it would be to establish an appointment, normal for a high official. Instead it was, 'Hey, come on in! Let's talk if you need. Let me make a call to make this happen.' The city hall, the cultural organisation, business organisations, they know each other. In order for this to work you need to deliver, but if you perform, those doors will still be open.

What about the history of this region?

Both the Saxons and Hungarians are proud of their history, proud of what they've accomplished. Romanians were excluded from the cities, they were really second-class citizens. The Saxons don't have any aspirations to re-establish their rule here. In Sibiu we don't have so many issues with the Hungarian minority, it's not very vocal here, but certainly there are Hungarians wanting much more autonomy, who would like portions of the country to simply become Hungary. I've heard some really incredible fallacies. Recently somebody was telling me that Transylvania used to be majority Hungarian. This is simply not a fact. This is a really disputed issue. I don't even know how to begin a conversation, if you can't even agree on some really basic statistics.

How about the Roma?

A lot of Romanians I've met feel that in Europe people have a negative perception about the country, primarily due to issues related to Roma or Gypsies. This is very frustrating to me in terms of conversation, not only in Romania but also in England, Germany, wherever. I find people polarised on this, blindly so, thinking in extreme stereotypes. Either they're all thieves, they're dirty, stinking people or they're all wonderful people going around playing their music and just misunderstood, given a hard time by everybody else. Both of these views are pretty blind to reality.

I've had the chance to spend 24 hours with a Roma family. They were working on the roof of the city hall. I was with my colleague, Russell. We were in the city eating and had extra seats at our table. We offered the chairs to a Roma family; there wasn't room at other tables and they needed to sit down. We struck up as good a conversation as we could with our limited language, got chatting and they invited us to come to their village, to their house for a meal, to spend the night.

We were received very well. When we arrived they washed our feet, gave us slippers, and gave us a really wonderful meal. They certainly have different customs to what we're used to, like the women served us but didn't sit at the table. They were very hospitable to us. They were also very industrious. We woke up at five in the morning, and they got up to milk the cows and cut the grass – when wet with dew it cuts easily with the scythe. It was the only time I've ever stayed in a person's house when they showed me the title to the property. People are accused of squatting and it was interesting they cared to show us this.

Talking of pieces of paper then, has the bureaucracy been very challenging?

You can have a problem or a challenge in Romania even if you think you know what the law is. Before I came in 2006 I had people here check the law. I could import anything – car, airplane, didn't matter, as long as I had already owned it for at least nine months. There would be no customs fees if it was my own personal property. I did not have the right to sell it for two years. That was fine. I just wanted my car to drive. I put it in the container, along with my other possessions. When it arrived, the customs listed all the items in the container, which were 48 boxes. The car was supposed to be the last item. They made 49 packages.

I was asking, 'Where's the car? I don't see the car on this form here?' The man showed me the note for package 49, the car, and I said there surely should be some separate form. He assured me this is the way it is. Finally I deferred to him and said, 'Okay, that's your job, you should know, fine.' When I went to register the car they gave me a temporary registration. Everything seemed fine. I had licence plates that looked like everybody else's but they were red; temporary, no big deal.

Next year I went to re-do my registration and the police said, 'You can't register this car because it wasn't properly brought into the country. You don't have the correct papers. You need to go back to customs.' So we went back to customs and they said, 'We can't do this because the receipt was made incorrectly in the first place, you don't have the right paper work. And we can't give you the correct paperwork. You have to import it now for the first time, and now the fee is €11,000!'

I explained the mistake was theirs. 'I don't want to cause any trouble, let's just make the receipt correctly.' They insisted that this was not possible. I spoke with the Head of Customs of Sibiu. 'No, this is not possible. We can't do this. The mistake was made and you have to pay €11,000.' I met with several other people, 'No, this is not possible, you have to pay the money!'

Finally, working through a lawyer I had to submit an application to Braşov, over 100 miles away, to get the right receipt made. I got the receipt from Braşov Customs. This said I'd imported the car on a specific date and everything should be fine. I thought no big deal, I'll re-submit this and have the car without the fee.

But I was wrong. Finally I had to sue them. I waited a pretty long time for the court case but finally the case happened. Oddly enough, despite everything I've heard about the judicial system being corrupt, we won the case without paying a bribe to anyone.

Immediately I was told the customs were appealing the case. I still didn't have the right to drive the car. We went to another city, Alba Iulia. I found a lawyer there and after a period of time the case came to court. I won again and it was definitive. The whole process took two years. For two years I didn't have access to my car.

At one point in this process, before I sued the customs, they called me and said they'd found a loophole. They told me I didn't have to pay €11,000; I only had to pay €4000 and everything would be fine and I could have my car…

A marathon! Going back to your photography, has that been a problem for the security people?

Many people of my generation, those in their forties or older who grew up under communism, are very suspicious of any foreigner. They're thinking they are here to gather information for their own country's intelligence service. The funny thing is, this hasn't created any problems for me, because there's also a generally positive view about intelligence services. They don't seem to have a problem with it. It's not making sense to them that somebody comes just because they want to do good work for people. If somebody came to run a dental clinic for a week, people would think, 'No, no, no. Maybe they have a good heart but they're also taking information back.' That's a pretty pervasive attitude.

In the States several times I photographed presidents. To photograph them during the presidential debates I had to give my name to them days in advance so they could do some sort of basic background check. Once my name was cleared I had to be given a certain pass. I had to be searched multiple times; dogs were used, magnetometers, all this stuff. This was my experience in America;

it's a big deal if you want to photograph the president, but it can be done.

In Romania one day I was photographing a festival, and somebody I know came up to me and said, 'Would you like to photograph President Traian Băsescu?'

I said, 'No, not particularly.' I thought, I don't have the time to go through all of that hassle right now, I'm in the middle of a job. They seemed rather surprised by my statement.

'He's sitting just over there and if you want, you can go over and photograph him.'

I said, 'Well okay, fine, if it's that easy.' They told me I needed to stay about a metre away from him, basically arm's-length.

'Don't get right in his face!'

Jonas Schäfer

Cund

'We have come to a level that is remarkably high but it's local women, who've never had a fine dining experience in their life, who are cooking their heart out with amazing food.'

My father came down here in 1990 for the very first time to bring relief goods, Christmas time, to the children's hospital in Sighişoara. That was the start of a long love affair with Transylvania for my father. Three years later my family started running a small social project in this village. And when I turned 30 I really wanted to change something in my life – I'd been an executive in the German music industry and just felt there was something lacking – and I came to see my father down here in Romania and absolutely fell in love with the village. This was 2003, November, the ugliest time of the year to come to Transylvania, and I still loved the peace and quiet, the warmth of the people. My mother was taken quite ill at that point. For about nine months my father had to stay home with her and I said, 'I can take over the charity for you for that period of time.' My girlfriend came to visit me from Germany and also fell in love with Cund and Transylvania. We got married in 2007, here in the village.

Cund is a Saxon village but the majority of Saxons had already gone by 2003. It was mainly populated by Hungarians and Romanians who moved in from the nearby villages. Until 2007 there was a very wise old Saxon shepherd who was actually responsible for us remaining in the village. He was extremely well read, well educated, though he'd never really been to school. He had five or six years of basic schooling but had read more standard works of philosophy than I have.

Where does this love affair come from? Is it the character of the people, the landscape?

I've travelled Romania quite extensively and I was always very happy to say that the place my father chose is the place I love most in this very beautiful country. I haven't found an area that has moved me as much as these rolling hills. But also, after nine years of living here, the very strong relationships we have with locals in the village is of course an important factor for us in feeling at home in this place.

We are now sitting in the Valea Verde. It's the centre of our small tourism project we started pretty early on during our time here in Transylvania. We started off by renting holiday homes. At that time there were virtually no holiday homes available that were providing travellers with basic comfort and a nice house. We set up one holiday home and then the locals in the village started to follow our example. After year one of our activities we had five holiday homes we were marketing, of which we owned one.

After two years we found more and more a demand from the visitors to share their experience, their very strong observations of a life so completely different from their background, predominantly German, British, or American. We ended up talking with them on a daily basis, most of the time in the evenings. This took place in my flat, before we had the restaurant. In the morning when I got up, our one and a half bedroom flat here in a small Saxon house looked like a bombsite after hosting ten or twelve people there. We enjoyed it tremendously and it also enriched our social life but it looked like I was walking through a deserted pub in the morning. So I thought it would be nice to focus that somewhere else, away from my living room. We decided to build this place here and open it up for guests.

Once you get to know them people here are extremely friendly and very hospitable. I'm welcome in all houses in the village. In winter I really take time to visit people, to interact and invite them round to our home. I remain in contact with the local community, apart from providing work for quite a few people nowadays.

It's much easier to build relations here. I'm from the northern part of Germany and we generally don't like to talk to people, never mind foreigners – foreigners meaning not being born in the village. That's something that really struck me when I first came here. I was greeted by people on the street who I'd never met, but they knew I was the son of my father. They invited me to come round to their house, to have a glass of wine. With their very little command of the German language and my non-existent Romanian we somehow spent an evening together, eating some incredibly greasy food and drinking an awful house wine here. It took me a while to realise that I had to drink beer. As a wine lover, that was difficult for me.

I find a stark difference between the professional and the personal hospitality. Nine years ago professional hospitality was non-existent; they hadn't grasped the concept of having to be friendly to guests in restaurants and hotels. These days I think it has changed dramatically, though there is a bit of headroom for things to develop. This is in profound contrast to the personal warmth and friendliness of locals or anybody you get to know. Funnily enough though, as a foreigner living here, it's difficult to get past a certain level, of intimacy, of real friendship I would say. Our really close friends here are usually people brought up outside Romania.

It was a massive challenge to set up a restaurant in a village like this. It's a massive challenge to run it. We haven't paid any bribes ever, and I guess it's a unique thing that we got away with it, from what I learned from colleagues. The fact is we are so far away from everything else, we don't pose a threat to any neighbouring restaurants, and we are not competition for other places, nor for hotels, nor for restaurants. We are not taking any business away from other people – that's helpful. And we are so small that even the greediest inspectors who come here are seeing that these guys cannot really be making a lot of money from what they're doing here. They are somehow also moved by what we do, by the fact that we ventured into this crazy world of hospitality in a place like Cund.

Romanians must think you're really strange.

They think we are utter freaks! You must be a bit of a freak to set up a business like this in Romania, you must be a bit of a freak to move to Romania, full stop. Funnily enough, I know many experts who lived and worked in the country and who come as guests, and they're all saying, 'Listen, when I first got offered the job here, I said you're going to have to pay some real incentive for me to go there instead of Paris or Rome.'

On the other hand all of them are enjoying their time in Romania, and would like to stay on. The countryside does offer real benefits to people who like to get out and explore more of the world around them. People don't know the beautiful sides of Transylvania.

Do you have Romanians coming here as guests to Valea Verde?

Yes, we do. For most of them it's a very deliberate step to rediscover their own country. Our core group of Romanian guests are married, something between 28 and 45 and have been to Tuscany, to Provence, to Brittany. They've been to the Cotswolds and they know their way around the New Forest, often much better than they know Transylvania; so for them it's a deliberate move to rediscover their countryside. And they are stunned by the utter beauty of what's here.

Our restaurant doesn't have a menu. We have a very small selection of wines. We are providing a very fine dining experience without white tablecloths, without waiters dressed in black. It's an element of casual chic, or rustic charm paired with great food, that is hard to be found in Romania. Very often we are receiving extremely good comments about the fact that we are doing something in their country, and that they're grateful for people to bring that level of quality or service here. I'm always stepping back and saying, 'But listen, we have all our employees from the village, we have only locals working for us. Nowadays 70 per cent of the food that's being prepared here is not prepared by me personally any more.' After four years of very hard and very intense training and work, we have come to a level that is remarkably high. But it's local women, who've never had a fine dining experience in their life, who are cooking their heart out with amazing food.

What is your philosophy in terms of food?

Very simple. We are focusing on good flavour; for that we work only with the best of produce, and much of that produce is sourced locally. We sometimes have to drive for hours to find what we want. We have a network of small farms. We have one farm that supplies our cheese; we have another breeding Angus calves for us. We have another place where we go to buy our mozzarella from organic buffalo. And we do have large gardens, about two and half hectares, where we grow our own produce. We have three ladies who are now working full-time in the summer season just to maintain these gardens. But I'm not an organic freak. I'm doing this because it tastes better and it's nicer and it's also appropriate. It wouldn't be appropriate to serve lobster in a place like this with no sea around here. We could buy high-quality lobster and we could fly it in here; it's available, it's not a problem, but it wouldn't be appropriate.

Have you always been a cook?

Certainly not, no. I was a very passionate eater all my life, and wine lover, but I started to cook only when we opened the restaurant. I trained two ladies, one to be chef, one to be cook. One month prior to the opening, the kitchen was finished and I was going through the menu planning process with them. I met blank faces. I thought, I've paid for a year and a half of schooling for them so they should have at least some basic knowledge of what we were talking about. The results of their cooking were disastrous. They know their kind of food, the local cuisine, what they're doing at home but they had no experience whatsoever of fine cuisine, not even with the basic elements.

First of all I asked a friend who helped me with setting up the restaurant. He is a Michelin star chef from Hamburg who helped me buy equipment in Germany. I called him and said, 'Can you send down a sous-chef perhaps, anybody, a good line cook to train us and to help us in the first two months, to take us from A to B. I haven't got any money but I'll find that somehow, we'll sell something, whatever, just to make sure we can do that.'

And he said, 'No, I won't do that, because it's not right. You will have to learn how to cook. I know that you have travelled extensively, that you are a real foodie, so you know how it should taste. Then just get working!'

That was how I started to cook. I spent the next month in the kitchen, cooking 14 or 15 hours a day, small menus. After four weeks we had some beautiful food that we were presenting the first guests who came here. I was proud like hell, and hooked, and from that time on spent all my holidays travelling, working in different restaurants in Europe, reading cookbooks in my spare time and dedicating my life to that.

How do you see tourism as a whole in Romania?

I'm sometimes invited as a speaker on rural tourism here; I've done about ten conferences. I think I'm more the humorous part in the discussion. It's all about EU funding and how to attract that. I'm presenting Cund as a different way of doing rural tourism. And as much as people are fascinated by what we do, nobody believes it really does work. It's quite funny. Even after the tenth conference I said, 'I can see in your faces you don't believe we do have guests. My last chart here for you is the official occupancy rate and you can see here our *pension* has the highest rate of occupancy in all of Mureș County, so that might give you something to think about.'

You're in the middle of what was the Saxon area. What kind of relationship do you have with those still here?

Many of those Saxons who stayed behind are very old and not very flexible in their thinking. For me it is very difficult to relate to the Saxon community. I understand those who lived here for 800 years wanted to maintain their cultural identity and integrity. On the other hand there are common characteristics that I find problematic. They are not very open-minded towards other nationalities they live with. They very often have major problems with the Roma, and that's something I find very difficult to deal with. In many cases despicable. There's a very strong element of racism towards Roma in most ethnic groups and very much so among the Saxons, who had to preserve themselves and their cultural identity. That's the only way I can explain what makes them tick in that respect.

In this very rural area, what changes have you seen?

There've been major changes for the better, and for the worse. The major changes for the better have all to do with infrastructure. The newly paved road here is very good. The access to the restaurant was done by the local *primaria*. They have invested heavily in building an access for us, which we didn't think would ever happen, but it did. The whole communications side has changed, also for the better. We still have only six telephone lines in the village, but at least it's not a manual exchange any more, as it was nine years ago. My first Romanian that I learnt was, 'I would like a connection with Germany.' I had to wait for them to call back and establish a connection. After speaking for three minutes with my girlfriend, they asked me if I seriously wanted to continue the conversation, or if I was aware that it is expensive to talk with somebody outside the country. 'Yes, I am but still, please let me talk, get off the line!'

There is a very special, unique flora and fauna here – I don't know if you're aware that this part of Transylvania, protected by a Natura 2000 programme, has the highest biodiversity in meadows of all Europe. There's only eight different places left in the world, according to UNESCO, where you have such a valuable biodiversity.

We are now seeing a growing number of foreigners buying up land here to do industrial agriculture. So they're buying up huge pieces of land and coming in with heavy gear to farm this area. They are coming in with their tank-like tractors that can plough a field doing 65 kilometres an hour. It looks incredibly spooky from here, and that's definitely one of the things that is changing for the worse. It has convinced us that we need to move in the other direction, buy land as well and set up an organic farm. This is the project for next year or the year after, whenever we have the funds in place and are set up to do that.

We are a long way from Bucharest, but of course it's extremely worrying to see the political situation of this country. It's frustrating and very alarming to see the political developments and the lack of understanding of political basics here. We are resigned to make the little place where we live a bit better, but it doesn't mean that we are not appalled, and to a very large extent frightened shitless, by seeing what's happening in this country on a larger scale. The really difficult thing is to see that many people are choosing the easy way out, meaning they leave the country, and are not staying on to fight to make this a better place.

We had journalists staying with us for the last four days. In the evening they were opening up their hearts and saying they were fighting hard-core against corruption, against crazy politicians, against a way they think is not beneficial, that is ruining their beloved country, but in the end they are bystanders. They can show people, but even with the most alarming revelations people don't seem to take a real interest.

Is this because of this fatalistic Asta este! *– That's the way it is! Or we can't do anything about it.*

Asta este is the major challenge for us in day-to-day life. The willingness to assume responsibility and to follow through is there, but the capacity is virtually non-existent. We are now resigned to establishing procedures for nearly every event conceivable: if this happens do this, follow A, B, C; if that happens, call me, do this, do that. It's an absurd amount of scenario planning to compensate for a lack of focus on getting a problem solved, embracing challenges. The lack of initiative is definitely the most challenging and frustrating issue. It follows through in all parts of society. It's why we have this political situation. It's why the economy is not really as developed as it could be. It's why the schooling system, which is in essence not a bad system, could be a lot better.

How do you see things long term?

My mid-term perspective is ten years. We were at a point, before we opened the restaurant, of really thinking how long we can take village life any more. Now we're finding we are having so many nice and interesting guests around us, it enriches our personal life tremendously. It's a win-win situation for us. Hosting is not only a professional necessity, it is also pretty rewarding in many aspects. We have decided on having children. The only thing I think might be difficult for me and my wife is to see that in the current educational system, or the current cultural situation in Romania, a certain part of life will not get the right focus. We will not be able to provide our children with the great offers that a city like Berlin, or even my small hometown, is offering.

Paul Davies

Constanța

'There are many other aspects to HIV infection that are not being given enough focus... emotional, spiritual and psycho-social problems... This is where we come in.'

Everybody in the early 90s saw the television programmes showing the terrible deprivation of the orphanages here. My wife and I at the time were members of a church in Chepstow, South Wales, and decided to join an aid group. We all came with wonderful intentions of giving aid to the Romanians, thinking this would resolve all their problems.

I'd just become a Christian, and as part of this first aid trip we visited a church in Iaşi, a Baptist church. Here I saw for the first time the true meaning of faith and compassion to others. Seeing the depth of deprivation the people were going through, yet remarkably clinging to a faith with a foundation so much stronger than mine – it was really an eye-opening experience. I felt then that Romania had something to teach me.

The guy leading our expedition had been in communication with the pastor in Iaşi, who'd been asking for help for his congregation. We visited ordinary homes, hospitals, orphanages and schools... and without needing to exaggerate, I saw the most appalling living conditions I've ever seen, and I came from a poor family. They knew the meaning of shortages, every day, with little hope of change. This was another level of deprivation: normal people struggling just to survive day-to-day. What impressed me most was the persistence to survive shown by the children, who seemed to have suffered the worst.

I first witnessed this when we visited the hospitals and the long-term institutions, especially the orphanages. The shock to your system is numbing when you see 300 kids tied up in cots in a massive hanger-like orphanage, with three or four people trying to care for them, receiving little nourishment, and even less love. Yet the children had survived against all the odds. What hit me most in these institutions was the smell. The children had been lying in their faeces for days on end. And the silence. You don't expect to walk into a room of 300 kids and have silence. I remember the first child I went up to – I leant over the cot to hand a soft toy to the little boy and he just scurried into the other corner out of fear. Nobody on that first trip came out of those orphanages the same person as they went in.

There were about 30 of us in a big old bus, coming over the hill like the 7th Cavalry, to save the poor natives. We'd arrived with so many pre-conceived ideas, like what the conditions would be when we arrived and what we would do to alleviate their troubles immediately. But the silence that we met in the orphanage changed the mood and our mind-set. On the bus going back to our lodgings, nobody spoke. Everybody was absorbing what they'd seen. It changed my whole perspective on life. And that is where my Romanian journey really started.

After this initiation, I began to run aid-trips to another county, linking with priests there. Over two years we found the toys, clothes, and other materials were no longer there; they were being sold out the back of most of the institutions and churches, from whatever denomination. The people that really needed it were not receiving anything. For a while we made excuses to ourselves, tried to find explanations for the missing aid, not wishing to admit our folly. But the evidence was too obvious. The people, they didn't seem any better off at all. The pastors would greet us with warm smiles, but they alone looked to be faring better – one was wearing a fistful of gold rings and a new, expensive-looking winter coat. We eventually learned you couldn't trust anybody. If you were bringing aid, you had to physically put it in the hands of the people you wanted to receive it. It's a lesson I still carry with me today.

I first went to the hospice in Cernavodă in 1993, then went back and forth for four years. Here there was yet another level of experience, meeting and working with some of the thousands of kids infected with HIV. This AIDS hospice for 100 children was the only one in Romania. When I went there it was overflowing with kids; some had to be turned away as there was not enough space. They only took the very worst cases, those expected to die within a few months. They showed them the love and care they'd been missing. Even though there was nothing we could do at the time to prevent the AIDS carrying through its full effect and the kids dying – anti-HIV medicines weren't available then – we made their last days their best days. Nobody who visited the hospice remained unaffected by what they experienced. The toughest truck drivers who drove aid over from Yorkshire, seeing 100 babies or toddlers one step away from death, were humbled to the point of tears.

The kids were so hardened by the system in which they'd grown up. They were used to taking care of themselves, but never showed any self-pity. They showed us, the new kids on the block as we were when we worked there for the first time – they would take you by the hand and show you what to do, where all the stuff was kept. Where the toys were, where the best toys were of course, because they wanted to play with the best. They were street-wise, but compassionate at the same time. Though I hardly spoke any Romanian there were ways of communicating. Those kids knew how to touch your soul without saying a word. They would just look into your eyes and you were never the same person again. I felt that there was such a pull; that my work back in Britain seemed to be a preparation for what I believed God had planned for me later on down the road.

Children would arrive at the hospice from all over the country, basically to come and spend their last few days with us. Medical opinion at this time agreed that their life-span was extremely limited. But the kids sometimes had other ideas, some being more resilient than anyone could believe, lasting much longer than expected. For our part we'd build them up as much as possible with the best food and medical care we had, to give them the best chance of life. But neither they nor we could escape the reality that there were no anti-HIV medicines, and no palliative care available. For extreme pain relief you needed two nurses and a doctor at the child's bedside in order to give morphine-based drugs. This was almost impossible to arrange every time a child needed pain relief. So the kids were dying horrific deaths in those days, in a lot of pain.

You can't alleviate HIV infected pain with ibuprofen, it's just totally inadequate. So the noises in the hospice at night stay with me now. In my dreams sometimes I can still hear the kids screaming, and there was a period in the early days when we were burying six to eight kids every couple of weeks. The kids would come in, we'd build them up a little, and then they'd die these horrific deaths and we'd be burying them. Those who worked as volunteers then didn't really realise the effect this trauma was having on them. But when I talk today to friends who worked with me at that time, they tell me they remember that as the absolute worst time in their lives. There was nothing we could do about the kids dying, there was nothing we could do to prevent their pain; we just did the best we could with what we had. It wasn't enough, it just wasn't enough. And the feeling of frustration and not being able to take the pain away from the kids was a horrendous experience – one that drew us all together because we were the only support we had. Even though we couldn't talk openly about the way we were feeling, we knew by looking at each other that we were going through the same ordeal inside.

There was a particular incident that turned my life 180 degrees again. It began with meeting a little ten-year-old boy called Florin. He wasn't the type of kid you would put on a poster if you were looking to appeal to people to give donations. He was an ugly little brat, scabs all over his face, continuously snotty nose, couldn't talk, couldn't walk, just screamed all day, and most of the night. He wasn't the most appealing of kids, but when I walked on the ward the first time, he looked at me, I looked at him, and we both knew a bond had already been formed between us. Together with a friend of mine, Charlotte, we took this young lad under our wing and decided he would be our first save, as aid workers call it. We would do everything we could to make sure this boy survived.

Charlotte worked the day shift, I worked the night shift. At night, in order for the other kids to get any sleep, I used to have to wrap him up 'Welsh-fashion', an expression for the way you carry the child, for him to feel safe and secure. You can carry on doing your work with the kid strapped to you. I used to do this all night, so he'd fall asleep on my back and the other kids could get some sleep. He loved it, and waited each night with arms tight to his side for his comfort blanket.

We made that kid well again, without looking for any praise. I mean Charlotte and I turned that kid around physically, emotionally, spiritually by the care we showed him. We fed him up, made sure he was one of the best fed there. Within a few months we'd built him up into almost a normal child. It was wonderful to us to see this change in the kid. Then in the last two weeks I was there, he caught a wasting disease and died in my arms. A ten-year-old boy, and I was 40 years at the time. That totally rocked my Christian beliefs. I nearly lost my faith completely. How could I believe in a God that would do this, take this innocent life?

But there was a purpose, as I found out on my way home.

When I was driving back from Romania after that experience I felt a conviction. There's no other way to put it – unless you've had such an experience first-hand it'll sound weird and overly spiritual – but I felt this conviction from God that I wasn't doing enough, that this little boy didn't die for nothing. I was there to help him along for a time, but when he left, he left me with this conviction that I had to go back to help others like Florin; to go there to work permanently. So in 1997, after that fateful trip, I went back to Britain, gave up my job, sold my house and came out to Romania to live and work for the children.

I worked as a volunteer in the Cernavodă hospice for a year. Later I was made Team Leader in a sister hospice in a village nearby, Slobozia. While I was working there I met a child called Magda. I didn't know her very well, because she was in hospital more than the hospice. Although she had lived in the orphanage for most of her nine years, when she died we discovered she wasn't an orphan. Her mother lived just two miles up the road. Her mother had had Magda out of wedlock and the Social Services took her away, placed her in the orphanage and gave her the blood transfusion infected with HIV. We were able to re-unite mother and child, unfortunately after Magda had died, but her mother was so grateful and relieved to be able to at least say goodbye to her child, after not seeing her since she gave birth. We brought them back together, even if it was only for the funeral.

We thought that there must be other kids in the same position, living in the orphanage but not orphans, and with relatives still living in the area. So we started a community project in Ialomiţa County. With Noreen, a friend and colleague in Slobozia, we repatriated 30 children from the main orphanage and our hospice. As far as I'm aware, this was the first community project in Romania. The kids were delighted to be back with parents or close relatives, who in their turn were happy to have the child back. And grateful to have the support that we were giving them. Community projects were new in Britain then; they were an absolute innovation in Romania. The idea is simple enough – from a base like the hospice you support the family unit, to keep it together at home. That was the aim of it and it worked really well.

There still are a lot of bureaucratic complications working in Romania, but the corruption is by far the greatest hindrance to progress. When you're a well-intentioned but naive aid worker working in a system you don't understand, you get drawn into the system and the acceptance of corruption as a way of life. But there's a point where you say to yourself, 'I can't take any more of this!' At our hospice we had managed to change the attitude of care towards the children; we re-educated the staff, and we brought the care system in the hospice forward leaps and bounds in the short period we were there. But we couldn't change the corruption that was going on at higher levels.

The breaking point for me was the stealing of the Christmas packets coming out for the kids from Britain. People in the UK were giving these packets with love and trust, from schools, hospitals – a great idea that still goes on, now thankfully much more smoothly. But at that time a lot of the Christmas packets weren't arriving at our hospice when they were promised. They were being siphoned off by people on the way. The boxes that did arrive had been rifled for the best stuff, leaving our kids with the dregs of a wonderful gift. I complained bitterly about it to my boss. That was the breaking point for me. I decided this charity and I had to part, so I left.

With the help of a small group of friends in a local church in Wales, we formed our own charity in 2000 – Everyone's Child Romania. I knew the greatest concentration of paediatric HIV infection was in the Constanţa area. So in collaboration with an AIDS doctor, Dr Mătuşă, we established a community project there, supporting 50 HIV-infected beneficiaries within their family units. Dr Mătuşă had been working in one of the hospitals where the mass infections took place and had been documenting suspected HIV/AIDS infections since the mid 1980s. She found a nurse and a social worker for us, and the three of us, with the van I bought from the sale of my house, began the first community project in Constanţa County. Soon I discovered that there were over 650 cases in Constanţa County alone, and we only had enough funding to help 50. Nobody else seemed to be helping the other 600 cases. This injustice has often tormented me. But I have had to salve my conscience in the knowledge that although we are just a drop in the ocean, we are an essential drop for our families. We started delivering food packets to families in Constanţa County, a large area with many remote villages. We were the only regular, reliable contact those cases had with the care providers in Constanţa city, even though they had all been living with HIV for five or six years when we met them.

Because we're not in the news anymore, everybody thinks that the situation has been resolved. But that's far from the truth. The kids have had a lot of help since the early days. The Romanian state has admitted there is a major problem. They are helping in that they're providing two thirds of the anti-HIV medicines needed. They have to be applauded for that, although there are still a lot of kinks in the system. The other third of their anti-HIV medicine comes through the Baylor Black Sea Foundation which runs a clinic, so the medicinal side is taken care of to a large extent. But there are many other aspects to HIV infection that are not given enough focus. The emotional, spiritual and psycho-social problems that come with such a disease need constant development. This is where we come in.

We're talking about a horrendous drug regime, taking three handfuls of pills every day, with the 'bonus' of horrific secondary reactions to the medicines for some. On top of this you have the psycho-social problems of being treated like a leper all your life. Some of our kids have been thrown out of school because the others found out they have got this terrible disease. It's more understood now, but not to the point where it's accepted. These are still the latter-day lepers of the world. This often leads to attitudes of hopelessness in some of them… they just give up and stop taking their medicines.

We always support the family through a child's death, and in the months afterwards. Recently we buried one of the children who'd been with us from the very beginning, Marysol, and her new-born baby son. She caught meningitis after a very difficult birth; the baby didn't survive more than a couple of days. We had to pay for most of the burial as the relatives were very poor.

I've learned over the years to be very careful when I go to these funerals, to follow the Romanian traditions. You make sure you walk into the church with a lighted candle, you make sure when you say goodbye to the deceased in the open coffin that you kiss the icon, then the forehead of the dead person. I tend to stay in the background so attention is not drawn to the family regarding the cause of death, as we're quite well known for supporting HIV/AIDS children.

I've learned many lessons from the kids themselves, but I've also learned from mothers and grandmothers, about how to behave and to show the proper respect. You have to adapt and fit into their needs. Mistakes we aid workers have made have partly been due to the fact we think we know best. We think we've got enough experience in other disasters to come and show these people how they should be living. Every disaster has its own problems and therefore its own solutions. You come and listen and learn first, then perhaps you can offer some advice and help.

I've always relied on my Romanian staff, who are 100 per cent trustworthy, honest and committed people, to protect the beneficiaries and the charity from corruption in society. I always stress to them that if we don't follow the accepted system of bribes, and maintain this attitude, then little by little people will realise we're different and maybe they will change as well. We work in the way we believe is correct, and God-led. Everybody I've worked with has had to have the same ideal. Although it was hard at the beginning to establish ourselves as incorruptible, the fact that we've been here for over ten years, working in the same way, is confirmation for me that what we're doing is right.

Our attitudes are also rubbing off on the people we work with, in that their attitude of living only for themselves has changed. Now they would love to see changes begin in the government structures, as would we all. I've noticed a growing recognition among ordinary people that a society based on bribes and back-handers and working on the black market will not survive. There must be a fairer society for everyone.

From a religious perspective, if you went to non-conformist churches in Romania, you'd meet a level of spirituality I've never come across in any other country. The church I previously mentioned in Iași, on the night we were there, had a 400-strong congregation on a freezing cold Sunday night. In Wales, on a freezing cold Sunday night, most people curl up and watch Coronation Street. In that Iași church, I'll never forget this little old lady getting out into the aisle, down on her knees, pouring her heart out, the tears flowing freely down her face. I didn't understand a word she said but she was obviously heartbroken about something, and didn't care who knew it. She was there alone with her God, and that was it. I've seen that level of peace with my faith previously only in the faces of some Orthodox monks, but to see it in such numbers in a non-conformist church was an eye-opener. These people had such a deep spiritual faith that they believed God would send somebody to help them, and He did. They had a faith that was founded on a rock. No doubt about it.

Romanians in general have a resilient character. They've lived through hard times, they're still living through them. They never bat an eyelid about life being hard because it always has been –

mending and making-do is a way of life. They very rarely throw anything away that could be useful. Here, if the vacuum cleaner doesn't work, you take it three, four, five, however many times it needs, down to the repairers, or you learn to fix it yourself. They never give up, they never say 'Pity me!' They just get on with life. To witness this attitude is an inspiration. Their main goal in life, besides health for their family, is to have a house to leave for their children.

The sad part about this insular attitude is that you make sure your family and your close friends are cared for, but outside this circle of care there's little concern shown to other people's suffering. An attitude of charity hasn't been developed here yet, but there are signs of change. People's eyes are being slowly opened to the idea of giving something to somebody they don't know, a revolutionary idea to most people here, but not all.

In the early days there was a great mistrust of foreign aid agencies and charities. The people we were helping had seen so many NGOs come, stay for a few months, do what they thought was the right thing to help, and then leave. So the attitude of the families when we first met them was that they were going to take everything they could from us before we left, which is understandable. It took up to four years before people began to think maybe we were going to stay, and an even longer time to build up the level of trust where the families could confide in us. Now we have 55 beneficiaries, some from the original cohort of children, some new cases, aged between seven and twenty-three.

On a personal level, it is a tremendous support to have the encouragement and positive contribution of my wife Alina. We have a similar vision, but she is such a positive driving force that she lifts all the regular workers and beneficiaries with her optimism – 'Yes we can' being her mantra. So when I'm asked, 'Where is my adopted home?' I reply, 'Romania!' for all the above reasons, good and bad.

Carolyn Litchfield

Târgu Mureş

'The fact that I have two kinds of friends, to some people that means I've taken sides, even though I'm friends with both.'

Ed died six years ago, and is buried here in a village on a hilltop. We started being interested in living in a former communist country because of watching CNN in '89, with the collapse of the Berlin Wall. I can remember watching the library in Bucharest burning. We just wanted to see how it changed, how they accepted democracy, democracy and capitalism together. We ended up coming here and loved it. I think it was the people that captivated us. We loved the people.

I've always been a teacher; home economics teacher, a teacher of the blind, a rehabilitation teacher. Right before we came we had a bed-and-breakfast together, in Kansas City. Ed had always been in entertainment and worked on Broadway and in Hollywood, in management. He worked for 20th Century Fox. The bed-and-breakfast worked because he knew how to establish a set and scenery and be a host. I, with my home economics, could cook. So I did the breakfasts, he made the sets, and together we schmoozed the people. We were very successful together.

We first came in 1991 and moved here in '95. Over the intervening four years we came six times, just to keep seeing if this was what we really wanted to do. Almost everybody here wants to go west, but we came here. For a long time we were the only ones who came not associated with a church or a business. So yes, they questioned it. I don't hear that anymore, but back in 1995 that was certainly on everybody's mind.

We had our apartment broken into at one point. Somebody said the thieves were working for the government. They wanted to see what was in our place. I don't know if that was true, because they didn't take the computer or any of the discs. It was the biggest theft in Târgu Mureş at that time, and people said it was because we're Americans. It was '96 and we had all the electronics. When the police finally found the people, it turned out they had sold a lot of the stuff to the courthouse staff.

We made a choice at one point. Do we want to live in an apartment and travel a lot, get to know the area and even expand beyond Romania? Or do we want to get ourselves into a community that we can become part of? We chose to be part of a community. Though we were renting an apartment here in the city, we bought a house in a village and renovated it. It took us about three years. My husband designed the renovation and we hired local people to do the work. Americans come and say, 'Oh it looks just like Transylvania,' and people here say it looks so American. Who's to say what it looks like, but we made this house, which I still have and love. But I need to sell it.

How did you fit into the life of the village?

I didn't insert myself, I was just sort of there, like when I moved to any new community. You become friends with the people next to you, and then you expand from there. I had lived in St Louis, Chicago and Kansas City and every time I moved I had new friends and you settle.

The problem was we couldn't speak Hungarian, still don't. I speak enough Romanian to manage. The men had all been in the army, so they could speak Romanian. A lot of the women worked in the village and only speak Hungarian. I'm limited because I can't speak to the women. I needed to buy milk so I'd go to my neighbour to get it every night, fresh from the cow. I'd go to somebody else when I needed some vegetables. We'd sit in each other's kitchens and just talk, somehow, in this bad Romanian, which was a second language for both of us.

The village was extremely small – 45 people, mainly farmers and old people. When we moved in there were 35 cows and people would sell the milk. We lived there 11 years. There are no cows any more. The men have died and the women can't take care of the cows, so the whole complexion of the village has changed. The cows are one illustration of it. Because they can't go out and farm the fields, they don't have an income. Now an occasional tourist comes and likes the village. Some have bought houses and moved there. They're still all Hungarian.

One time we had some Romanian friends who wanted to buy a house across from us. I went to two families that I liked and said, 'Is it a problem for you if Romanian people buy this house?' and both of them said instantly, 'If they're nice people, it doesn't matter. If they're Gypsies, it matters a lot. We don't want them here.' In that village there was only one house that had Gypsies. They were gone most of the time because they were off working, doing tin work, making gutters on houses. They weren't there that much, but 'Romanians are okay, Gypsies aren't' was what we heard.

After a time we realised it might have been better if we'd moved to a Romanian instead of a Hungarian village. The Hungarians were always sitting around saying, 'Ain't it awful we are persecuted.' My husband called them all professional martyrs. However, it's how they perceive life in a lot of ways. They can give me examples of when they've been persecuted and why the government in some cases is not fair to them. Like getting property back. Some people are still fighting to get property back. Or their lives were affected because their Hungarian fathers were professionals or ministers in churches. Their children were not allowed to go to university, so they couldn't become a doctor, they had to become a nurse or a lab technician. You still hear some of those stories.

I listen and nod. Then I take these stories to talk over with Romanian friends. They say, 'yes, but this and this.' And in some cases, it happened to Romanians, too. So I just try to listen. I try not to take sides. But the fact that I have two kinds of friends, to some people that means I've taken sides, even though I'm friends with both.

Do you ever bring Hungarian and Romanian friends together?

I'll give you an example – when a researcher friend of mine was here. I'm friends with a really interesting Hungarian couple and a Romanian couple that enjoy talking to him. I had them together for dinner one evening. I know these Romanians are very open and support Hungarians in their work, in their professions, and vice versa. Ethnic topics never came up and I asked them why, afterwards. 'I didn't want to get into it. It just wasn't appropriate.' Now, when he comes, they do want to talk to him about the ethnic topics, but I don't have them meet together. These two couples live next door to each other just down the block from me; they've known each other longer than I've known them. I feel very often as though it's the politicians that stir the things up. People live next door to each other and get along fine.

I had a man who helped us with the renovation. We got to talking about how we all live together and everything is good. Then one time he said, 'If there's a war between the Romanians and Hungarians, I will push my sons into the Hungarian part and I will let them fight. I want them to fight.'

'Really! But I thought you got along with everybody?'

'No, those Romanians, hmm. Another people! You can see it in their eyes. They're different, they're not good.' And the Romanians say it about the Hungarians. I've just tried to sit and listen.

I don't teach many children but I had a young student called G, the little nationalist bigot! He kept saying, 'Those Hungarians, they're just different. You just know they're different.'

I was so upset I wanted to stop working with him. Finally I decided no, I would do my part to get this out of him. I knew him from fifth grade until he graduated from high school. He would say, 'Carolyn, I know you're going to say I shouldn't feel that way, and that's one of the reasons you've stayed to teach me.' He knew what my agenda was. I talked to his mother about it. 'I worry about G, he's just a little bigot.'

She said, 'Yeah, he got that from his uncle.' I keep challenging that. That's my little thing I want to do. I don't do it with adults very much, but I feel as though I have a little bit of power over kids.

How do you keep up with what's going on?

I don't read the newspapers and I don't watch TV at all. I do listen to people around me. I feel as though everybody would just like to get rid of the politicians and start again. There doesn't seem to be much hope for the country with the current people in control, almost on any political level, and that's a shame. Somebody I trust said that years ago Nokia wanted to build a factory here and the mayor said, 'If you give me €50,000 I'll allow you to build it in our city.' Nokia said no. The word is that people enter politics to get rich. That's just a given. Nobody thinks that people become politicians for any other reason.

How do things get done here?

People we met – this was years ago – were operating a foundation and they had brought a car in from another country. Well, everybody knew back then that you couldn't get a car licence unless you paid somebody to help you at the licensing place. We brought a car in and we did just that. A friend of ours at the police department excused it, saying the police don't get a big enough salary, so he considered that this was supporting them with their salary. We put money in this officer's drawer, right in this guy's desk. Some people believe politicians don't want to make the laws better or easier because then they wouldn't get money on the side.

Another thing I'd say about people here is they're extremely creative on how to wiggle through stuff. Art is very interesting, the music is interesting, their writers are so good, and the writing is creative. But it's also how you deal with making it through regular life. You have to be flexible.

Do you get preferential treatment because you're a foreigner?

As a foreigner I had to get my car licensed every year. People there began to recognise me. I went legally one time and sat in the line almost all day. When I got up to the head of the line the man recognised me. 'Why did you wait all day? You know me. Why didn't you bring your car round the back?' He wanted to help me.

Used to be they'd insist we went to the head of the line. Doesn't happen as much now, but it still does from time to time. And then my husband got sick. We would go into a hospital, and it was in his nature to create a bit of drama. He would kind of collapse or look extremely pitiful, and I'd ask for help. I would speak in English, and people would just push us to the head of the line. I used to have to take people with me to help, but now I can manage with the language. Some of my friends call me an honorary Romanian now.

Visiting Americans, when they get to talk to people, realise there's something special in the people here. It's the *sufletul mare*, which is the big heart, the big soul. They're very kind to foreigners. Sometimes they're not as kind to each other, but they're nice and open to foreigners. When my family came to visit I said, 'Look around to see how things are! You're coming here to see something different. You're not coming here to find a McDonalds, you're coming here to experience a different place. Come, but don't expect service in most cases, because service is still not great. And don't expect American plumbing. But expect people to like you!' Romanians still like Americans.

I have a little bit of a personal philosophy, why I haven't learnt to speak the language real well. If I stumble on my words people are nice to me, because 'at least she is trying to speak.' I'm embarrassed sometimes, but I can walk in villages and get invited into houses, and get to see things and meet people. If I have tourists with me we all get invited. Some of it's because I don't speak like a native. But they do have this expression about all guests, not just foreigners, 'We will give you the last piece of bread in the house although we may not have any later.' That's how they treat guests, and that's very obvious.

You must get some good insights. Do you find much frustration in the town?

A doctor I know had opportunities to emigrate to some other countries, but circumstances didn't work out and he chose to stay. He says, 'I have to stay here and keep trying to make it better, but I'm so discouraged.' One of the things he says is the government is not helping the medical profession. For example, they are still delivering the same quantities of supplies to the different hospitals as they did during the communist times. There is a small maternity hospital nearby. The supplies that are always delivered to this little hospital are the same as previously. They can't use everything there, but at the big county hospital, there are shortages. They can't change this because the Ministry of Health won't change their paperwork.

That must get to him. What are you doing with your time now?

I've been teaching English since I came. It's keeping me alive but I can't quite live on it. I have a little bit of a pension from the US. Here's the problem – it's not enough to live on there, and I may end up staying here because I can't afford to live in the US.

When I first came I volunteered at one of the college preparatory high schools. I did a course in conversational English with two classes, and one of the things I had them do was plan a company. I divided them into groups. 'You're going to start a company. You have to think about what your business activity is going to be, and how you're going to market it.'

One of the things that some of them didn't understand was, 'It's not correct to buy something at one price and sell it higher.'

'How do you think the shop can pay their rent?' I asked.

'I don't know, but this isn't okay.' That was at the beginning – now they all understand so that is a positive change. The role of an English teacher is to get people to talk, so I get to have these wonderful conversations with people. That's one of the ways I feel I have picked up some insight.

In one of my English lesson books was written: 'hard work pays off'. When I first came… people had a lot of trouble with that. 'No it doesn't!' That comes from the communist time, when it was who you knew, it wasn't hard work. They also told me, 'Everybody knows that if you have a job you can't make money.'

'What? Explain this to me!' When I first came everybody worked for the big companies, basically state-owned companies. They hadn't privatised. Everybody still got low salaries. If you worked only for them you didn't get enough money to live on. If you were a plumber for one of these big factories, for example, you had to do plumbing at night and at the weekend on your own. That's how you made your money. People will still say, 'He's rich but he did it honestly.' They're proud of those people.

I also have a book club. I started it because I read a lot and I was lending books out to all my friends. I thought, wouldn't it be fun if we could read some stimulating books and then discuss them. We meet once a month. It's a group of people who range in age from about 25 to 72 – Romanians and Hungarians. That's another way I fit into the community. I also teach a group of older women who have been meeting together for 15 years. It's like a club now. We meet every week, but not in the summer.

Do you know a book that was made into a musical, *Wicked*? It's about the green witch in *The Wizard of Oz*. The Wizard drops in to Oz, in a basket on a balloon, and he didn't plan to go there. He says, 'Because I came in this kind of magical way, people expect me to be wonderful. And so, I'm wonderful.' I feel the same way here. I'm a little bit special here. I was always just nobody. Mousy brown hair, a nice person. Not an A student; only a B student. I was never a standout. Here people remember me and this gets heady after a while. I personally try to be better here, and therefore I think I like myself more because of it. I don't know if I can go back and translate that in America. In all honesty, it could also be because I've grown older here. Maybe it would have happened in the US as I aged. I'm 67, and you hope that you have learned a little bit in these years.

Craig Turp

Bucharest

'The quality of life I have here is available at a price which I can't really get anywhere else.'

I now consider myself an ordinary person here, living an ordinary life in an ordinary Romanian apartment in an ordinary block. I don't consider myself privileged in any way. I'm not going to pretend I live like an average Romanian, because I don't. At the same time I'm not earning the kind of money that high-end expats are. Our children go to an ordinary Romanian school. I'm not and never have been a particularly ambitious person. I can be happy with very little, to be perfectly honest. I don't have that drive to go after more money, a big car, a bigger house or apartment. When you accept what you have, you're more willing to accept what's around you.

I'm an Englishman in Romania with a small publishing business. We publish the city guide *Bucharest In Your Pocket* – for people visiting, people here on business, people here on holiday. But you can't really give your opinion in a city guide. People aren't interested in that anyway, so I started the blog Bucharest Live. It was a place to dump all the stuff I was writing anyway but didn't have anywhere to publish. That's how I started, in the summer of 2007.

The blog has changed as I've changed. At the beginning I was a lot more critical about Bucharest and Romania in general. I've mellowed over the years. I like to think I've not lost my edge, but

I'm a lot more laid-back about things which really got on my nerves and made me sit down and write the 'angry man of Bucharest' type of thing. I was very 'Romanians do this or Romanians cannot do that.' I knew I shouldn't have been using these stereotypes, but I did anyway. And there's no way I would do that now. The city still has many problems, but there's no question that it's a much nicer place than it was five years ago. Life is far better for most people.

Do you accept the driving?

Well, they are terrible drivers…

That'll make you popular!

No, you don't need a foreigner to tell you that. Most Romanians will say it about themselves. They will not obey the laws of the road. Again I'm being stereotypical but there is a general given rule that the bigger and more expensive your car, the fewer rules of the road you have to obey. The reason for that is they can pretty much get away with what they like, because the police are relatively weak. You can drive the wrong way down a one-way street and nobody will do anything. You don't have to stop at traffic lights if you don't want to, you can park your car wherever you like and people do – everybody does. Probably I'm as guilty as anybody.

But if you take the same person to Britain or Germany they will obey the rules of the road to the letter, because they know they can't get away with it. There's a stereotype that Romanians are by nature a people who will try and get away with whatever they can, they're a bit shifty, a bit crooked – that's completely false.

I live here because I genuinely believe the quality of life we have cannot be replicated in England. I suppose it comes down to the life that I can offer my children. Primary education here is fantastic. Even the poorest schools do very well. Secondary and university education is an entirely different subject.

Also I enjoy the fact that I'm two hours from the mountains, two hours from the seaside. In the summer we go there as much as possible. The cost of living remains relatively cheap, although it's going up. My wife's parents own a house and a large parcel of land with animals and crops close to Satu Mare, right in the very north. The children are able to go up there for a month or two each summer. We also go for a few weeks at a time. When I think what it would cost me to replicate those things in the UK, it's frightening. The quality of life I have here is available at a price which I can't really get anywhere else.

My in-laws are fantastic. From day one we hit it off. They're wonderful people, they come and visit us as often as possible; my mother-in-law arrived this morning in fact. It's a shame they live so far away, at the other end of the country, 18 hours on a train. With Romanians in general, I've never had any problems. We go away with a group of friends quite a lot. They're a cosmopolitan bunch. One of the most vocal of the group is a merchant seaman who's been at sea for 20 years. He's got a story about every country and some pretty forthright views, after which anybody else's opinion always seems relatively reasonable. Nothing is taboo.

Are you treated better as a foreigner?

I find the more you're integrated, the more likely you are to be taken advantage of. A couple of years ago I had some problems with the electricity company. I went through three or four days in a row, arguing my case. Someone needed to come and do something. I went there speaking Romanian and nothing was getting done. On the fourth or fifth day I went there as a foreigner, pretended I couldn't speak a word of Romanian, and got it done.

Amongst themselves Romanians will talk themselves down;

with foreigners they will talk themselves up. It's this idea that our house is a mess, but nobody from outside can know what it's like inside. One of the things I dislike is the rather craven attitude they have towards foreigners, saying nice things about them, or for that matter, saying something nasty. When Romania appears in the foreign press it will be reported here. They are obsessed with the way they are seen abroad. That's why everybody has an opinion about how the country should sell itself as a tourist destination. The fact that the country has been dominated by foreign powers for so long, that's got something to do with it.

They certainly believe that they do not get a fair hearing in the foreign press. They think they're misunderstood and that people have to come here before they can have any opinion about their country. Having said that, if you criticise something about Bucharest, or Romania, there are those who will turn around and say, 'You're a foreigner. You choose to be here. You have got absolutely no right to criticise!' I find that attitude appalling, always have done, but unfortunately it's prevalent.

The literature of Romania is not widely known abroad. It's a shame that people outside the country have never heard of Eminescu or Sadoveanu. These are great writers. Try and find something by Caragiale in English. He has been translated but it costs £100 a copy. They would tell you something about Romanians. It also tells you something about this place that they are not available in translation.

What do you feel about the place of religion here?

To me this is not as religious a society as it would like to think itself. For many, religion is a ritual. I do not believe that they are genuinely faithful, as it were. They use the church as a crutch. They will have a predefined opinion about homosexuality, for example, and say, 'That's what the Bible says. The Bible says it's wrong, so that's why I think that.' Far too many Romanians take their virtues and vices from the Bible. They use the Bible as an excuse for their prejudices.

The country was so far behind the rest of Europe it's playing catch-up and will continue to play catch-up for a long time. That's a process that's going to happen whichever prime minister is running the country. Now we have Victor Ponta. I'm not a fan of his. In my opinion it's been proven beyond doubt that he did plagiarise his doctoral thesis and in any other country in the world he would have resigned. The biggest problem about that whole scandal is that in Romania he didn't feel compelled to resign. There was no groundswell of public opinion saying he needed to resign. It comes back to this 'everybody does it' attitude because, let's be honest, there are many people here who happen to have cheated at something at some stage in their life – whether it was in high school or university or taking their driving exam. There is an acceptance that plagiarism is a part of life and that's the real scandal, not that the prime minister plagiarised his thesis.

But the face of Bucharest has changed, wouldn't you say?

A journalist from a UK newspaper came here two years ago. I was showing him around. We came to this area here, in the summer, and all the terraces were open. It was a fantastic day; there were loads of people on the streets. He looked around and said, 'This is horrible. It could be anywhere in Europe.' He was genuinely disappointed that there weren't poor people or beggars or people with guns. He was expecting, hoping this would be a really edgy place. And the fact that it was just like anywhere else in Europe was a genuine disappointment.

There's continuing poverty in the countryside and I'd really like to see something done about that. Westerners romanticise the countryside. People seem to think that the Romanian countryside is full of happy peasants living wonderful lives on their subsistence farms and they're there because they want to be. They go to certain Potemkin villages which might look idyllic, but that's not true. People do backbreaking work, 12 hours a day. Unless you would swap places with them for the rest of your life, you shouldn't be saying, 'This is something that's wonderful, that we should be taking forward.' We should preserve village life, yes, but let's make it worth living first.

Krishan George

Bucharest

'The service isn't the best in the world, but they are students, they start learning and they start getting into the philosophy of the place.'

I was first here in December 1995, as a consultant. I had a two-year contract working with the Ministry of Finance and the Ministry of Agriculture, looking at the development of a privatisation policy. Today I'm doing a range of things. My latest venture is a water buffalo farm. I bought an old state farm in 2006, located in the middle of Transylvania about 15 kilometres from Rupea. I saw it from a distance; at first look it had two or three roofs on buildings. When I went back two months later everything had disappeared; electricity lines going into the farm, all the roofs, bricks – half the walls were demolished…

So your property had been stolen.

Absolutely, but now I have buffalo on the farm, water buffalo, about 150 for their milk. I find the animals fascinating. I'm selling the milk to a local sheep farmer, who is making cheese with it. I don't have the facilities yet to actually produce my own cheese or bottle the milk, but that's the intention, to bottle raw milk on the farm. There's this huge raging debate on raw versus pasteurised milk, and I'm getting involved in that slowly. I also started a permaculture programme, planting a 'food forest' and an integrated garden system, to look at ways of using permaculture systems in our own production process. I've been looking at these traditional food systems, in Romania, in India, South America; especially fermented types of traditional foods.

Like pickling in autumn for the rest of the year?

Yes, these are traditions that people have had forever – how to store fresh foods – common throughout the world. I would say most of the food products in the supermarkets or in shops today have nothing of their original food value. Rice is polished, sugars refined. Preservatives, binders and even tastes and smells are added to food products to make them cheap, last longer and travel further. We take the good things out, put questionable stuff in and then sterilise everything! We planted about two and a half hectares of what is referred to as food forest. You find examples of these in Morocco, in India, in Asia. These systems have been growing for centuries, without any sort of mechanical maintenance, chemical fertilisers or annual planting.

Is this a commercial enterprise, or is it an idea that you are trying to propagate?

It's an idea – an idea that I really like. It reminded me of my grandfather. He was a retired school principal. He'd had some land in Kerala around the family house. The back garden was always a mess. We'd walk out and he'd make me sit down and observe. Then we'd go and dig up something here, move something there. It looked like a mess but everything had its place, and I realise now what he was talking about. I always thought, because I went to a very British school in India, everything had to be organised. Lines of crops. But he didn't have it like that. He had it as a traditional food forest. It really brought back these memories of my grandfather's land. It's a very personal journey – and also making the link with what I think is one of the major problems we have in today's society – that we depend on somebody else curing us from illness, rather than being able to cure ourselves. I am talking here about the health benefits of traditional diets.

This comes from a man from Kerala where Ayurvedic ideas are prevalent?

That's right. I think a lot comes to us subconsciously. How much was absorbed through interactions with my parents and grandparents… there must be something in that. There must be an explanation of why I'm in the middle of Transylvania trying to do all this stuff. Although I do have other companies, my main focus is now the farm. I live up there and it's wonderful. It's one of those places where people will leave me alone. I'm not bothering anyone. I have a cluster of buildings, some land and no neighbours. I ride regularly, and at this time of year when the leaves are changing – oak forests – it's spectacular. There are no fences in Transylvania, so you can ride and ride for kilometres and kilometres without seeing anyone. So it is a dream.

I'm trying to find a way forward now in terms of a research project that we can do here. I'm thinking – can we not get somebody to do clinical trials with raw milk, or fermented raw milk products? If this research can be done and has some sort of positive result, some correlation between the intake of these products and their curative value… imagine if we had clinical trial evidence, data to empirically prove this correlation. Amazing!

So you've set yourself a bit of a mission.

I have actually. I think it's going to be a long journey, but it's one that gives me the opportunity to live in an amazing place, to do amazing things, to meet amazing people.

We're sitting here in the Barka Saffron restaurant. This has been going quite a while.

This has been going 13 years almost. I lived around the corner for a long time and it was a derelict building – no roof, burnt out. Homeless people used to sleep here on cold nights, build fires; it was quite a scary place. I made an offer to the owner, 'If you rent this to me, I'll clean it up, do something here.' That was in '99. He's my neighbour upstairs – used to work for some authority at that time. I started working on the place, doing it up, and he came along and said, 'No, no, you have to make the walls thicker. Consolidate the walls, the structure is falling down!'

'It's not falling down!'

'No, no, consolidate the walls!' All he wanted was to build another floor on top. He sent along his friends, the inspectors. Basically they stopped the work for about six months until I agreed to consolidate the walls, so he could build another floor on his building. After we got over that I put the place together. I always wanted a bar on the beach to look out on this turquoise water, palm trees, that sort of thing, but I didn't get that here.

So now you look out on this boulevard with the trams!

I'm not a restaurateur so I didn't know what kind of food to serve. It started out as Italian. I had an Italian chef; he didn't last very long. Then an Indian guy walked in one day and said, 'Can I cook?'

I said, 'Kitchen – go ahead!' Then there was a Cuban guy so we had a bit of tapas moving in. There was another Indian after a few years. Somebody from the Thai embassy called me and said, 'Look, we have this lady here, she'd like to work.'

I said, 'Carry on!' It became a bit Thai, a bit Indian, a bit Mexican; it was an eclectic mix of food. I just let them carry on.

A variety of people come here. Used to be a lot of the advertising crowd, the bankers, embassies, ex-pats, Romanians, a lot of writers, artists, people that wanted something different. Every time I come in here I'm fascinated to see what people are writing on the walls. Barka works in a very different way because there's no manager. There's a lady that does the accounts but the students run their own show. They hire themselves, fire themselves. They can only stay three months maximum after they graduate. Barka will pay for their education during the time they work here. We've had about 25 or 30 graduates from the Barka system. They always find somebody else. When they leave they have to replace themselves with somebody to whom they would entrust the key to their grandmother's house. That's how they find new people. Not many people know it and we don't publicise it. The service isn't the best in the world, but they are students, they start learning and they start getting into the philosophy of the place.

How did you come up with the idea?

Kerala. You know Kerala has a lot of grassroots organisations, a lot of empowerment of people. Everyone said, 'You're mad, this is a bar, there's cash, they're going to steal it from you.' I don't have the key to the safe, I don't have the key to the door. I said, 'If you give them responsibility, they will take it.' It's an experiment here. It's a working living experiment; it does work.

Do you keep up with the graduates?

They come back all the time. They bring friends here, they bring family. Staff get 50 per cent discounts, for life, so they all come back. Anyone that's worked in the bar here will have some sort of affinity to the people that are working currently. A lot of them have gone outside Romania, living in Italy, France. Sometimes I help people find jobs. We've just had one girl leave. She'd been here for three and a half years, graduated. I had a big discussion with her, said, 'Look, it's easy, but you have to leave, you have to find another job.' We went around and looked but she found her own job in the end. She's now working with a green solar energy company.

They are stronger people. It takes a bit of time and they think in a very different way. They have to take responsibility. They're a little bit more creative. It's funny because when I walk in here and they are busy doing things, and I haven't been here for two weeks, I can see bits and pieces are out of place – the lamp's wrong, the bulb is touching it and I think maybe it's going to burn the paper. I'll walk in and say 'That's wrong, what's that doing there, put that right' and they are scratching their heads and saying, 'What? He's only been here for two minutes.' After a while they start noticing things.

Working in a bar is a very good experience of life. You're dealing with all sorts of people. You're dealing with money, you're dealing with how to please a difficult customer. You have immediate gratification if someone is enjoying something – you get a good tip. There's immediate responses and you know their moods, you can see if they're getting angry or annoyed, you have to have one eye on this person and another one on that one. The bar teaches you a lot.

All this goes very contrary to the opinion that Romanians find it difficult to take responsibility.

I agree. They are not given the chance and I think there is this fear of failure.

So how about the business of trust in Romania?

I've made my mistakes. Sometimes I do get burned, but the

majority of times I'd still like to keep an open mind and think that we can trust. We have to trust, otherwise your whole philosophy has to change. You then become a paranoid individual that doesn't trust anyone.

Trust between one Romanian and another is a bit more difficult. I think there is a complete lack of trust there. The other day I had a horse to be sold to somebody, up in the farm. This chap was supposed to be coming down to buy it. I said to my Hungarian, a young guy, 'Look, why don't we just give him the horse because we need to move the young animals in and we have one horse too many. He doesn't have the money now but maybe next week he'll bring the money.'

This guy says, 'Absolutely not. No money, no horse.' There is no trust.

I think there's a lot of jealousy also, there's a big element of that. I see it in the city, where a few years ago it was all about the money and the cars and the big watches, the big everything, and the show. Now people are hurting. There is that human side coming back. The things I remember in '96, '97, those things died in the period of rapid accumulation of wealth here, when people got rich very quickly. Now they're starting to search for those intangible things that I felt when I first came here... time spent talking with friends, doing things. We used to go to the park in the middle of the night. There'd be a group of ten people; we'd raid the kitchen and walk into the park, in the middle of winter, ten or fifteen people, just messing around in the snow.

Do you find Romanians very passionate, focused on particular things?

I've had the privilege of climbing with top climbers here. They're passionate about it, being out there in the wilderness, on a rock somewhere. There is that passion. I got involved with a guy called David Neacşu. He had this dream of taking a Romanian team to

Everest. He came to me and I said, 'Great, let's put this team together. The only request I have is that I come with you as a member of the team.' I went around raising money for this from all the corporates and he went to the government. Basically it was the 50th anniversary of the first ascent of Tenzing and Hillary on Everest. I got involved with this project in 2002. It was exciting. We managed to raise the money. We did it on a shoestring budget, scrabbling together all the equipment. We had 16 people and first climbed a 7000 metre peak, Aconcagua, in Argentina. It's a very good climb before you do the Everest climb, because of the latitude. Then we went off to Tibet to climb the old Mallory route. We got to Kathmandu, then the Chinese border.

At the time I was arranging for PRO TV to come out – they had a satellite dish. I'd organised the media people to send live broadcasts from whichever stage we were climbing at, with David Neacşu speaking. It would be quite an exciting time for Romania. At that time it was about building personalities, building heroes. There were no heroes in Romania that were worth anything, only footballers and money. I was very excited at the whole idea of helping to promote these people. There's not many times in life when you can die for your country. Let's go stick a Romanian flag on the top of Everest, and meanwhile one in eight of us might die. It was a great way of publicising some other spirit in Romania, some other national trait, and I thought that would be a fantastic thing for the public at that time. If we could show faces with icicles on their beards, struggling away, that would give the country a sense of national pride.

The TV crew filled in the visa application for Tibet. Where it said occupation they wrote in journalist. The idiots didn't realise that the Chinese hadn't let a journalist into Tibet for the last 50 years. Anyway I tried to sort it out at the border but no, we couldn't, so the TV crew were sitting on the border. Now we had to change the strategy and the climbers had to carry the cameras.

We climbed. Four got to the top. There were no major incidents, except for the fact that everyone started fighting with everyone else over food. It was always a fight. The food would start over there and the person sitting here would get nothing. And that went on and on. Then nobody would carry the cameras. At about 6000 metres they all turned round and said, 'No, you're making money on it,' pointing the finger at me.

I said, 'No guys, we got you the money to climb. You're climbing. If there's any money left over, we split it between all of you. The film is about promoting Romania, promoting what you're doing.'

But they had the impression that somebody was making money on it, and that was it. There was fighting between themselves, fighting with me; it was a mess. The fact was that somebody was going to benefit, and it wasn't going to be them. Eventually, we got the Sherpas to carry the cameras but they had no idea what they were doing so we had very little footage. They all came back.

In terms of a team it wasn't a success?

It wasn't a great success. I still climb with David and I will with individuals but not as a group. Individually they're great guys. When you put a group of climbers together it's all ego. After a certain height it's every man for himself; there's no one going to stop and help, you can't.

You're not just talking about Romanian climbers here.

No, all climbers. But I know what you mean, about a team. Having also worked in the ministry, there was always a lot of fighting, a lot of backstabbing, a lot of trying to get the better of the situation, and there was no trust between anyone.

Your students here are working in a self-managed team. So 'Romanians aren't able to work in a team' is not necessarily correct.

Not necessarily correct. I also think it's about age. The younger ones have a much greater ability to work together.

You've been married to a Romanian?

Yes, I was married to a Romanian. We divorced a few years ago. Two children, two boys. Lucas was born 27th October 2003 – goodness, that's his birthday on Saturday. He'll be nine years old. They live in Bucharest. It was difficult at the beginning. We didn't know each other very long before I started climbing, that was in 2002, 2003 – I went away when she was pregnant. We didn't really know each other very much. I was thinking, well, arranged marriages in India, why not arrange it yourself. Didn't work.

Getting to know women in Romania, is that like anywhere else?

Romanian women. Best I don't talk about that. It's always been quite difficult. Maybe it's the very different expectations. Now not so much but before, that trust within relationships, that was an issue always. I think more from their side. There was that feeling maybe they didn't trust their partners to be able to talk to another girl. All of the conversations had to be very limited or they had to be a part of it. The element of trust between two people wasn't normally there. There was a fidelity issue all the time, and I think it was more the point they didn't trust other girls or somebody who might be a friend. Nobody actually knew how to behave at that time, in the early 2000s. They were quite wild times in Romania. I think also girls had expectations of acquiring more. That material side was a bit difficult.

What I can say is that the people I've worked with, or have

climbed with, or have socialised with, they've been fantastic friends. I've had fantastic relationships with people; they're not closed. Most people do open up, I find.

So where is home today?

Here, definitely. I've got these kids and I need to stay close to them. I'm 49 this year. I don't know where life is going to develop, going forward. I'm the product of an institutionalised upbringing. My close links to family have disappeared at some point, and these are the feelings that I think I want to bring back in my own life. I don't have the opportunity to see my children growing up on a daily basis, but I would like to be around them. So, I'll be here…

Charles Bell

Cluj-Napoca

'Bloody brilliant Romanians, as I call them. But it just takes... to tarnish everything.'

Where am I from? I'm a stateless person, I'm a refugee at the moment. I'm a prisoner here and I cannot live in my own country. What brought me to Romania? The UK's Department for International Development – member of a small team assisting reforms of the criminal justice system, with regard to the sentencing of people and the development of the probation service. That would have been 1998. In 2001 my boss thought I was becoming too Romanian, because I understood what was going on in this country, because I was exposed to it rather than exposed to five-star hotels and the Ministry of Justice in Bucharest. I bounced around the country and started to understand the cultural, economic and socio-political situation.

In 2001 I started up a recruitment business. That was a big story, because people thought I was crazy. But it was extremely successful. I was recruiting Romanian social workers to take up employment in the UK. In 2007 I moved here on a semi-permanent basis, setting myself a target of promoting Cluj-Napoca. I remember speaking at a press conference here, saying some polite things about the city and its people, and in conclusion saying, 'I could almost say that Cluj was my second home.' I had four Romanians chirp up in the background saying, 'No Charlie, Cluj is your first home.' Well, the predictive powers of Romanians!

My objective was to put the city on the international property market map. So I did some research, went to a conference and decided that a particular company was a good bet. I went to a seminar in London where the debate was where best to invest, Romania or Poland. I can speak passionately about Cluj. Four weeks later the chief executive was out here, quickly followed by two of his brokers, and they marketed over 30 apartments.

[And then, let's just say, the difficulties began, but to avoid libel charges we won't go into the details.]

The apartments should have been completed in the autumn of 2008. That still hasn't happened. I had to sell my home in the UK. I had no money to pay the rent, so I got made homeless last year. I also had to sell my boat, which I could have lived on. Now my apartment, a place that I hate, is going to be sold, despite the fact that I paid for it back in 2007.

What about the justice system here, then?

It doesn't function. I'm appalled. I have a lot of experience in criminal justice. I worked in the criminal court for over ten years in the UK. I've been involved in police investigations, ensuring that the alleged offenders are treated fairly and in accordance with the law. I know a bit about this. This system doesn't function. I first put matters in the hands of the police back in October 2010. Very little has happened. Six weeks ago I put in a complaint. Last week I phoned up and said, 'Look, nothing's happened on this, I need to pay you a visit.' They said, 'All right, come in tomorrow.' Well, the bloody police, the bloody prosecutors just don't investigate! It's a system that doesn't function; it's as simple as that.

So, where next?

Somebody once said to me that things will never change until the last communist is dead. I think that's true, because probably the justice system more than any other aspect of Romanian society just doesn't function. It protects those who are rich and very corrupt. That's where serious money is made – corruption. It's not a justice system as far as I'm concerned.

The only other thing I want to say is that I've had some very positive experiences over a long period of time with Romanians. Bloody brilliant Romanians, as I call them. But it just takes… to tarnish everything. It's not representative of them as a people.

Tell me more about your recruitment enterprise.

People thought I was mad. There was a shortage of social workers in the UK, but I had all sorts of prejudice when it came to Romanians – do they speak English, it's not ethical to recruit from Romania, images of Ceauşescu and orphanages. All that changed very quickly. I started up and after the first three years everybody got a job at first interview. They did their homework, they were bloody brilliant.

Back in 2005, I met a girl, Ana. I thought, she's got a brain. She'd had 18 months' child protection experience. I remember about six weeks later I had a group of nine coming over for interviews. One dropped out. I phoned Ana and said, 'Right, pack your suitcase, update your CV.' Ana failed her first interview. Other people had told her to be serious, so she wasn't her natural self. The second interview she got a job. This was in Lincolnshire. People were told, 'Yes, we want you to go to Louth. Yes, we want you to go to Stamford.' When it came to Ana, it was, 'Ana, you can have a job anywhere you want.' To cut a long story very short, she now heads up the Children and Family Courts Reconciliation Service for a region in the UK. Worked hard for it, deserves it too. I've got an ability to spot talent.

A very small number return. Two have gone back into social

work, working for a British funded NGO up in Baia Mare. There's one in Iaşi who came back. She happened to have about eight apartments, so she's okay. Yeah, a small number come back. I think nearly all of them are happy in the UK. They've got new lives, they've got futures, financial security – which they certainly wouldn't have in this country.

What I find with Romanians, and this goes back to the mentality that developed under communism and the *Securitate*, is that initially there are barriers, but once you gain their trust, then they're very open and direct people. You don't start a conversation with the weather. Not like the British. You go direct to the point, which I really enjoy. In the context of my social workers, it was a win-win-win situation, which helped many people change their lives for the better.

Getting things done in this country? We're in Ardeal – Transylvania – and Ardeal has a certain reputation for things happening slowly, if at all. It's extremely frustrating getting things to happen. The concept of working to a time scale or a schedule is not understood by many Romanians. There's a lot of frustration in terms of daily life. I had an experience recently. I was trying to set up a stockbroking account with a British company, who wanted evidence consistent with EU money laundering regulations. They wanted evidence of my identity and my address. So I went to a notary and they did a copy of my passport, copy of my registration certificate. But the stockbroking company wanted a simple form which had two questions. Well, the notary isn't allowed by law to stamp a form that isn't in Romanian, so I went to my bank. I've had a Banca Transilvania account for seven years, but banks are not allowed to stamp forms that don't originate from themselves. So, how do you function? I ended up opening up an online account with the Danish Saxo Bank. That's how I got around that one. So simple things which would take two minutes just can't happen in this country. I think the majority of Romanians have a lot of frustration, and to survive you have to be a bit of a snake and live on the edge of the law.

One of the things I notice is that there's an element of a must-have culture in the society here. You have to go to Kuwait or Qatar to see as many big cars as you do in this country. With some people there's no concept of money management. There's a significantly high level of debt. It goes down to very little things, you know. The women are always dressed in something different. One of the best businesses in this country is second-hand clothes, a lot of which come from the UK, and are sold here at double the price.

Has your experience here affected the way you do things?

I don't think it has. I'm still very much me. I might be 58 years old, but I can certainly say that life does begin at 40. I still hold on to my principles and my values. I don't think it's really changed me. I've had some very negative experiences and very positive experiences, neither of which I'd probably have got if I'd had a mundane nine-to-five job and career in the UK. It's brought excitement to my life, let's put it that way. And challenges.

[A year later Charles gave the following update on his situation in an email.]

The update is that I continued to live in poverty, returned to the UK at Christmas to see my children, and after being convinced by a friend, abandoned the return part of my ticket. Fifty-nine years of age and not able to get a job, but thank God, no Romanian stress!

Nobody has attempted to gain entry to my apartment. I have recently written to the executor but have had no reply. The police have still done very little. I just spoke to my lawyer. The prosecutor has apparently asked for land registry documents relating to all the blocks and all the apartments, so the case is still open.

Greg Helm

Brașov County

'Nothing is half-assed about Romania, nothing at all.'

Pitch black, that's my first impression. I got dropped off by a lorry driver somewhere on the outskirts of Bucharest, an unlit city apart from a few streets. Very austere, very dark grey and bloody depressing. But an interesting city. Not like it is today, of course. I probably spent most days doing about 20 or 30 kilometres walking around, just taking a lot of photographs. I saw things I'd never seen anywhere else in Europe, a lot of weird stuff. On the Metro, some of the strangest things you ever saw: beggars, street dogs, street children, a lot of chaos. The buses you could hardly get on, they were just chock full. I'd been to a lot of places in the world, but at that time Bucharest looked very strange. You still see crazy stuff today in Romania.

I came to visit my girlfriend. She was working in Bucharest, an English girl working with an English charity. So I came out for a holiday, and I've stayed ever since. That was 1992. I worked in the orphanage near the Arc de Triumf where she was working. That's when I first started seeing street children and going down to the railway station, talking to the children through a translator. That was an eye-opener. Most of the kids I spoke to were begging me to get them out of the station, to take them somewhere. A lot of them had run away from children's homes. The youngest was around five. They all wanted to get out. Heartbreaking and sad.

I moved to Braşov a year later. I worked for three months for a charity with a holding centre for children, *Centru de Minori*. During that time I met a German lady, and we set up a project for street children, and with that I worked nearly three years in the Braşov railway station. A lot of the children from the *Centru de Minori* used to run away to the station. Or vice versa, they'd go from the station to the centre. I was going down to the station in the evenings, helping the kids, taking them food, taking them clothes, taking them to the hospital. Used to go sledging and all sorts of crazy stuff. I found out there was this play therapist who was angry with me because she was doing similar sort of work in the railway station. The children hadn't told me, because they were having the best of both worlds – myself and this therapist. So she ordered me to come to the children's hospital to meet her. Very scary interview I had with her. 'Why are you messing with my children? They don't even want to eat my food anymore.' So yes, that's when I first met my wife. That was 1994. We got together not long after that, married in 1998. I didn't speak much of the language when I met her. It took me a long time to suss out living in a different culture like Romania; an interesting, challenging culture. She was a great help and support.

I worked at the railway station when it was in its heyday. What a place! What an education for Romania! I lived just up the road in an apartment block. My God, they were kings in their element. That's why I used to enjoy taking them out... used to go camping, going off on walks, getting them out of that environment. These were hardened kids. Taking them camping in a tent in the middle of nowhere, they'd shit themselves, but in the railway station they were surrounded by the weirdest things. In any city it starts at the railway station.

One classic morning, two blonde brothers – T who was eight, and M seven – they were late one morning. I went to where they were sleeping under this railway bridge; met them halfway.

'Greg, guess what we've seen?' Nothing could shock me by this time, but this did. 'We saw this guy with his head cut off!'

'Ah, fantastic, where is he?'

'Come on, come and have a look.'

'No, I don't want to see a guy with his head cut off.'

'And his hands are cut off!' It was in the newspapers not long afterwards; it was a teacher who'd committed suicide by putting his head on the railway line, and his hands.

I said, 'What the hell did you do?'

'We had a right laugh!' They started to mess about with his head – played football with his head, put his head on his stomach and as a joke put his hands in his pockets.

I remember walking down to the station one night and thinking: you've stopped being shocked. I stood watching the trains coming, waiting for this friend of mine who worked in Bucharest. The train was going pretty fast, but slowing down. Somebody opened the door outwards; smashed into one of the older kids probably doing about 30 miles an hour. He went ass over tit. I didn't know the kid – he was quite new, an older kid, 18 or 19 – and he was out of it.

'God, he's dead!' I said, and sent one of the other kids up to the station doctor's office. He came back and said, 'She's not coming.' I went up and told her he'd been hit.

'No he hasn't, I saw it, he collapsed.'

'He hasn't collapsed, he's been hit by the bloody door, he's out of it.'

She came down, picked him up, slapped him round the face, sniffed him… 'No, he smells of aralac – this aluminium paint – he's collapsed, he's out of it, he's stunned.'

I said, 'No, he's been hit, I saw it with my own eyes. Can you phone the ambulance!'

'No, no, no. I'm a doctor! Who the hell are you?'

Very weird. She wasn't accepting what I said because he was a street kid and she didn't give a shit, basically. This is the thing I found most difficult working in Bucharest and in Braşov; the complete apathy, lack of care or wanting to address a problem.

When I first started working in the Braşov railway station, I went in to the head of the railway police – took him a bottle of whisky and told him what we were doing. He just looked at me and said, 'Are you crazy? These kids are like rats. They'll steal everything from you. They're a problem.'

'These kids aren't a problem. Come to England and see an 11-year-old open any car within two minutes. We have child criminals you wouldn't believe. These kids are petty crime, they may be doing a bit of pickpocketing, bit of stealing here and there, but on the whole they're damn good kids. But in the future? Holy shit, you're going to have a problem!'

'Okay, do what you want!'

I have hundreds of stories. Some of them went back to my wife and she wouldn't believe me. When my German sponsors used to come, it was, 'Nah, that doesn't happen in the world.'

S is famous. When he was 15 or 16, he and his friend, completely stoned on aluminium paint, crossed the road from the station and got hit by a car. His friend was killed and S had a shattered femur. He had a metal plate. He was still growing and it had to be changed. I met him after a year and he was 16. Got him into the Children's Hospital where my wife was working. When she left her shift at three o'clock, I had to stay with him till sometimes ten or eleven o'clock at night. Me and my friend, an English volunteer, were taking it in turns. That's how I got to know S. While he was in hospital, we knew we couldn't take him back on the street because of the infection risk, so we phoned all over the country, trying all these different NGOs who had houses. We eventually found the best place in Alba Iulia. It was a fantastic place. It had 40 street kids on this floor of an apartment block, so we got him into there. It went okay, but he relapsed, went back to the streets. Ran off, came to stay with me for a bit. Every time I used to find him back at the station he would just break down – this great big, muscular 19-year-old kid, absolutely crying his eyes out because he'd screwed up. He knew he should have stayed in Alba Iulia – he could have kept his nose clean. Guilt, despair. Where the hell's he going to go now? What's the future going to be? He phones me regularly. Being abandoned by your mother, the mother being a complete alcoholic, a father he doesn't know… Damn good kids, but three of them are dead. Let me think of one success story. None. One or two… and it's not a success, it's just getting by. Most of them went to prison. I'm in contact with most of them still. They're all in their late twenties or early thirties. Strange lives, wonderful times. It was fascinating, and at the same time it was very sad.

And how did this house here in Cristian come about?

Our German organisation based in Heidelberg was very small. They were mainly students at the time when they started, around six active members, and they raised most of the funds and supported us up until four years ago. We had an English charity helping us too. When we started this place in '96 we thought we'll get it ready quickly and bring the street kids that we knew. We were naive. Working with street kids takes a lot of support. You couldn't do it in this village; you'd have been drummed out. And it took nearly four years to finish this house. By this time a lot of the kids were 18, 19 or 20. Quite a few of them were in prison, so we decided to change. We decided to work with abandoned children, smaller children, taking them at an early age. We had ten children in all, and two of our own, and it's worn me out. Now we only have P, who you saw last night. She's 17 next week. She's in high school, so she's the last.

What were your main challenges here?

Working with the authorities, the local authorities, and trying to keep in line with everything that's required of us – health, safety... Basically we were bombarded non-stop, and sadly that took a lot of our time, and a lot of stress and effort. We could have used that, spent more time doing what we should have been doing.

One example: for this family-type home for abandoned children, the health and safety people wanted us to put seven sinks in our kitchen. Seven sinks! 'Why's this?'

'One sink for washing eggs, one sink for preparing vegetables, one for... ' I measured the smallest kitchen sink, multiplied by seven, and there was no working space! But she stuck with it, she didn't let go. We just had to go against the laws.

She was fired. When we finished the house in 2000 the new director came and said, 'It doesn't comply with regulations, but I congratulate you on the cleanest, most functional children's home I've seen so far in this county. And there's no way I can make you comply to the regulations because they're not practical.'

Şpagă? No. Doesn't exist in Romania! Well, it does, everybody knows that. It's one of the first words you learn. It's just an everyday acceptance. No, I don't pay it. I refuse outright. You're never asked directly. A lot of it's petty, a lot of it's just small *atenţie*. We've always found ways of getting around things without having to pay. If you make a *mică atenţie* – a little tip, it greases the wheels.

The money that doctors are paid is a joke. There was a documentary on the radio last year: Does Corruption, or *Şpagă*, Exist in the Medical System? Well, officially there is corruption, but do you want to see doctors leaving left, right and centre to all the other countries in the world, because they're paid $300–400? Most of them do a damn good job, and it's a shame that the government can't pay them a decent wage. The wages here are abysmal. If you're working for a foreign company there are a lot of advantages, higher wages. My friend in the village, his wife has perfect English. She's an English teacher in the best high school in Braşov, and her salary is €200 a month, I think. It's just not possible to live on that money.

What are you doing these days?

Since 2005, on and off, I've worked as an equestrian guide in probably Romania's top trail-riding centre. We do centre-based rides, where we come back to the same place at night and stay at our guest house. We also do treks across central Transylvania, a large loop of around 200 kilometres, stopping at different villages, most of them Saxon. Very exciting stuff. We have a lot of return clients and a lot of good feedback. It's definitely the best riding I've ever done anywhere in Europe. It's all sheep grazed, so you have an amazing riding surface with long, grassy canters. The landscape is unbelievable. There's vast open meadows, rolling hills; it's incredible and unique. It's open, no fences – there's no other place like it in Europe. Over 200 kilometres we open one gate. You get an idea of what Transylvania used to be like, until recently when you had a mass exodus of Saxons in 1989, which changed things dramatically.

I enjoy showing people the country. Not many people know much about Romania. Normally Hagi, Ceauşescu, Dracula… that's about the extent of their knowledge. Obviously people Google it quickly, or we have a few clients who are really interested in Transylvania and Saxon or Hungarian history, so they come not just for the riding, also to see and find out. Most are pretty blown away by Transylvania. Romania gets a lot of bad press in the West, so it's nice to show them something really positive.

Are there any subjects you find you can't talk about?

There's a lot of people who don't like to admit what their positions were before the Revolution, especially because many of them in their fifties or sixties were obviously involved in the Communist Party or the *Securitate*. That's a taboo subject. I've sat at tables with guys that have been *Securitate* officers. You'd never bring the subject up. Everybody seems to ignore it. I find that a bit strange. Sort of brushed under the carpet, let's forget about it, which is maybe a good idea. Get on with it. The future is the future.

It's a very macho society. But you look behind any Romanian family and it's the woman who runs the show. Leave any Romanian man on his own for a week and he'll starve to death. You never touch any subject like the gay scene. 'Oh, are there no gays in Romania then?'

'Absolutely not, it's definitely a Western illness!' to quote someone I know. And then there was someone else I knew of who was gay.

When he died, the locals said, 'Maybe that's the wrath of God? God doesn't beat you with a stick, but he beats you in other ways.'

When I first came, this anti-Gypsy racist stuff... I couldn't believe it. A woman in the *Centru de Minori*, end of '93, said, 'Why do you come from these foreign countries and help? All these children are Gypsies!' Probably in the holding centre it was half and half. 'They're all Gypsies!'

'What about this guy with blonde hair and blue eyes? He's definitely not Gypsy.'

'No, no, even if they don't look it, they have Gypsy blood in them. Maybe his father, maybe his grandmother.'

I've employed a lot of Gypsies here and I've had problems, some amusing, some dangerous, all of them downright frustrating. I employed C for 12 years. A damn good worker when he was here, but he'd disappear for three or four months at a time. But I loved the guy. For me this was the epitome of this Gypsy mentality. We integrate them into society. What society? Our society? *I* don't want to be part of it! What the hell for? Sat at the wheel of a big BMW I can't afford? C was fantastic. If he got a whiff of the forest, that was it! Adventure. Like trying to tame a kestrel. There's no point; you're trying and trying and it's impossible. He was a real Gypsy guy. Brilliant, loved him.

I employed his daughter. She was okay, but she used to borrow things – not big things – and it got a bit frustrating. I employed his two sons. His younger son, I always said to him, 'P, the only way out of this is education. Get yourself a trade.' He saw his father was an alcoholic, and he couldn't cope with it. He didn't go to school because he didn't have any identification papers. I got him into school when he was 14, but being 14 and in a class with 6- or 7-year-old kids, he was rather embarrassed. He stuck it out for two years and I said go anywhere, just to learn a trade. And he did. Now he's an amazing guy. He has his own house that he's built just outside the Gypsy village, he has a driving licence, he has a motorbike and he's a very respected tradesman.

On the whole I get on very well with people. Yes, there's a lot of cultural differences, but Romanians have got a good, ironic, black sense of humour. It's a good country to live in. People behave a lot more civilised than I see in my infrequent visits to the UK. But I get accused of being very cynical and pessimistic. What I do dislike most of all is this romantic, wonderful idea of Romania. Any country you go to you get ex-pats saying it's fantastic. It depends what you're doing. If you're actually living and working in the country, dealing with all types of people and all types of problems, this 'everybody's wonderful, everybody's friendly' – it's bullshit. Depends what you do.

Take Bran, which is legendary, not only for Dracula but for difficult people. But some of them are very fine. This is a perfect example of Romania. Some of the evilest mother-fuckers on the planet are from that area, and some of the best. Nothing is half-assed about Romania, nothing at all. I bought a house there. The night the old guy moved out – and he was a legend in that valley anyway – he said to me, 'You have to move in straight away, because if not, the neighbours will start!'

I said, 'What am I supposed to do?'

'If you don't live in the house, or get someone to live here, you'll see what'll happen!' And he was right, but I'll leave it at that.

Marrying across cultures? Yes, there's a lot of differences, which, rather than being quirky and interesting like at the start, will start to annoy the crap out of you after a few years. I've learnt a lot of things from my wife. She's a lot more laid back than me. Romanian; Latin mentality. Don't worry so much, sit back, enjoy today. Now I'm more for not making plans, but I worry about the future. At least we're healthy, and you hear that all over. *Sănătatea-i cea mai importantă; suntem sănătoși* – Health is most important; we're healthy. If you haven't got your health, you've got nothing.

In the Holbav with Greg Helm

Travelling in a Landrover

As the crow flies, we're probably six kilometres from Braşov. Not more than that. Maybe ten. Like going back in time. There's no electricity. Lot of the houses you'll see have no electricity, no water. And the water's sometimes down in the valley and half a mile away.

So how do they get it up?

Horse and cart. Oxen. I forgot to bring the solar charger for Domnul N.

Who is this guy, Domnul N?

It's where we camp with our horses on our centre-based rides. We do an overnight trip and we camp on his land. He's a typical resident of this area. Works very hard and drinks extremely hard. I've never caught him sober yet. Once, he was ill. The whole of this area, it's not actually a plateau, it's rolling hills. But you're pretty high up, between six and eight hundred metres high. Follow these hills. You'll see it better when we get to the top. And you have houses dotted…

Dotted around? They're essentially subsistence farmers, presumably? Not too much state assistance up here. They've got cars?

No. Horse and cart. Most of the areas we'll see you can't get a cart up there. Some people try. You can get a Dacia up there. It's a shame it's not sunny. From round the corner you can see the Bucegi Mountains and the Piatra Craiului. It's an amazing view. I've had clients up here on the horses in tears: two Swedish women.

Do you have a problem with the dogs?

Basically, yeah. I have an electric prod. It makes a horrible noise. It's a really powerful one and most of the time it scares the dogs off. I've only had to touch one once.

So you're my answer to getting my wife out into the hills? Because she won't. She's frightened of the dogs more than the bears, but bears also.

Bears aren't a problem. You see a bear, it's only running, and it leaves a big pile of steaming shit to prove it. A friend of mine was ripped to pieces last October. Yep, bitten straight through here, backside bitten to pieces, knuckle joints bitten through, scalp ripped off, not too badly, but... another guy in the village where we ride, when you cross the Olt, he was badly bitten, his arms ripped open, his legs. He was just walking without a dog on his own. Depends, depends on the shepherd. Some of them are very good, some of them are bloody awful. While this friend of mine was being ripped to pieces, the shepherd was standing there watching, a young guy, a bit retarded I think. Would have died if it wasn't for being rescued. You have to be very careful. Bangers are a good idea. Firecrackers.

Quite a road, isn't it? It's beautiful down there.

This is a highway, this isn't bad at all. People come up here with Dacias, small cars. But you'll see quite a lot of houses empty, falling to pieces. This is probably the last generation of people living up here. The kids just don't even want to hear about it. Imagine the postman – the fittest guy in the world!

What about people buying in and coming here as a holiday cottage?

There's a few who've bought places here. There's a German guy on the next ridge. Who else is here? A French guy, but only part time… he's coming every now and again. That's where we used to camp with the horses. With five hectares all like this, you need crampons to walk up it. There was an old guy where we used to camp, and he wanted me to look after him. I couldn't. I had no possibilities, but he wanted, I think it was, around £3000 for his house and his land. But extremely inaccessible. This is okay, but you can imagine when you have snow drifts…

One guy lived here all the time, a German guy who was a bit of a hippy type. But he realised how bloody hard work it was, walking up and down. And again, his friend was attacked by dogs. He fell down a ridge and broke his pelvis, and we had to go and rescue him. It's a beautiful place, a place to visit. I'd never like to see it covered in holiday homes like the Bran area. Bran and Moeciu… this is what it used to look like before.

It's now covered with new housing.

Yeah, with plaques outside, EU funded. You know how much work it is getting the funding? This friend of mine got €40,000, I think it was. Thirty odd trips to Alba Iulia and back, just to get this. He paid for consultancy and ended up with about €30k. It's completely not worth it; a waste of time. That's why I didn't apply for any funding. Far too long, far too…

Bureaucratic?

Yup. I don't know whether I told you, my pa had a place in Ardèche, around 16 hectares. They're trying to get people to come and settle in the area, and the grants there are amazing. Even on the first day you move in, they actually phone you. They come, give you advice. In Romania, imagine one of these guys trying to apply for funding? There's absolutely no chance whatsoever.

[On the track we meet a couple of locals moving logs with a horse and cart.]

He's got a handshake and a half. Looks a tough character.

Hmm. Forestry, scything and drinking a lot – three main activities.

What about the women? They've gotta be tough ladies.

The guy we're going to see – if he's sober or not cutting trees down, if he's at home – we camp there normally once a week when we do centre-based rides. One night we'd run out of beer. We were sitting round the fire. Called his daughter – she was 14 at the time – chucked some money at her and she had to run.

'You can't send your daughter now at ten o'clock at night!'
'Yes, not any problem.'
'Right down in the village? It must be five or six miles.'
'It's no problem.'

Off she went, back in 45 minutes with a big bag of plastic bottles of beer. And all the kids, they go down to the school. Starts later, at half past eight, because the kids have to walk down to school. And walk back up again. They go to the Holbav school. Long walk. You imagine, in the middle of winter? I was up here once with a Swedish biologist; she was recording for Swedish radio. There's a problem in Sweden – wolves coming back there. They bought cages for the kids to stand in to wait for the buses, because they were frightened of the wolves eating the kids. She came to this area. Little kids, seven or eight years old, on their own, walking down to school. And I said, 'This area is full of wolves and there's never been a recorded wolf attack, ever.' In winter you see them more. I've been here 20 years; I've seen them four times, and that's riding sometimes 500 kilometres a month.

[We meet a shepherd with his flock and dogs in the forest.]

Do you want to get out and see if they'll attack you?

No thanks, I'll believe you.

You're supposed to sit on the floor, look down and put your hand up. I've never had the courage to try that one out.

That's submission.

I've seen it done, yeah, with my street kids. I took them on a day trip up in the mountains.

'Let's go and see the dogs.'

'Not a chance,' I said. The dogs were coming, so I said, 'Look, we're going to go for that tree!'

'No, no. Don't run, whatever you do!'

I ran for the tree. Up in the tree, turn round… the kids, they're playing with the dogs!

Quite often we get hassled by stallions when we're on the rides. And I had to prod a stallion unfortunately, on the nose. He was mounting one of our mares with a rider on it, and it can get pretty nasty. And if the mares aren't in season he comes anyway, and the mares start kicking the hell out of him. The stallion, he can also kick. We've had three broken legs so far, horses kicking other horses. Do you ride, Nigel?

No. Wish I did, because these cross-country treks must be something.

The best riding in Europe, on these trails we do.

And what's the accommodation like when you get to the village?

It goes from luxury to bloody dire.

Depending on the house of the villager?

Yeah. They're difficult to find. You can be in the middle of nowhere, these villages, a bit like Viscri. We normally stay in the church, or what would be the vicarage. Some of them are bloody awful. Stay with a German lady in a fantastic place, she has a wonderful guesthouse. That's the highlight. We warn our clients, 'Eat well tonight, because tomorrow it's terrible!'

Okay, this is the place we were looking at buying for a couple of thousand quid. The guy wants four grand for it. It's one hectare. It goes right down to the forest, up round this little barn. The problem isn't buying it, but to keep it running. That's the big problem. But this is a typical sort of farmstead here. The water is down there in the valley. You have to carry it up 200 yards; no electricity to pump it with. Apart from that, it's all right.

You ask the kids here, the teenagers, 'You going to stay here and carry on scything?' Most of them, when they get to eighth grade, go to a bigger school – either Codlea, Brașov – stay with relatives or stay in an *internat*, call it boarding school, and that's it. So what with the future? Who knows? And once you stop scything these places, within four or five years it just goes back to scrub; within seven or eight you've got the trees back. Who knows?

Pietro Elisei

Bucharest

'In Romania we are not in post-communism, we are in late-communism. Tardo comunismo!'

What I'm doing now? Currently I'm working as a town planner and a researcher in urban policies. I do the same as I did in Italy before coming to Romania five years ago, more or less. The difference now is that I do many things for myself, I'm not in the university, and I'm not in a research institution.

I started my company last year, October 2011. I succeeded in launching it as a partner in European Union projects. The company is Romanian, working here, but taking money from European Union funds – you can apply directly to Brussels. My aim is to apply for European Union money distributed by Romanian institutions, but in this case it is more difficult. Time for public procedures is very long. It's very difficult to make a business plan here. I still have a project in evaluation, from a previous company, and they are two years in evaluation now. I don't know if one day I'm going to receive an answer or not. This is still one of the very important problems here.

To keep my family and the business here, where financial continuity and stability is hard to achieve, I also take contracts outside the country. I prefer those in Italy where I come from, and in Germany and Austria where I've been a student. There I have my networks – places I was working before coming here. Integrating contracts in these other countries with my work here gives me the continuity that's otherwise difficult to find.

So working abroad is financing your development here?

Yes, we can say that, together with some contracts I have in Romania. But the total value of projects in Romania is normally not so relevant. If you make a comparison, the same project pays more in Italy and the rest of Europe than here. It was very important for me to keep the feet in two different sides.

I come from the academic world. My university in Rome was calling me back in 2007. I said I wanted to stay here for family reasons. I got to know my wife in 2007. She's Romanian. Also because I was doing very interesting things in terms of town planning. It was a really important period for Romania. They had a great opportunity to invest a good amount of money for urban regeneration. We are speaking about €1.5 billion. That is an impressive figure for urban regeneration, even in other developed nations in Europe. It was interesting for me to be a consultant for the ministry. My work was direct to the cities to create, together with city councils, strategies for metropolitan areas. The cities and the Ministry for Development had a great opportunity, but my impression is that this opportunity was not used in a good way.

Of course there are many reasons. At the local level they still don't have a good planning capacity; and they normally do not propose ideas for sustainable and coherent development. The level of political conflict is extremely high, and this is probably the most important brake on development. Then there are minor things that we can call corruption. I'm not convinced that this is impeding development, even if it's triggering a very important delay in the process. In the moment that you have corruption, you have development. It's before the corruption, it's the political conflict and the lack of ideas.

Another problem was that everything tends to be controlled by the central level here. Extreme centralism does not permit proper local development. That's not to say that people at the central level are the best people to do that, I'm quite convinced about that. To change development here, this is something we have to fight for.

We should be using funds through a more collective or cooperative strategy, where other small actors can participate. We should be more horizontal in shaping, designing and planning processes and not allow a few people to just do what they want. I believe it's possible. It's a question of time. I'm optimistic because I see in Bucharest and other major cities there are grassroots movements, a lot of people who propose a different way of doing things. But the political and even technical power of these movements is really weak. Because it costs to participate, to be active. There are no instruments that facilitate people's participation in public decision-making. These movements don't have continuity and they are not so well structured.

This happened in Western nations in the 60s, with advocacy planning in the States. Thanks to these experiences we changed the way of shaping urban policies in Europe. We don't have planning instruments in Romania that take into account the issue of bringing local communities into the planning process, to have a more sustainable approach to projects – to define projects the people really need. This is a big problem. In many of the cases we are not dealing with the real needs in urban planning.

With a design group we made a proposal in Pitești to work on public space in between apartment blocks. As far as I know the design is ready, but the project is still not approved. In the evaluation they were only looking at small bureaucratic points, formalities, not the real function. This opens another door on things that should be changed – to be more strategic in economic and financial development. We have too many laws. If you have too many laws with a lot of details, everything can be outside the law. Maybe something to do is a reduction of the thesaurus of laws and make them less deterministic.

What do you mean by deterministic?

They are ruling every small thing, even the number of square metres you have to have in a single garden. It's extreme. You lose the sense of the project, and you focus on a brick that is not important.

Could there be other reasons, such as they wanted to disqualify your proposal?

Just for approving the design we were wasting one year in contestation. We got eight contestations. We won them all. But of course we were people coming from abroad, working in a city where local people did a lot to block our project. They didn't succeed in the design phase, but probably were succeeding in the implementation phase. This is the way of losing European Union money because once you have a good project with the design approved you can start something new.

Do you see this inability to get to the strategic as something that's going to take a long time to change?

Yes, absolutely. I see it as cultural heritage in the bad sense of the meaning. I see it not just in public procedures but every day in informal discussions, even sometimes with my wife, with the family. I see that my Romanian friends and family sometimes approach questions, issues, problems just looking to the very short period; not strategic at all. As an Italian it was difficult for me. It's important for us as Italians to have results tomorrow, but actually we like to fit results in with a long-term perspective.

Even at the level of the family doing things like investing money, like buying something, I'm the only one that is stopping the process before making the investment – let's take a look at what is our income in the future, what are our plans for the future, what are we doing now. I see that sometimes they do things without calculating. But banks are not giving you money just to have fun. Romanians don't know the bank systems properly and I know stories of many families who are really in trouble now. They had to sell houses or goods. Many banks did good business here because there was an ignorance in how to get access to financing. They have objectives, but sometimes they don't know the way from the desire to the real achievement of the objective, even at *famiglia* level. You have to pay a lot of attention to that, because they are beautiful people, they are great people.

One of the reasons I stay here is because I like how Romanians are, because I found here some values I can't find any more in Italy or the rest of Europe. The enthusiasm they have. They are open, the way they like you, the way that they introduce you in the family, the way they are friends, simply the things they do. They sometimes seem to be really crazy but they are still very beautiful. For example one thing I like, they always go around with flowers. Everything is with flowers and I find this simply great; it's a small thing with a lot of non-material value behind. I also really like that they have a celebration of the day of your name. When it's St Peter's Day I receive a lot of SMS, a lot of telephone calls; people remember this is your day. They want to keep a relation with you and they don't lose the occasion to demonstrate to you that you are important for them. This we don't do in Italy any more. I like that they pay attention to this human dimension. This is something very positive for me.

I really started to like this city. It was very difficult at the beginning. It's a shock when you arrive. I remember my first day in Bucharest. I say, 'What am I doing here?' It was a really rainy day, very grey, all people screaming, lack of respect in the street, crazy driving – I mean even for an Italian it was crazy driving. You can imagine! Then I started to discover that there is something beyond this surface. At the start it's not easy at all, but you have to resist and then you discover very beautiful people.

Something I don't like – Romanian society is very oligarchic. This is probably coming from the past. There are a very few people that are incredibly rich, very well educated, while the mass of people is not so well educated. There still remains the issue of creating the middle class, this important topic of discussion in Western Europe, in Italy, to keep the middle class alive. In Germany after the war they created an institution for the middle class, to protect it. After 2007, thanks to availability of money because of the EU financing, a sort of middle class is starting to create itself. In Romania we have to protect this and we have to help it develop.

Being married to a Romanian presumably provides you with a guide?

Yes, she was my Virgilio, my guide to Romania. Of course it's a big advantage. The language is another key to open the doors. When you start to make jokes in Romanian, even in official important meetings, they start to look at you as one that can use the language. They come to you, 'Pietro, you know how things are running here' – so you have an advantage in comparison with other people coming from abroad.

I've changed a lot of course. Many things that five years ago were impossible for me to accept, now I do. There are many things that are Romanian in my life, even in my behaviour. I'm not screaming in the street and not driving like crazy but I start to be… for example, every time I had to pick up my luggage in Băneasa airport, I was always the last. Now I'm not the last because I can fight to get my luggage. It's not positive at all, but I started to behave in order to survive. I do many other things that are very Romanian that I didn't consider positive five years ago. I'm very close to Romanians but you always feel the distance. It is very difficult to be completely Romanian and I don't know if I want to be.

It's a very sad period for me as an Italian and as a Romanian. It was a period for me having Berlusconismo in Italy and having here the disaster of the Romanian politics. Politicians are essential for a town planner. You have to make the job with politicians. If you don't have the other part, you don't have the dialogue with the people that are the decision-makers. Generally we don't have politicians capable of mediating development, and we need the mediation. In Romania we are not taking very seriously the opportunity of being inside the European Union. We cannot trust our Romanian politicians. If I had the right to vote, I don't know the person that I could vote for in this moment.

I prefer to work with young people because I see that they can change things. But even if I was working with people who were very smart, very quick, there are other ones, same age, still with a deterministic background. We cannot say 100 per cent the new generation are better, but I can say that I met a lot of capable young people. They can see things in perspective, and they have a good university education sometimes.

Asta este, asta este! Okay, it's an expression that I don't like at all but it is very common. It would be nice if we could delete it from our thesaurus because I prefer *panta rei* – everything is going to change and must change. Young people are less *asta este* than in my generation or the older generations. I'm 43 years old. I see people of my generation – they're taking care of doing all possible businesses in order to make money tomorrow, without any form of perspective. I prefer to go out with these people that are 30, 35, because they have more ideas and more perspective.

Asta este is something atavistic. In the Romanian culture it's very difficult to move the *asta este* philosophy. But this is not just Romanian, it's in the Italian Mezzogiorno, Calabria, Campania, less in Sicily. In all the underdeveloped regions in Italy there is a lot of this philosophy. Probably this *asta este* has roots in Latin culture. The drama of the Greek tragedy – nothing is going to change; we have seen everything and life goes in this way. But this is not the right way of facing things; it stops everything from the start. This is something to fight, *asta este*.

I see many similarities between the Italian Mezzogiorno and the Romanian situation. Many politicians are capable of building on this feeling of *asta este,* like *Il Gattopardo* in Sicily, to change everything in order to keep everything as it is. This was just a way of keeping the same people in the same position of power. It's changing the form but not the substance. We say in Italian '*cambiare tutto per lasciare tutto com'è* – to change everything to leave everything as it is'. This was the philosophy of *Il Gattopardo* and here in Romania it's *gattopardesc*. There's a lot of *gattopardo* even in Romania.

1989 was only changing clothes?

Exactly. I like to say with close friends that we are experiencing '*tardo comunismo*'in Romania. Thinkers like Zygmunt Bauman of the London School of Economics say that we are not in post-modernism, we are in late-modernism. I really like this definition. We can transfer this. We are not in post-communism, we are in late-communism. *Tardo comunismo!*

Can you discuss any subject with anyone?

Some people are still scared about being completely open-minded but it's a minority. Generally you can speak freely of everything here. But I've been working in Sicily and in the Italian Mezzogiorno. They are also very open-minded people, but you have to pay attention to the way you speak about some person in the public realm, in the public context. This is the same in Romania. I can do it as an Italian. I can always play the role of the fool that doesn't understand the situation and it helps. '*Oh, n-am înţeles* – I didn't understand – *Am greşit* – I made a mistake.' But I see Romanians don't have that possibility. In some meetings I see it's better not to speak of some people in the wrong way.

The future of my family is between Rome and Bucharest in this period. My daughter is now eight months old and she was already taking the aeroplane ten or twelve times in seven months. This is commuting between Rome and Bucharest – it's possible. It is difficult but we are not capable in my family at this moment to make a decision. So we have two cars, we have two houses, we have contracts in Italy and in Romania. We see many things possible in Bucharest, and we are not scared to educate Ingrid here. We are not speaking about public schools, we speak about private schools. In Italy it is possible she could go to public school.

I was once in Craiova. The taxi driver was stopped in front of the Town Hall and a policeman came over, 'You cannot stay here!'

The taxi driver said *'Lasă-mă în pace!* – Leave me in peace!'

We Romans have the same expression, *'Lassame 'n pace!'* – in our dialect. This was one of my first days in Romania. And these people are speaking my language, my dialect! Then I started to notice that many sentences, many words of the Roman dialect are in the Romanian language.

This is an exception of history, Romania. These are a group of Romans that more than 2000 years ago remained here. They have been contaminated from many different cultures, but the basic language is still the Vulgar Latin that was probably spoken 2000 years ago in Rome, with some integration from the Turkish and Slavic languages. The structure is Latin and they still use some expressions that we use in our dialect in Rome. This was impressive for me and helped me a lot to stay here.

Johan Bouman

Bucharest

'Maybe they shouldn't try to imitate the West but do things in a Romanian way, with their talent of improvisation and spontaneity.'

In the Netherlands I was bored and looking for something different to experience, and my wife wanted to go back to Romania.

Here I used to work in IT but didn't really like the job so after a year and a half I quit and decided to become a translator. That's what I've been doing since. Over the years I specialised in pharmaceutical work. I've also done a lot for the European Parliament, translating from Romanian into Dutch. I'm trying to do more legal translations because I'm studying law here at the University of Bucharest.

Being a translator has many advantages – I'm extremely flexible and have Western rates and Romanian costs, but it's a lonely job. I don't have any colleagues, so I already know I don't want to do it for the rest of my life. Going to law school is my way of preparing for another career, and maybe I can also contribute to Romanian society in some way. If I want to contribute to this country it's no use without any expertise.

So you selected a fairly difficult area – justice.

You could call it difficult. I first have to pass the bar exam, which is very difficult even for Romanians, but if you can't be a lawyer, you can always be a legal counsel. I already did a very short internship in a law firm here in Bucharest. I liked it very much. I really see a future for me there but of course we'll have to see. I hope it will not be disappointing after a couple of years, but that's the idea, to work for a large international law firm. I'll probably be the only Dutchman who has a degree from Bucharest University.

Good luck! Do you see any difference in relationship-building here to that in the Netherlands?

I do. I think relationship-building, if you're from Western Europe, is easy in Romania. People here are interested in Western Europeans. They find you exotic, and most of them are open-minded and very warm and helpful. At least to me. Anyway, we made good friends in a relatively short period of time. The Dutch in the same situation would be much more superficial, less warm, and less connective.

What about integrating into Ana-Maria's family – same thing there?

We were living together in Holland for many years and married in 2005. Her parents have been in Holland, my parents have been in Romania. The integration process was already well underway when we moved here, which was a big advantage. They have been and still are a great source of information and help. They took care of our daughter when we didn't have a place to live. The first year we lived in a very small one-room apartment and didn't have room for her, so she stayed with her grandparents. We still go there often in the weekends, and in the summer season when they move to the countryside.

So having come here, are you happy with everything?

No, I'm not happy with everything, but I wasn't happy with

everything in the Netherlands either. Romanians complain a lot about Romanians. Many say that a lot of their countrymen are uneducated, loud, and egotistical in a brutish kind of way, especially in traffic. Many have a life philosophy of survival of the fittest, instead of live and let live. I try to keep an open mind and not have any pre-judgements or expectations in a positive or negative way. There are differences, but at the same time we're all Europeans. Of course there are differences between the generations and you hear a lot that the older generation is very nostalgic and wants the Ceaușescu age back; that the younger generation is very materialistic, thinking only about making money. So there's a gap there but it's really an eternally recurring theme, not just Romanian.

The Romanian language sets them apart from their neighbours. They have always stressed this point, but they really are different. They're like Italians. They are a Latin people and I like that, the hot-bloodedness. They have a poetic way of speaking and an artistic way of looking at things which I also really like. It's funny sometimes. The Dutch are very business-like and to the point, and Romanians find that offensive. However, I don't get the feeling that people don't like me because of my Dutch traits. I'm exotic to them and they forgive me for being blunt and rude and unadapted. They are open to Western Europeans and for me that's a warm bath – a Dutch expression. It feels good to be around Romanians.

It's difficult to generalise when you talk about Romanians with each other. They have these regional differences. They say people from the south are Balkanised, people from Transylvania are very slow, people from Moldavia are dumb and aggressive. But they never fight. It's more like a game of words. There's an exception – I have met quite a few Romanians who had a deep personal dislike for ethnic Hungarians from Romania, without being able to explain why. They dislike them but when asked for the reason they can't come up with anything concrete, except general things like 'All Hungarians are aggressive' or 'Hungarians have been given almost total independence and they still want more.' And with the Gypsies... nobody likes Gypsies. And nobody knows any Gypsies.

Asta-i viața! or *Ce să facem?* I hear it a lot. To many Romanians themselves, it's like the essence of Romanian-ness. I do feel that they have a tendency to auto-victimise themselves, to be passive, to complain without doing something about the problem. I've heard that's a very Slav characteristic.

But they wouldn't want you to say that.

No. Romanians don't like it when I say that they're Slav, because the fact that they are not sets them apart from the surrounding peoples. You never know to what extent it's a myth or reality – the island in a sea of Slavs. It's just a very nice way to describe Romania.

How do Romanians feel about right and wrong? Most values are universal for Europe but Romanians are much more expressive and convinced about them. In Holland there is a tradition of tolerance, or at least simulated tolerance, towards other opinions, beliefs, and cultures. This doesn't exist here at the same level, which makes me feel that they are more honest in a way. If they think something they will say it, while the Dutch will try to hide their true feelings and put a little political correctness on their views.

How do you see the position of the Orthodox Church here?

They say that only old women from the villages have respect for priests, but at the same time priests are notable figures in their society. They are judged as really being a part of life. There is an officialdom about religious practice in Romania which is there just because it's always been there. And because the church has such a powerful position in society, not because Romanians really think things should be done this way. I do think they are religious people – certainly compared to the Dutch – religious in the way that it's part of their everyday life. Maybe because in general, life here has more uncertainties. God is a bigger factor here – because he has much more to do in Romania than in the Netherlands.

So they call on him more often?

Yes. God is a solution in Romania.

Does that make them more spiritual?

They are a spiritual people in the sense that they like to be poetical and philosophical and think about the meaning of life. Many of them are very much into nature, in the way that they like to go to the mountains, just to experience them – that's a spiritual thing to me.

Apart from calling on God, how do things get done here?

In my experience, all sorts of plans get made and the making of them is a very interesting process. Romanians really like doing them. Plans are complex – long-term ones with the procedural aspects very well-developed, after which nothing happens until around the deadline or past the deadline, and then suddenly there's an enormous amount of activity by everyone involved. Suddenly a result which you didn't see coming or expect. That's how it was in the IT company where I worked, and for me as manager it was extremely frustrating and gave me a lot of stress. But looking back, it's an interesting way of doing things. I really like Romanians being spontaneous – they are good at improvising and that's a character trait which clashes hard with the traditional Western way of running a business. Maybe they shouldn't try to imitate the West but do things in a Romanian way, with their talent of improvisation and spontaneity.

I'm happy to say that nobody ever asked me for any *şpagă*. I never gave it but I still got treated in state hospitals, I still got a permit for parking from the city, and I've been able to sign a contract for the apartment and all sorts of things where people usually say that it's involved. I'm very proud of this because I think it's unfair and unjust.

On the other hand *şpagă* is also a cultural thing. Doctors accept it because their salaries are low, but if someone wouldn't give it to them they would still treat that patient. I'm convinced this is true for the large majority of doctors. They aren't evil people who only want your money, but it's so ingrained in the culture. The same with the kindergarten. We never gave anything to the teacher and she is very good and treats her children well. But I'm lucky, I'm not an entrepreneur that has to buy land for his living. I know that would be quite another experience.

Are there other things ingrained in the culture you can't talk about?

Homosexuality is something they are allergic to. And many Romanians don't like to talk about cultural relativity issues – like you can be Orthodox but you can also be a Muslim. For many it depends where you are born. For many here Orthodoxy is the thing – and all other people will just go to hell.

I like to talk about communist times a lot, just because I'm curious. I like to ask questions about how things were then. Many Romanians don't like to talk about it – younger ones because they don't really know. It's very obvious that those times have influenced Romanians and their society in a profound way. Whether they want to speak about it or not, it's a subject that's still very important.

The *Securitate* is most definitely an issue today in Romania.

They say half of all adults have been in some way connected to the *Securitate* as informers. I don't know if this is true, but they say it was the toughest and meanest and most comprehensive security organisation in all of Eastern Europe. Romanians are conspiracy theorists because there really were conspiracies everywhere.

Today many people are still being judged – it's like how it was in Holland after the war. One person could not be trusted because his father was in the SS. Another person was a hero because his father had been in the resistance. It's like that in Romania as well. If your father was in the *Securitate* you cannot be trusted. Many politicians have connections to the former *Securitate* and there is still a residue of fear among the population. Many people think that they can't say anything to anyone because the wrong people might hear it. This is how it works in Romanian society; there is always someone who will spy on you.

They have a lot of faith in their family. Maybe also that's why Romanian contacts are very much person and network-based, not on formal structures or procedure. They will be not trusting at all when it comes to people they don't know, which is sad because it blocks change and progress and cooperation. They are great takers of initiative but I don't think they are very good at working together in teams or in an apartment building, because there is a lack of trust. People always suspect the administrator of stealing money. People always suspect someone who comes with an idea, that he will profit from this. They never take anything at face value. Romanians just don't do that.

Who do you feel runs the country?

Like in any country it is run by an elite. In the Netherlands it's an elite of civil servants and industrialists. In Romania it's an elite of people connected to the former regime and the entrepreneurs, and it's not necessarily a bad thing. Someone has to run the country. It becomes a bad thing when, because of lack of information, voters don't have a real alternative. If you don't really have a choice, this is bad for democracy and bad for progress.

The other day I took a walk in the park with my daughter, and there was a politician speaking. He was like a Messiah, surrounded by a group of elderly people who absorbed every word he said. Even if it was complete nonsense, without any backing from reality. It was like a show. I am absolutely convinced no politician at any level in Holland would get away with such blatant nonsense, but here they didn't really seem to care what he said. They were all watching his presentation and his gestures. They didn't ask any questions – about how do you want to pay for all these plans – they were there emotionally. It was not a cerebral event and that's exactly what theatre is about. It's about the sharing of emotions, of feelings, about an experience – it's not about facts. Facts, statistics, rules, they are much less important than in the Netherlands. And maybe it's good, I don't know.

I've been interviewed several times by press and TV. They all want to know why I'm here, what I like about it. They are all after the same cliché, which I am happy to confirm – that the Netherlands is a very organised country, while Romania is very unorganised; Romanians are good at improvising, the Dutch are good at structuring things; the Dutch can be boring, Romanians are always lively; Dutch have flowers, clogs and Rembrandt, Romanians have… other things.

We were at a party. A satirical magazine organised a table tennis tournament and I won. There was a journalist there and he said, 'Look, there's a Dutch guy who likes to talk about things, let's interview him.' I really like the crew and I'm doing volunteer work and writing for them now. I write about my experience, how I look at things here from a Dutch perspective.

Romanians feel they are living in a country that is not well known, not well respected, and they like it very much when foreigners come here to live and declare that they are happy. It's something they really need. It's not very nice to be the arsehole of Europe – an expression I've heard. What they need is a large dose of optimism, a can-do mentality and just by being here, and saying that Romania is a great country, I hope to contribute to that in some small way. And it's true, I do feel that way.

So you think, yes they can?

They can. But they have to believe it. *Asta este* is not going to work.

Israela Vodovoz

Maramureș

'The mentality starts to change with two and a half generations – it's the story of Moses, Moses coming out of Egypt, after 40 years of slavery.'

1964 I went to Israel with my parents and my family and my sister and my brother-in-law. It was because my family is Jewish. After what we know about the Holocaust maybe the reason that we went to Israel was because a Jew, even though he's feeling okay in his country, he has to pay his debts to his ethnic country, and to serve in the army, and to be able to take care of himself if, God forbidden, something like the Second World War will come.

The first time that I came back, it was in 1977, after the earthquake in Bucharest. I had a cousin who lived in a building ruined during the earthquake. I came with some help and medication. The second time was at the end of '87. I came to Vatra Dornei where I lived before, with an idea of a project of stomatology (dentistry). I had to fix a lot of work on my teeth. You know that you're going to the dentist, he's doing five minutes today and saying to you, 'Come next week,' and I don't have any patience. So I got in touch with one of my colleagues in Vatra Dornei, she's a dentist, and I say, 'Can I come for three weeks? You do whatever you have to do. I'll bring materials, whatever.' It was before the Revolution and they didn't exactly have the conditions to do it but she said okay.

I arrived in Vatra Dornei and we did whatever we did and from this I got an idea. Maybe there could be a collaboration between

Israel and Romania in the field of dentistry and tourism. I developed this idea and went to the Romexpo on medicine and dentistry in 1988. There I made my first contact and the project was accepted. Even the headquarters of Mrs Ceauşescu approved it because it was semi-scientific. We started to build the project with the Health Ministry and with the Tourism Ministry and it was supposed to be in a place called Lebeda, in the lake of Pantelimon in Bucharest. We started with very small groups that were receiving the treatment here and also a little bit of tourism. Then in '89 came the Revolution. I was supposed to come at that time but the airport was closed.

So that was a complete upset?

It was and it was not. I didn't believe at that time that this is a Revolution since I'm very interested in politics and I think that I know how to read between the roads. I knew exactly about *glasnost* and everything. I was sure it was a plan to change the system, just the people made it in a little bit of a rush, the ordinary people that didn't know about the plan. From my point of view it was good for me, that I was there in Israel and not here, because it upset me what happened, when you cannot help. After the Revolution they changed the head of the project. He didn't understand that the moment you don't have a governmental insurance for malpractice, you cannot work. I tried to explain that we have to get something from Lloyds and so on but he didn't understand. So I finished with this idea, the dentistry, I gave it up.

The people of Romania, they like chocolate. I see that they like chocolate and, in parallel, I see that they like very much exotic fruits and almonds. I said to myself, maybe I'll make a chocolate – good quality but also for a good price – filled chocolate with the taste of exotic fruits that they like. I went back to Israel and met there a South African Jew who had come not many years before.

In Africa he had a chocolate factory. In Israel he was at the beginning and was making chocolates in his backyard, but he says, 'Yes, why not?'

We worked on it and developed the idea. I had a contract with Loredana Groza. She is a pop singer, the first pop singer of Romania, and the chocolate was called Loredana with her photograph on it. It was a big success because the taste was okay; it had eight kinds of tastes. And the chocolate was good, the price was good and the market was empty. It's unbelievable but the Romanian people at that time, they had money. As little money as they earned, they didn't have anywhere to spend it. They had money, and they liked the chocolate very much. We made a release of the chocolate, like a release of a perfume, at the Sofitel hotel, the first five-star hotel in Bucharest, with the Ambassador of Israel and the Ministry of Tourism of Romania.

For about five years it was on the market, until I heard that Suchard is coming to Romania. I cannot fight Suchard and even though my chocolate is a brand registered, they could make it the same, a little bit like this, a little bit like that, doesn't matter. They could not call it Loredana so they called it Laura. They could not use pictures of Loredana so it's without pictures. But it was the same idea; so I said okay and moved aside.

Parallel with the Loredana chocolates I started to bring raw materials for Bucharest producers of chocolates and sweets. We continued with the raw materials. Somewhere in '93 or even '92 the government had a lack of sugar. The sugar was at that time only ordered by the government. It was sold to the people with a subsidised price in the early 90s. I was asked if I would be interested in importing sugar. I said, 'Yes, why not? It's okay,' so we got the license. From Israel every week we brought sugar in containers, which is a little bit expensive. Also we brought almost a whole ship. This was a great headache and I will not do it any more because the stealing was so bad. At that time I hired the first detective company of Constanța, with dogs, to guard it. They were also stealing.

I'm an optimistic person, very optimistic; I refuse to see the empty half of the glass. And since I have a little bit of a background in psychology, and since I was born here, and since I have the opportunity to educate myself in the West, I can understand where they are coming from, the stealing. For many years, for 50 years, they had to steal in order to survive. When you steal once, twice, three, five, ten times, somehow, somehow it becomes a habit. Okay. And even after, when you don't have to steal just to survive, you can steal in order to improve your level, so I can understand where it's coming from. I do not accept. But it will pass, in a generation to come.

When you left in 1964 you were speaking Romanian presumably?

I was speaking Romanian, German, French, and Russian, but Romanian was the main language. My father was born in Austria, and he spoke German with me before Romanian. My mother speaks French.

And in Israel, what were you speaking then?

It was a big problem. First of all I was raised as an atheist. I knew that I'm a Jew, but my father was an idealist communist. I was not educated in a Jewish style. I didn't know anything about Israel. I just knew that it's my ethnic country and that I should be there. And that I and my future children should have the opportunity, if God forbid the Second World War will be repeated, to fight and not to be taken like sheep. I didn't know English. At that time in Romania they didn't speak English at all; just in Bucharest, in one school.

Here I finished the tenth grade. Israel was very well organised to teach the language, to change or to retrain professions, but this started particularly in the 70s. At the time we arrived they had special schools in kibbutz for Hebrew, but just for adults. I went to school the first day and I found someone to speak French with me. 'What's your name?' And my name was Isabella. He said, 'Isabella. Isievel.'

I said, 'Who is Isievel?'

He said, 'When you know Hebrew you will be able to read the Old Testament so you will know who is Isievel.' I already had an Old Testament in Romanian so I said to myself, I'm going to go back home and I'm going to see exactly who the lady is.

I talked with the manager of the school, and he said, 'You know, we have to put you back in the ninth grade at least, because if we put you in the eleventh grade now, at the end of the year you will have already two of the graduation tests and you won't be able to catch up.'

I said, 'Listen, you're not going to put me back in the ninth grade when I'm supposed to be in the eleventh grade. But we shall make a contract. Give me six months, and after six months, test me. If I don't achieve at least the passing qualification, do with me whatever you want to do. But if I pass, you are going to leave me in the eleventh grade as I should be!' And for half a year I almost didn't sleep; about one hour per night.

I was very lucky that in the village where they sent us to live, the wife of the mayor was a retired teacher. Even though in this area there were many newcomers, she heard that I had said 'let's make a contract' and so on. She liked me very much and said, 'Listen darling, I am ready to teach you every day after school as much as you can take.' A wonderful lady, she was sitting with me every day, hours and hours for the Hebrew. I didn't know the history and the geography, I didn't know Talmud, I didn't know the Torah. Her daughter-in-law started to teach me English. In parallel, I subscribed to all the youngster organisations in order to speak all the time Hebrew, even though with mistakes. I refused to speak Romanian, just with my parents and only when strictly necessary. After half a year I did a test, and I stayed in the eleventh grade. I then graduated from university in Tel Aviv.

How do you identify yourself now?

When I came to Bucharest in '77 I believed that I am very Israeli with Israeli roots, with Israeli feeling. I was a volunteer in Israel, I was in the army, I have children born in Israel. I defined myself as an Israeli, born in Romania. When I came back the first time in Vatra Dornei, at the end of '87, I didn't announce when I'm going to arrive with the train. I didn't want people to bother. But by chance someone heard that I'm arriving with the train from Bucharest. It arrived about six in the morning, and all my colleagues that were still in Vatra Dornei waited for me at the station, with flowers and so forth.

At that moment I felt different, I felt that I am born in Romania, I'm a Romanian Jewess. My roots... if we can describe it as a tree, my roots are in Romania, the other part of the tree, including the leaves and the blossoms and so on, are in Israel. Today I can say that I am equal, but really equal, a Romanian in Israel, an equal patriot of both countries, with equal feeling for both countries.

The first of December is the National Day of Romania. From one TV station they applied to have a direct transmission from our guesthouse here on that day, so they arrived with all the team. There were many people and we prepared traditional food and the transmission starts. The moderator says, 'Can we start? Do you have beer? Do you have *mititei*? Do you have this and this and this?'

I said, 'Sure we have, but we are in Romania and my education says that before we start having a party on the National Day of any country, it will be nice to remember the ones that fell, wherever they fell, so we can celebrate this day. So I would like to ask you to stand up for a few seconds in the memory of the heroes of Romania.' Before this, I had about ten minutes and I wrote a poem for the Independence Day of Romania. After the people sat down, I asked the moderator for another two minutes – 'I would like to read something for Romania. I call it a little bit of a patriotic poem.' The reaction was unbelievably positive. They told me they got thousands of SMS and mail to thank me, that I remind the people that celebrating the Independence Day of the country is not only *mititei* and beer.

What about your Jewishness? How much are you in touch with Jews here?

I'm involved in the Romanian Jewish community. I help as much as I can to rebuild or renew the old synagogue of Chabad in Bucharest. Liviu was raised here in Vişeu, that's how we came here, and I didn't know that before, in this area, were about 70,000 Jewish people. Vişeu, before the Second World War, was one third Christian, two thirds Jewish.

In life nothing is by chance. We wanted to build a holiday house. A woman phoned to Liviu's mother, then called us and said, 'I have 5000 square metres for €10,000.'

I said, 'Okay, tell me where it is!' I asked her to tell me about the land, a little bit of the history.

She said, 'My grandparents bought the land in 1952 and I have the papers from the Jewish community.' So I said, 'Okay, we'll come.' This was Jewish.

I'm involved in the Sighet Jewish community as much as I can be. The Romanian people, they're making a difference between Jews and Israel. Whatever anti they had before, was anti-Jewish. For in their eyes the Israeli is something very sparkling. In time they understood that Jewish and Israeli are the same. They understand something else from the stories of the eldest people, that in the time the Jews were here, it was not bad. They understand that the Jewish people, most of them, usually tried to improve the community.

I feel very good here. I was accepted. At the beginning they were shy a little bit. I come from Bucharest, from outside, but when they understood that I don't show off, it's not my way, and I can feel very well cleaning the stairs and washing the floor, I feel they respect me and appreciate whatever we did here. This place didn't exist before. There was no electricity at all. We put it in. When we first opened the streetlight on the road the eldest from here, they fall and they cry and they pray, and they said they didn't believe that they would see light on the road in their life. The city hall didn't have the money for this.

This is a wonderful area. We have to have the infrastructure to get here. But you cannot change 50 years of communism. The people were taught not to think, not to have imagination, not to have initiative and not to have anything to buy. Now they would like to have it all, at once. That's why they are not optimistic, even the young ones. For 50 years, you need 50 years of transition. The mentality is very hard to change. The mentality starts to change with two and a half generations – it's the story of Moses, Moses coming out of Egypt, after 40 years of slavery.

Duncan Ridgley

Maramureș

'I can buy a house in an afternoon. And have it delivered, put it up in a few days. No paperwork, no problem. Try doing that in England!'

Why am I in Romania? The short version is – a big wave pushed me here. I spent 25 years in London, I'm a bit of a maverick, I'm an entrepreneur and so it's like, let's go travel, let's go do something. Went off to Sri Lanka to live there, to set up Somewhere Different. Lasted 24 hours. Got caught in the tsunami, horrendous time. Back in London, washed up, didn't know where to go. On the way to Sri Lanka I had wanted to buy somewhere in the Balkans, and Romania was on my list. I bought some land here, never planned to live here. To cut a long story short, we ended up living in Egypt in the winters and Romania in the summers. So I'm here for lots of reasons, to do tourism, to have a way of life.

We do cultural holidays. We had land around Piatra Craiului in the south. Our neighbours there were driving brand new Range Rovers and had gold watches, all from Bucharest. I asked people, 'Where's the real Romania?' All said the same thing, 'If you want the real Romania, if you want the traditional, go to Maramureș!' I came up here, took one look at the place, like this is amazing. When I came round the corner and saw this village – it looks like the village that Santa Claus comes and drops his presents in the winter – I looked at my wife and said, 'This is it!'

How did you set about finding a place in the village?

We call it land fishing. We've done it for years and it kind of works in every country. You never know if you're going to pull a salmon out of the river in a second, or if you're going to catch nothing. There's no real estate. Nobody sells anything. You walk around, you find the hill you're interested in, you sit there and eventually someone goes, 'Oy, Vasile, there's a foreigner sitting on your hill. What the bloody hell's he doing there? Try and sell it to him!'

And you negotiate. Romanians are unbelievably good negotiators. No one is buying anything here so there's no buyers, there's just me, and they've all got balls of steel. They all ask €30,000 for anything, for months, and it's like, 'How can you? I'm the one who sets the market.'

'Oh no, no, no, you're the foreigner, you very rich.' The attitude that I've seen all over Romania is – I'm foreign, I'm rich and I'm stupid. And so you're the stupid rich foreigner.

They're not in a hurry to sell?

That's the thing. I've no problem with some guy trying to make as much money out of me as he possibly can. It's fair enough. Land is worth what someone is prepared to pay. It's all negotiable. But there are no prices here because nobody buys. So no one has a clue. It took me months to establish a price. Eventually I was shown a piece of land that was perfect. Walked away and luckily for me about a month later they rang up desperate. They said, '*O sută milion, teren*' so I bought one hectare of land for a 100 million, as they call it. Romanians are a nightmare: they negotiate in euros, they talk in millions – old currency – and they look at you like you're slightly confused when you have to give them RON – new currency. It's like you got three bloody currencies going on there. If we just talked and negotiated and wrote and spoke in RON it'd be quite easy.

So I paid about €2500 for one hectare of land, 30 trees on it, right next to the village, when everyone was asking €30,000 for anything. Once I'd bought that it was, 'Fine, you can have mine for €2500.' I'd set the price by that one person desperately needing the money. That's when it's actually for sale. Until then it's a game and I can't blame them.

Did you build the houses yourself?

Yes, I've done it with my bare hands. The way it works here is that people don't want old wooden houses, they want new concrete ones. The fact that the thermals in the new ones are ten times worse than the old is irrelevant – it looks good. They want a flash house – they sell their old house. These houses are all tongue and groove, no nails; the whole house just fits together. You number the timbers; they come down in one day and they go up in three. It's crazy to make a new house. A lot of people have bought houses and exported them to Italy or wherever, just for the wood. I try to buy from other villages and bring houses here, to keep up the number of wooden houses in this village.

Are people in the village speaking English now?

The kids are learning. The problem is that a lot of people will understand but they've never spoken English so they're too shy to use it. It took me a while to realise. If you say, *'Vorbești engleză?'* they'll say, 'No, I don't speak' and then you'll be telling a joke or something and they'll laugh and it's like, 'You understood that, didn't you,' and they'll nod. They've learnt because of the television, specially the youngsters. Satellite television changes everything. The kids are growing up with satellite TV, with Hollywood. That's the culture now, that's why Mum and Dad are stupid and I'm not going to cut the grass. I'm going to go and live in Hollywood.

So the children are leaving once they've grown up?

There's lots of reasons. One – if you're from this village they see themselves as the lowest of the low; they really are the peasant. Maramureş is seen as where the peasants live. They don't like that, they're embarrassed about it, they have a bit of a complex and so to leave the village means that you leave that stigma behind.

Another reason is – 'I don't want to cut the grass.' That's what they do here, they cut grass, manual work. And to them that's what Dad did and he's a loser. There's the big foreign dream; anything abroad is good and all things here are bad. That's a huge hangover from Ceauşescu. If you could go abroad it was amazing and for those who did leave it was pretty cool.

The other reason why they're leaving is – it's medieval here. The attitude of men to women. If a woman walks into a bar here on her own, or with another woman, in the evening, it is socially seen she's a whore. And if she got raped it was her fault. This happens. It is seen by the women here as being her fault. She shouldn't have been out after dark. 20, 30 years ago it was arranged marriages; women do not go out.

That is the attitude here and so if you're a good-looking girl you want one thing, you want to get out. If you're a 20-year-old young guy, where are you going to find a girl? They left. That's a huge problem. In the cities, if you go to Bucharest or Cluj, it's a fashion parade. They all get out because in Cluj they can walk around with a miniskirt on and everything's fine. In the villages girls are only allowed out during the day. Or for three or four hours in the bar on Sunday. So they all dress up on the Sunday and go down to the bar. It's the only time they go out. My guests are perfectly safe if they stick to the rules. I have had single girls staying here and I've just told them, walking around during the day, it's absolutely fine. If they want to go out at night, I go with them.

The parents still rule with an iron fist. The way I see it, it's all to do with television. America went through its cultural revolution in the 50s, England in the 60s and 70s, and I've seen it in lots of other countries. Romania's going through it now with Satellite TV, so the younger generation is completely different to their parents' generation. The parents just don't get it, they don't understand. 'Why don't you go to church and just marry a nice boyfriend down the road?' Their parents grew up in a way of life that had not changed for hundreds of years. My neighbour, I don't know how old she is, she's probably younger than me, but it would have been suggested that she married the boy she married. She would have been a virgin. She can't understand that her son wants to go abroad for a little while. Why doesn't he just do what I did? There's a huge divide in the culture.

What sort of problems is that giving the village? Is it a dying community then?

No, that's the weird thing. One of the main reasons I moved to this village is that it is still very much alive. There's a school here. People are still having babies. A lot of people can't leave. There are people who are happy with that way of life but expectations are now huge. You got these princes and princesses, I call them. When I interview people for a job I realise this one person has six people, grandparents and parents, taking care of them. They're the most spoilt people, a nightmare to work with, and this village is full of them. So you have some people that are hard grafting, salt of the earth, getting on with it and happy with their ways; and then you have these others. We have a problem trying to find people to help change the sheets here. You speak to the young girls and say, 'Would you like to learn English, you'll be talking to foreigners?' and you get, 'I'm studying. I don't change sheets, thank you. Mother does that.' They're just not interested.

Because of the financial crisis a lot of people are coming back too. A few years ago I couldn't get anyone to help me build. Now I'm getting asked all the time, '*Eh, domnul, muncă?* – Hey mister, work?' Yeah, people are coming back but there's no big success stories. There's such a strong culture here that they just lock in. You don't bother to try and change it. You leave and when you return, you do as your mother says. Mother clicks fingers and goes, 'Oy Vasile. Do the pig!' and he's going, 'Oh God, what am I doing?' He just slots back in because he knows that's the way it is – there's no point in trying to challenge the old guard because it's still very alive and strong. Which is why I'm here, because people want to come and experience the culture.

There's an old couple, he's 68, she's 70, and they've got no kids. I call them Hill and Billy and they're just amazing. They're a walking museum. I bought their house and they're still living in it, and when he walks with me he's telling me, 'Look at this land, it's kept so well, he's smart.'

But most of the time it's, 'Look at this one, look at these trees! He's just let this go, it was such a nice piece and now look at it.' He gets quite depressed as we walk up the hill because he's showing me that a lot of the land is going by the wayside. The mountain is growing over.

There used to be great pride in the way the land looked?

It's the peer pressure. It's exactly the same as if you're in London and your primrose fence is kept well and your car is washed on the driveway. It's all about prestige and your job. Here it was how well you kept your field. There are still hectares and hectares... they're like golf courses because it's everything to them and they take such pride. The second the snow melts they're up there burning and clearing. The youngsters don't want to do the scything to feed a cow.

The shepherds are alive and well here. We've got thousands of sheep up in the hills. We do have bears and wolves. They're not really so much of a problem as we have so many shepherd dogs that keep them away. When we do walk up the hills we take a horse and cart to deal with the dogs. If you have eight dogs coming at you it's pretty scary. We do a shepherd safari and people like it. They see the hills are alive and there's a whole code of conduct up there. Once you're on the inside of the circle of dogs, with the shepherds, you feel safe.

One thing they're very proud of here, there are no Gypsies. One family, and now they've gone. There are hardly any Gypsies in Maramureş. The attitude of Romanians to Gypsies – they are unbelievably racist. I've had several what I would call very normal, liberal Romanians, openly say stuff that's really shocked me. It's very different when I talk to the Gypsies and say, 'What you think of Romanians?' They never say a bad word about them. 'Well, they hate us, so I don't really have anything to do with them.' The Gypsy culture is fascinating. I've had nothing but good experiences.

I found a Gypsy girl who speaks English who is helping me in Târgu Mureş. The whole thing is like, 'I've got ten people who want to learn how to dance, can you teach them?'

'Yeah, of course we can.'

Give them respect and they're laughing at us. I've had Gypsies just rolling around at the stupid foreigner. 'You don't dance like that, you idiot!' Breaking down all the barriers. These are people who don't work in the tourist business. Most of them have never seen foreigners before. These girls, 15 or 16, it's just the sexiest dancing I've ever seen. Amazing. Fantastic.

To Hungarians, the Romanians are the Gypsies. I'll often have conversations with people and think, why is he saying that? I've learnt to tell if someone's Hungarian, when people just go, 'Ah, these people!' It's when they blatantly slag off and say everything is absolutely useless.

'Are you Hungarian?'

'Of course. Why?' It's 'We're Hungarian, we're from the Empire, we're organised.' I've met a lot of Hungarians in Bucharest. It's a lot more watered down there. When you get right out into the villages, it's blatant racism against Romanians.

What are the other big differences between here and Bucharest?

Politically it's very similar. The local political level is interested in dealing with local businessmen, wheeling and dealing and doing a few things. And the people... who gives a damn about them! I'll do a deal with you and everything's good. It's exactly the same at the top level in my experience. I run a paparazzi agency in Bucharest so I'm photographing senior government officials on a daily basis. Bucharest is a big village.

But huge differences with people in the city. In the city they moved on with their cultural revolution a long time ago. They're pretty liberal, open-minded people, whereas the traditional country ways of life here are still very much alive. In England the culture is the same, if you're in Birmingham or in a tiny village in the middle of nowhere – it's kind of all one culture. Here I really feel the difference. You're going back in time. When I get off the train in Sighet I have a different etiquette and I will say hello in a different way, *'Să trăiți!'*

The *primaria*, the mayor's office, is everything here. Bucharest is another country, it's another world; they couldn't give a damn. To them, life stops at Ocna. The municipality is in Ocna. Everything is done up there. When I started registering and legalising my land I went through a professional lawyer, and he had one question, 'What is your relationship with the mayor?'

'I think it's okay, it's not good, it's not bad.'

He went, 'You will have no problems' and left.

That's all he wanted to know from me, how do I get on with

the mayor. If I am an idiot I wouldn't be able to legalise my land, I wouldn't be here, I would be kicked out of this village. It's human decency and it still works. Of the local politics, people say, 'Ah it's terrible, it's corrupt,' but it's called common sense. To do it with new EU regulations, that's going to cost you five times in legal fees to legalise that piece of land. 'That's bollocks, we'll do it this way!' And it makes sense. I'm being very honest here, the local mayor is fine, he's never expected a bribe from me and they've helped me a lot, and I'm not just saying that, they're absolutely fine.

They want to do everything correct because you're the EU. 'I'm not the EU, my name's Duncan.'

'Oh, he's a foreigner, we'd better do it the correct way. Vasile, what is the correct way?'

Vasile: 'I dunno, I never done the correct way.'

'We'd better do it the correct way. Can you come back next week?'

'Why?'

'Because I'll be on holiday.'

They don't know how to do the correct way. There are laws in this country that are changing all the time. They all make it up as they go along, so they don't even know what their system is. Sometimes it makes it easy. Fine, just go do it.

Land registry is a huge problem. We got Austrian land registry which is 200 years old. It's all written by hand in Hungarian, doesn't match up to GPS. It's all over the place. To legalise land here we had to take dead people to court to prove that they should hand over the land to their children. Yes, I've done this. Then the children finally own it, it's in their name and we can buy it off the children. You need a local lawyer, a good lawyer, who understands the local systems and has the connections.

Buying cars – that's an absolute nightmare in this country. But I can buy a piece of land, I can buy a house in an afternoon. And have it delivered, put it up in a few days. No paperwork, no problem. Try doing that in England. Some things are easy, some things are not.

They don't know how to deal with foreigners. There's still a fear that you're a foreigner, you're a spy. I'm not joking. The secret police ring up here two or three times a year to check on what the Englishman's been up to. 'I'm a hippy,' I say. 'Oh, no, no, that can't be right, he's a foreigner.' I've lived under a secret police in Egypt and it's their job. You're a foreigner, keep tabs on this guy, what's he up to, he must be a spy. They're paranoid, and that culture is still alive and well in Romania.

Has running your paparazzi business taught you something about Romania?

There's a huge fear among journalists and there's a fear in the village here. Step out of line and the system will get you. The bad guys are all watching you. I saw it in Croatia, I've lived in two ex-communist countries, and communism has the exact same technique as religion. There is no God in communism so the secret police are watching you, all the time. I've done this job for two years now. We're doing corruption, we're doing all sorts of stuff. I haven't had a single phone call, a single threat, my kids and I are still alive, nothing's happened to me.

The sad thing is I advertised for a secretary for a paparazzi agency, €300 a month, a crap salary. I got 800 CVs. A few months later I put in the same place, 'Undercover reporter. If you're pissed off about the way things are going in Romania and the corruption, don't complain to your friends, email me.' I got no replies. Everyone will tell you, you don't understand. This is Romania.

Are they more religious? They all go to church. You have to be seen to be going to church. When I ask, 'Do you believe in God?' how do they describe it – 'I believe there's a God, not in the way that it's portrayed but I believe there's something.' They kind of know that the Bible is not the be all and end all, as it was written 2000 years ago, but they still have the fear of God. I was in the Boxing Day tsunami in 2004. Every other family on that beach that day didn't walk away as a family, they lost somebody. I was pretty damn lucky. I'm convinced I did that because I made a hell of a lot of good decisions that day, but mainly I'm bloody lucky, nothing else. Any Romanian would say, 'Ah, you were chosen.'

I was hitch-hiking the other day and Vasile, a priest, gave me a lift. I told him about the tsunami story. 'Why did we live?'

'You were chosen, of course. God saved you.'

Gianluca Falco

Bucharest

'They start to realise what is important. When you're playing in a team you learn many rules. You're not the only one. The ball is not just for you.'

I would say Bucharest is becoming like Prague ten to fifteen years ago. It's a town that for young people and students is close to perfect. It's not so expensive, there are lots of things to do, life in the centre is dynamic. It's absolutely amazing what happened in the last four or five years. It's one of the best capitals all over Europe that offers to the young generation concerts, lots of theatres for very good prices and for each kind of taste. There are exhibitions weekly, there are cultural centres of foreign countries like the Czech Republic – the best one I think – which are organising events all the time to promote their culture.

My hometown is Caserta, a small town close to Napoli. I studied political science at Naples University and then was one year in Prague where my work for graduation was about the Prague Spring of 1968. I married with a Romanian I met there in 2002 when we were both studying Czech. We lived two or three years in Italy then decided to move here where we've been almost seven years.

I'm press correspondent for the biggest press agency from Italy, but from the financial point of view the best part of my income is from my translation and interpretation agency. I'm the director and owner of this company.

A big plus for my integration in the Romanian community is the Latin language, very close to Italian slang of the south. There are many words and expressions that are similar. Also the mentality is very similar to the Mezzogiorno. I mean in the way we relate to other people. We are Latin. That is probably why I felt quite good in my six plus years here. You can see also in the politics there is the same chaos. From this point of view I never had problems in relations with Romanians, and the language I've learnt quite easily. I would say it's perfect for me.

I'm also supporting an NGO. I was a basketball player and coach in Italy and I'm teaching basketball to Roma kids once a week on a Saturday. The main goal is to let them spend one hour and a half playing, just forgetting all their problems. Some are six years old and I've heard all kinds of problems, you cannot imagine. Ten-year-olds already had a bad experience with drugs, and now thanks to the help of this association they are getting out. People whose mother is a prostitute and the father is in jail. The environment is absolutely awful.

I went also to their apartments. What I saw there I'll never forget – the way they are living in a room like this, without even doors, six or seven of them. It's clear they need to be cared for, because when they meet me they are so happy, they come to me, they hug me, they want to talk with me, they play with me, they take my hand. It's something that makes me happy, it makes me proud.

They start to realise what is important. When you're playing in a team you learn many rules. First of all you are together with the others. You're not the only one. So you take the ball and you have to pass to the other. The ball is not just for you. This makes you linked together with the others. If I say for instance that before shooting you must pass the ball between you three times, this is another rule. It means that life is made to be shared with the other people around, that you have to get used to, respect and enjoy the people around. It is the base for building a community.

I think that they improved from this point of view. They learnt how to act together with the others better. They also became very nice, very kind. The simple fact is they thank you. They were not used to that. Or to say good morning. Also to speak openly.

Valeriu is the director of this NGO. I met him last year. I was searching for something like that and I was also collecting sportswear for them. I played basketball in Italy for 12 years so I had a lot of teammates. Last time when I went to Italy it was seven or eight boxes like this which I sent through a bus company. When they opened the bag, for them it was like gold. I would like to dedicate more time really, but unfortunately there's no possibility. I have to think also of my family.

Will you continue living here?

I'm not sure of this because I started to face the first problem, education. The problem basically is the way of teaching and the relation the teacher has with the kids. I think that most of the teachers here are still at communist times. They remain with the same system of teaching and style. It's hard for a young person to decide to be a teacher, considering the salaries. To start with you cannot get more than €200, and to put everything, all your passion, in teaching, when you know that at the first occasion when you can improve your financial situation you will move from the school, you will choose a private school or something else.

Here the problems are with public schools. Go to the British school, you solve the situation, but for me, I believe in the state. I was born like that and I simply believe that at least the basic education must be granted by the state.

Bucharest is perfect for the young guys and the students but it starts to be hard to live here when you have a family. After education there is health. I don't know if you ever had the experience of being in a public hospital. The majority are in really bad conditions, and always you have to keep your hands in your pocket to give money here and there. At this point I don't know why I'm paying taxes if I have to go to the hospital and pay anyway in the black. I have to pay. Simona giving birth had to give some €250 to the doctor because it's the general rule and for the nurse 10 lei. So what's the point of paying social taxes for healthcare?

Justice also. I hope I will never have problems with the justice because you can be innocent but find yourself the guilty party, without even knowing why. The trials are extremely long. I would never wish anyone to go to trial. That is one of the reasons why Romania is not still in Schengen. These are things that can affect you in daily life.

How about getting things done?

You have to know that the things you're asking for will not be done immediately, or not in the time they said. Or it won't be done at all. If you go to an Internet provider and you tell them that you need a connection urgently and they say, 'Okay, in two days', you will be waiting the second day but he will never come. You will call him and say, 'Today I had an appointment. I was waiting for you.'

'Ah, sorry we forgot. Five days.' You will be waiting for another five days. Probably he will not come even on the fifth day. So you have to fight with them and start to shout. Then probably things will start to move. This is typical. You cannot count on anything, I would say. I cannot understand this. It's this lack of respect. If you're living in a society, a group of persons living together, sharing the same thing, not necessarily the same ideas of course, I believe there should be more respect for each other.

But what is positive is that people are quite happy. They like parties, life is beautiful and there is always a solution for everything – probably not so professional, not so moral, but always a solution. You never give up. This is something positive. They really never give up.

John Ketchum

Bucharest

'I've long felt that Romania is a bit of a secret that one day the world will figure out.'

We met at a dinner party in Bucharest in 1997. Her father had daringly escaped the country in 1985. And because Ceauşescu was feeling the pressure internationally by that time, the family were able to join her father in Chicago. She grew up there from the age of 14. At university she applied to Budapest for an exchange – she spoke Hungarian. She fell in love with Hungary and eventually found herself opening the Romanian headquarters in Bucharest for a Canadian real estate company. I had arrived here the previous autumn with the telecoms company CONNEX – now Vodafone – for a six months contract. My plan at the time was to return to Canada after the contract ended and enter the world of film, a lifelong dream.

In the end, I spent three years as a director of marketing for CONNEX. I quickly fell for the country and its Latin culture and people. The company grew rapidly, providing opportunities for those who stayed on. I then spent two more years with the sister company in Prague and in 2002 chose to return to Bucharest to pursue a career in film here. I knew from my previous work in marketing it was the perfect place: the competency, skills and education levels in the film industry were very high, not fully appreciated by foreign productions. With my two partners – one English, one Irish – we set up a company and finished a feature film in 2006.

Since then I've spent my time on a wide variety of film-related projects. I'm fascinated by the changes and opportunities the digital age has brought to the world of film. I'm inspired to be living in a place with such a fantastic atmosphere – and legacy of powerful storytelling, demonstrated by the success of the Romanian 'New Wave' of films. I'm probably best known for Filminute, the international one-minute film festival I co-founded in 2006. The festival, which showcases the world's best 25 one-minute films each year, now attracts submissions from more than 70 countries and audiences from over 130. It acts as an accelerator for new global film-making talent.

Have you had many Romanian entries to Filminute?

In each of the seven years we've run the festival, Romania consistently ends up in the top five countries in terms of quantity and quality of submissions. A Romanian film won best Filminute in the inaugural year, and their films have won numerous awards ever since. It's not surprising if you live here and know a bit about their film-making and storytelling history.

The first films were screened here less than five months after the first Lumière brothers' film screenings in Paris. Romanian cinema was then very active through the silent film era and early talkies, and even during the communist period. Like all industries it struggled in the early 90s, but then found its footing at the turn of the century. Following the 2002 production of Cold Mountain the floodgates opened, and this country enjoyed a period of intense inbound production. This dramatically increased the technical skills and crew base here, key elements for the growth and success of the domestic film scene we see today.

The success of the Romanian New Wave of films, which really kicked off with Cristian Mungiu's Palme D'Or-winning film *4 Months, 3 Weeks, and 2 Days*, has continued to deliver awards and accolades of the highest order, right up to the present with Călin Netzer's Golden Bear win in Berlin earlier this year for *Child's Pose*. Many other directors are building on a long and rich tradition of storytelling here.

I suppose I really first saw that rich vein of storytelling in CONNEX when we hosted a black humour contest. We were overwhelmed with submissions of an incredibly high degree of quality. Since then I've seen the black humour thread run through so much of the storytelling, including the New Wave films. More than a few people have compared Romania's gift of the gab to Ireland and perhaps the Irish in me connects with that. It's a storytelling culture through and through. From the taxi driver to the old woman in line at the supermarket to the legions of writers, playwrights and poets, many still waiting to be discovered by the wider world.

We also have to recognise the severe budget restraints these film-makers work with. Long engrained into Romanian film-makers, this forces a high degree of creativity and originality. These two traits – focusing on story and working with low budgets – are very important in today's world with its global economic downturns.

I love the attitude of Romanian film-makers. Before coming here I had the opportunity to be on the sets of a number of films in Canada. What struck me there was the jaded attitude of the crew, the power politics amongst the people in charge, the general inefficiencies in production. Perhaps that was just early 90s film-making in Toronto. No doubt it's gotten better. However I remember feeling how counter-productive much of it was.

For a film to have the chance of really working, of obtaining the magic that the great Japanese director Kurosawa calls cinematic beauty, it must have everyone working together as a team, towards a common goal. Most of the Romanian film productions I've been part of here have had this. I'll never forget on our film the constant early November morning wide-eyed refrain, 'We're making a movie!' When the person in charge of food on set tells you this, with a big grin on her face and excitement in her eyes, you can't help but be inspired and energised.

Do you think of Romania as having a well of creativity?

Definitely. I remember a taxi driver in my early days telling me that every Romanian is an artist, that there is something in the water here that makes it that way. In marketing in the early days at CONNEX I saw it taken to the extremes, where campaigns would change almost daily as people flexed their creative muscle.

Dennis Hopper was filming in Romania, and then returned to work on a script he had optioned from a friend. I had the chance to spend some time with him. He didn't have to be here, and he had no connections, no family history. I asked him why he'd chosen to work on the script here, when he could be anywhere in the world. He gave two reasons. First, flying into Bucharest he felt a strong sense of coming home. Second, he said he felt very creative when he was here.

I too feel creatively inspired here in a way I've never felt in other cities and cultures. And film is just one part of it. The theatre, music and avant-garde art scenes here are strong and fearless and it rubs off. It's a unique culture, and there's also something to do with it being a Latin culture, which was one of the big pulls for me coming here initially. That and Ilie Năstase.

You're a tennis player?

I am.

Have you met him?

I have, and there's a funny story there. Prior to coming, a Canadian

TV producer and I were throwing ideas around and he said, 'You love tennis and Năstase – why don't you do a documentary about him? You could make it about how tough it was to meet Ilie Năstase. About your many attempts to meet him and then, finally, succeeding.' We laughed about that and then I put it aside to concentrate on moving here and starting the new job.

On my first day in the office, a Monday, my new boss said, 'Listen, they're opening a Canadian exhibit at the World Trade Centre. You're the new guy here. We want you to come and meet President Constantinescu.'

So we went and quickly I find myself squashed in a crowd, with the Romanian president slowly making his way towards the Canadian exhibit. The idea is that I will shake hands with him. There's a bit of a crush and I get thrown against someone. I turn round and it's Ilie Năstase! So of course I started talking to him, and in the process forgot to shake hands with the president. Eventually my new boss turned me round. So in the end it only took three days in the country to meet him. I sensed things were going to be great from that moment. And indeed I've had the pleasure of playing and working with him a number of times since and remain a big fan.

What about getting to know Romanians in general here? Have you found that easy?

One of the reasons I've stayed so long is the people. The ease with which one interacts with Romanians, and their openness to new ideas, especially the younger generation, is a huge part of why I enjoy living here. There's often a division when you're an ex-pat in a country. I experienced that in Kyoto, Prague, Phnom Penh and Nairobi. But that division is something I don't feel here. For me there is a real transparency, a real openness here. They are some of the most human of people I've lived amongst. Even in

Bucharest, a city with such amazing contrasts and influences. They are open to connection and want to communicate and I like that.

Like any place there are many challenges. But again I want to emphasise that the human element I find so prevalent here is often the overriding factor, and makes it all tolerable. Of course there's corruption and political issues to work through. And a degree of cynicism that can be deflating, but overall, slowly, it's improving. And there's no sense of a giant conspiracy – just turn on the television or radio and you can see and hear it all.

The day-to-day corruption one comes up against is often understandable, given the extremely low salaries that so many professionals are subject to, and the lack of opportunities that a heavy bureaucracy places on enterprising citizens. But again, as Romania continues on its path towards real independence and partnership in the European Union, I'd like to think that much of that will disappear. I'm sure many would argue with me. But that's my take. For a good understanding of this, I recommend Alexandru Solomon's documentary film *Kapitalism*.

It's also clear to me that 40 years of communism left a big gap in the world of leadership models. So I struggled with that in the beginning, when I was promoting people at CONNEX. Sometimes I had to deal with huge character shifts after a person's title changed. And you still see hangovers from this experience gap today. But certainly less. When I understood why it was happening I adjusted and things worked out.

There's one thing I can say about Romanians at work – if it's something they enjoy they will apply themselves fully, and learn quickly. Traditionally they are a highly educated and industrious group with lots of incredible and important inventions and firsts to their credit. In management terms I've always enjoyed the fact that the focus here is about containing and channelling energy, which is much more fun and productive than trying to find and inspire it! Again, it's not surprising to me that Romania is home to so many great inventions and inventors.

They often refer to themselves as lazy and not liking to work. I really don't see this as the exaggerated characteristic it's made out to be. Like anyone, if you clearly explain the goals behind what you're doing, they're as motivated as other nationalities I've worked with – often more so.

They can be very explosive and verbose in both their spoken and body language. This is especially visible when they're driving. I see this bother others, but I don't mind. For me it's a way of letting off steam, of expressing frustration, returning to some kind of equilibrium. Thankfully it doesn't last long, and they don't seem to hold grudges.

Romania could benefit from a regional leadership role in a number of areas, including the start-up or small business sector, as well as my industry, film. It's a proven fact that start-ups are the real engines of an economy. Societies that promote this and work to motivate activity at this level are the leaders of tomorrow. With their intelligence and willingness to learn, you have the perfect conditions. The film industry itself needs leadership and a strategy, because there you have huge opportunities to leverage the success of the Romanian New Wave films and quality initiatives like the Transylvanian Film Festival to create a sustainable, growth oriented industry. The time is ripe.

For me the positives greatly outweigh the negatives, and that's why I stay. It's also such a safe place. A big part of being Romanian is the strength of the family – the immediate family, the extended family. I have young children and this is a fabulous place to bring them up. The love of children is everywhere. Yesterday I took my four-year-old daughter to Piaţa Matache – a market – and for every single thing we bought an extra one was given to Ana Sofia. I also love rituals like spitting on children to ward off curses, or being reprimanded by older women for having young children out in public before they're baptised.

The sense of family is also very attractive to people like me, from cultures where consumerism has been allowed to run rampant and unchecked. Capitalism or communism, these are things that come in and invade, and Romanians figure out how to adapt. It seems clear to me that not many people here were ever really communist tried-and-true; instead they were simply adapting in order to survive. But what never changed was the love and respect for family and enjoying the moment and limited time we're here.

I go back to Canada almost every year and talk to Romanians there – friends, and friends of friends. It's been very interesting to watch the evolution over the past 12 years. In the late 90s the ones I spoke to were just so happy they were in Canada. They couldn't understand why I would choose to live here. In 2003 and 2004, this was still very much the thinking, but there were more genuine enquiries into how it was to live in Romania. Today, it seems to have reversed. Canada's not that great, they tell me – and they really want to get back.

I still want to make more films here. There's something in Ilie Năstase's great autobiography I'd love to capture. Ultimately, I've long felt that Romania is a bit of a secret that one day the world will figure out. But until they do, I'm very content to enjoy all the amazing things, and the incredible vitality it has to offer.

Italo De Michelis

Miercurea Ciuc

'What's the difference between the Italian Regioni Autonome *and this place?'*

My first impression was, I go back in time, because here was something I remember when I was young. After two or three times coming to Romania, the owner of this restaurant made an offer to me. I moved here. I've been six years in this restaurant. I pay the rent and I do what I want, but is good. The first work that I made was to teach the cook my home *cucina*. I knew what I have to do, because I learned this from my father and mother. I changed all the menus. We made Italian food here, just Italian food. And the people, they're coming. We buy many products from Italy, and I know that many people that come from Italy like this *cucina* and say it is the same as in Italy. There is a firm that every week takes some things to north Italy and brings me back what I need – crudo Italiano, parmigiano, salami, speck.

Many people come here. I pay much more for the food because we use the best quality of food that we find, but we must keep the same price of the other restaurants, so the profit is very small. We think we are the best, even of the county. We have people come from Brașov, even from Bucharest. All around they know San Gennaro. We had ministers of the government come here, a judge. We are even known in Hungary, because two or three times in the year we receive a visit from the Minister of Foreign Affairs of Hungary.

What about developing local taste?

I had a little difficulty the first year, because the people don't know *cucina Italiana*. Just pizza or carbonara or spaghetti. When I come here I teach the people, offering each day different *cucina*. I say, 'I want you to try this. If you don't like, you don't have to pay.' And the people know that on Thursday and Friday we have fresh fish from the sea. I buy in Braşov fresh: we have shrimps, *dorada*, shellfish, *bande mari*, *scoici*, *vongole*. The people like, and after, we have a reservation every Thursday for the fish. After, we tried with the wild mushrooms from the forest, and we have many recipes. We use about 50 kilograms of wild mushrooms all the year; in the summer fresh, and the rest of the year frozen.

Where do you buy the wild mushrooms?

Here, because there are two or three firms exporting this kind of mushrooms into Italy. And after I tried to use even the truffle, and see if the people like. We use two kilograms per month, with just ten or fifteen grams per portion. It's not so expensive. I buy here and the price is around €100 a kilogram.

Is Romania good for truffles?

This kind of truffle, the black truffle, is good. I like. We have the best kind of truffle in Italy and France, the white truffle type, and this kind of truffle in Italy has a price of around €1200 to €1500 per kilo. But is like the diamond. Every year the biggest white truffle is put into an auction, and last year the biggest was sold in Japan at €200,000. One piece, just one piece! White truffle. But now I prefer this kind of truffle, the black.

Where do they find these truffles, then?

In a forest with particular trees, oak and beech. This is the best for truffle, not the pine. People who do this job know secret places where they go with the dog to find, because it's a business.

What kind of dog?

Any kind. You have to train them when they're young. A dog of my friend, a golden retriever, we train him in three weeks. In three weeks is a smart dog. We take some little metal balls you can open, with holes for tea, and inside put a piece of potato – we keep it 12 hours in oil of truffle so it has a smell. We put it inside the ball and hide the ball at home. Then we say, 'Hi, hi, hi!' and he finds it, brings it to us. We give him a piece of biscuit. After one week we try outside in the grass. 'Hi, hi, hi!' Then we put it underground, four centimetres, because the black truffle you find it under maximum ten centimetres. The white quality, sixty or seventy centimetres down. For that white kind of truffle you can use even a pig. When you see the pig start to dig, you go there and you stop him getting there first. You get it out first. If you use pig for the black kind, he gets there too quickly, so we use dogs. The truffle is not everywhere. Where you find it, if you come back there after one week, you get more. So when you know three or four different places, you go one by one and collect.

So you're a truffle hunter. Do you hunt anything else?

I'm a hunter too, just for partridge. I have a dog here. I did the Romanian hunting examination, and I like it, because for this kind of hunting I am alone. Nobody is interested in partridge. Here the people are going for deer, bear, wild boar, not in the forest, in the fields. Even the wild duck by the river, this is my hunting. I have a shotgun here. I like nature, and when the season is off for the hunting, I go for mushroom. In September time for truffle.

I know that in this forest are living bear, lynx, wolves. It's incredible. Just yesterday there was a newspaper report about a boy who was attacked by a bear – not bad, just the shock. The dogs are more dangerous than the bear, because there are much more. And I must ask to carry a pistol, because when I go in the bush for mushrooms, I was attacked by dogs.

I was with a friend two years ago near Miercurea Ciuc. When I come out of the bush in the fields, I saw six or seven dogs that were looking after some sheep. One start to bark at me, and the others come. They came all around me like a band of wolves. I have just two bags with mushrooms. One tried to bite me and then another one. I was lucky the shepherd was not far, and he come running before the first dog bite me. After that I speak with somebody, and they told me buy a spray and fireworks.

Last year I was around the same place. When the first dog bark at me I throw one of these fireworks, and all the dogs, even the sheep, run away. And after comes the shepherd, and said, 'Why I do that?'

'Why I do that? It's better that I do, because next time I come with my gun and shoot all, even you, because your dog must stay there. I'm not a wolf, I'm not a bear.' Now I buy this pistol; it has a rubber bullet. Up till now I haven't used it. One month ago I was with my dog looking for partridge, and there were some of these dogs coming, barking, and I shot in the air and they went away.

And have you seen bears?

Three years ago, in the same place where the dogs attacked me. I was looking for mushrooms. When I looked up, I saw in front of me, 20 metres away, a small animal, brown colour. At first I thought it was a little cow, but after he got up on his feet I saw it was a bear. I was surprised and immediately it was a shock for me, because where is the child, there is the mother. Maybe the mother's watching me. I was with two other persons who are a little further away. I shouted, 'Bear, bear, bear!' and I run away. This was my experience with a bear. I was lucky.

What about your relationships with people here? Is it the same as in Italy or more difficult?

Like in Italy. Maybe the first time someone moves here they think it's a different place, with a different thinking. But I think everywhere in the world where I was – I was in many parts – after a time you understand people everywhere are the same, even here. Now here I have no problem with anybody. Just sometimes a small trouble with the *primaria*, the mayor, because I am not in agreement with the politics of this municipality. Sometimes I write to the *primaria* what I think, and sometimes to the newspapers about his social policies. They have another vision. People here come from the communist time, and until now don't think like us. They accept everything.

So you challenge, and what happens?

Sure, sure. I get some results for small things. One of these was about every time a firm of electricity or water or public water or gas has to do some work, they make this work from eight o'clock in the morning until seven o'clock in the evening. I don't want that, because I must close the restaurant. No, so I speak with the chief of different firms; I write to the newspaper. And after that they change, they work in the night now. I'm happy for that. Many people are happy.

Does that give you a problem afterwards?

No, no. Now many times people come to me and say, 'Italo, can you do this, this, this?'

I say, 'Why you don't do that?'

'Ah, because you know very well what to do, it's better you do it. They know you already.' I was the same in Italy. I just exported it here. People prefer to be quiet, but they are happy when I do something.

What about personal relationships?

When I come here first time I got to know my girlfriend, Monica, but she was with another man. She had trouble with her boyfriend, and at the same time I had trouble with my girlfriend in Italy. We meet here and we start a relationship, and after one year when I moved here permanently, we stayed in an apartment together in town. We were talking about working the restaurant together. Now my occupation is the *cucina* and the guests; her occupation is all the paperwork. It's harder for her than for me. She is very good. I'm happy that I found her. She resolves many problems. I couldn't on my own.

When I come here for the first time, they are all Romanian. After, I understand there are big differences. You know, the Székely are much more nationalist, and different from Romanian people. The culture of the Romanian is from the Latin, and the Székely are Hungarians and completely different.

Are they are a Latin people, the Romanians?

Yes, but it's not a Latin like Italian or Spanish, but nearly. Even the language is somewhere the same, coming down from Latin. I think these are not Latin people, just the language is from Latin.

They say they are Latin.

It's not true. Because Latin people are people from South America, from Spain and Portugal, from Italy. The people from here are different, but I think that the mind of this people is near the Latin people, you understand – near. They are more open, a little bit like Italian. The Székely are more cold, even when 80 per cent of my friends are Székely. They take much more time to accept you, but after, they do accept you. In the small village where I live, 100 per cent are Székely. It's just four kilometres from Miercurea Ciuc, and the children there don't speak any word in Romanian. All my neighbours are my friends now. They invite me for a grill, or when they kill a pig they send me a little gift.

The adults, they speak Romanian not very well, but we understand. When I buy the terrain – the terrain belongs to the Catholic Church – the priest, before he decides, I must talk with him many times for him to sell me this piece of ground. I want to make a small house to move here.

He said, 'Okay, I promise you, but I have to take some time, because I have to talk with the people around to see how is their mind here.'

So after a time I'm going and saying to the priest, 'I pray you, I want to do it now because we are in springtime and we want to make the house in the summer.'

And he say, 'What's the hurry?'

And I say, 'Monica push me to do this.'

He changed face, expression. He say, 'Monica is Romanian, and Romanians must be the other side of the Carpathian Mountains, not here.' I told him I'm Italian. 'Okay, the Pope is Italian, okay.' And after he sell me the terrain. But the mentality here is they are much more open with foreigners than with Romanians.

How is it for Monica in the village now?

Very good, she's okay. In the last two years it was even better. She is not Catholic, she's Orthodox, but for two years we go to the church on Christmas Eve. All the people of the village are there. We brought hot wine and *gogoşi* – doughnuts – which we made here. We put them on the table outside the church, and me and Monica offered them. All the people know Monica. They accept Monica, even because Monica speak a little Hungarian, and with the church this is better.

Do you talk politics at all?

Yes, sure. Here we had just one political party, UDMR. Now it's changed because they made two different Hungarian parties. This was not a good idea, because before they had around five per cent, and this was enough to enter into the government. Now they are divided, no Hungarian goes into the government. This is the problem. In the 22 years after the death of Ceauşescu, UDMR has always been in the government, always. But the people say they don't do anything for this part of Romania, they made many wrong actions.

In Italy we have four regions that are autonomous. We have Alto Adige where people are speaking German; we have Val d'Aosta where people speak French; and then we have the islands of Sardinia and of Sicily, *Regioni Autonome*. They can do the same thing here, but the politicians don't make this. In 22 years they haven't got anything.

You're thinking they could be similar to Sicily or Sardinia?

Yes. What's the difference between the Italian *Regioni Autonome* and this place? I speak with the minister of this government from

UDMR, with Kelemen Hunor, and they say it's very difficult to do. This is politics. Kelemen Hunor is now the leader of UDMR, and he come maybe one time every week here and we talk. When he is not in Bucharest he comes in this restaurant.

Moving on to your future, do you have any plans?

In the village we made this wooden house for me and Monica. We have a garden, and on the land near the house we have a barn. My idea is to transform this barn into a small restaurant for maximum 20 people. Maybe I begin next year, then I move there and stay there. It's not too far from the centre of Miercurea Ciuc. I think that many guests of San Gennaro will come because they like my *cucina*.

I want to make a different kind of restaurant, just for reservations, just for 20 people maximum. A kind of restaurant – there are many in Italy – where people make a reservation and I prepare what I want to serve to them; seven to ten different kinds *antipasto*, and after two plates of pasta, just a portion so they can try different ones. And after, two kinds of meat or fish or chicken, prepared at that time. Dessert could be apple pie, another time could be something with cream. People come, they know me, they know my *cucina,* they just choose the wine and what they want to drink. I open when I have a reservation. Is typical in Italy, there are many restaurants like that. I can offer a good service because with few people it's easier to have quality food. Even the price could be a little cheaper because I don't have so many employees. This is my dream, this is my dream.

Philip O'Ceallaigh

Bucharest

*'Places where things don't work are necessarily more spontaneous...
you find yourself feeding off that kind of stimulation.'*

I decided I wanted to write. I wanted to simplify my life, win a
little independence, to find a place that was messed up enough
that I could live cheap. I would've preferred if it wasn't messed up
but yeah, basically economic reasons. For $5500 I was able to buy
a one room apartment in a neighbourhood called Titan, out
toward the edge of the city. I didn't have to worry about money as
much, and I was able to write my first book. It took about four to
six years. I'm from Waterford in the south east of Ireland and grew
up in the country. I've come and gone a bit, but basically Romania
has been my base since 2000.

   With time the writing became the only thing that was really a
constant. I kept writing one story after another. All I could do was
keep writing and keep hoping. I was very conscious that I was
learning a craft and that it would take time, and I never felt that I
was possessed of some tremendous talent. Bukowski, writing about
a life I could relate to, which was a life of frustrations, problems
with money, instability, inspired me to be a writer who could make
something out of simple things, the daily struggle with life. I
wanted to escape work, and writing, when it's going well,
resembles play rather than work. You give yourself up to something
unconscious and something happens. It's nearly magical.

   The first few years I edited a business magazine. Very repetitive, just correcting English, but kept enough money coming in. I had a transitional period when I was translating a lot of stuff, including Romanian films, one of which, *4,3,2*, won the Palme D'Or in Cannes. That was interesting, to be able to see these new films coming through, to see this totally unexpected burst of creativity and storytelling about the country, about the country's present and its past.

The films made in the 90s and the kind of literature Romania was producing then never seemed to me to connect with daily reality. I went around for a good few years scratching my head trying to figure out why this was, why Romanians couldn't represent their own country in writing or in film. I'm talking about the 90s, the early 2000s. Now, of course, there are a lot of different directors telling a lot of different stories and you really do see the past debated, as you saw in *4,3,2*. That's something that wasn't there at all in the 1990s and I think it's only beginning in literature now.

Cărtărescu? In my opinion he'd be an example of the kind of literature that was allowed to appear in the 1980s. His first book of prose was published in 1989, and it's a work of fantasy. All the stories are set in Bucharest, but you wouldn't recognise the suffering that the city was undergoing. I'm talking about having to queue for food, being cold in the winter, having to deal with the secret police prying, the backstreet abortions because there's no reproductive freedom. These things were not registered in Romanian literature in the 1980s of course, but this somehow carried through into the 1990s, this inability to register ordinary experience. Now I'm not saying that writing has to be about social problems, political problems, but to ignore all these things is extraordinary, because it creates a sense of unreality in the prose.

The breakdown in storytelling under communism is still felt today. The recovery started first in film. *The Death of Mr Lăzărescu* – you know that film? I remember the shock of the opening sequences because it was the first time in a Romanian film I saw an ordinary apartment that looked like the apartment where I lived. That was released in 2005. The reason it broke first in film, before literature, was because there was finance there. Any young person thinking about telling a story is also having to think about making a living, and thinking about a potential connection with an audience. To do this through writing is harder; you can't make money out of it. In most places you can't make any money out of it, but that's especially true in Romania.

My *Notes from a Turkish Whorehouse* was received very well and it got a lot of attention for a book of short stories by an unknown writer. It won some prizes, sold thousands of copies. Maybe because it was an unusual sort of book. It was translated into Romanian and drew a lot of attention over here too, but for different reasons – there was an element of 'let's see what the foreigner has to say about us.' There's this curiosity Romanians have, a sensitivity to how they're seen by foreigners. It's a kind of national narcissism. Like teenagers with mirrors, constantly having to check out their image.

There's a massive difference between generations. It's the only real change that's taking place. You see all the reforms attempted from the political level that didn't go anywhere. The culture has to change before there can be any reform. The young people here, they're much more self-confident, they've travelled. They access information differently. They get their information from web blogs which they can set up with absolutely no money at all, communicate through Facebook, send articles back and forth. The free flow of ideas is there among young people in a way that it's never been before, and that, if anything, is going to change politics.

Politics has been utterly stagnant since the Revolution in that there's been no political movement that represents the needs or aspirations of ordinary people. The political parties are associations of business people. They do deals among themselves, go through the motions of politics and at the same time control television and newspapers, the entire media. And they all derive from the old communist *nomenklatura*. Publicly they talk dirty about each other; you'd think they were at war. They're not, they get along very well, they do their deals behind closed doors and publicly they make a theatre of democracy. You have disputes, you have name-calling, you have scandals. It really has the quality of a *telenovela*, of a soap opera, in that there's no substance to it, there's no progression. It's all about the personalities sniping at each other. It's not about principles, it's not debating issues. What we call politics in a mature democracy is about working through the issues, defining problems and coming up with solutions. That doesn't exist here. Salvation isn't going to come from politics.

Change can only come from the ground up. You're seeing now for the very first time activism by young people, in lots of different areas. People are seeing that they actually have to do something themselves. You get a little bit of satisfaction in working with other people who feel the same way as you do, as opposed to just complaining, which is all anybody, including myself, has done until now. So it's a matter of time before that bears fruit. I don't expect it to make a change fast. Real changes don't occur fast.

People are still very suspicious of each other. You see it in the street, in the casual rudeness, which is such a contrast to the consideration, even exaggerated courtesy, that people display in more personal contexts. In the street, people don't trust each other, don't like each other. You see it in business too. I steer clear of doing business in Romania. I haven't the stomach for it. Where there's money involved, Romanians need to begin by establishing the power relationship. It's not like two equals coming together to make a deal which is advantageous to them both. The style is different. They immediately start to mess with each other to establish who is more powerful in the relationship. This style spills over into other things too. You know you'll see it any time you have to deal with the state bureaucracy, even to access basic services.

Traditionally it is a hierarchical society. Under communism this expressed itself in the smallest relationships. Everything was a transaction. If you had power it meant you were in a position to help someone or hinder them. Someone gives you a little present and that establishes that you're in charge. And of course the importance of the deal, the difference in power, determines the size of the present.

In those days nearly everything that you needed to get done you had to do illegally. You're both caught in an illegality. The one who is facilitating, the one with the power, receives something from the other person, so you begin by humiliating the person who needs your help. Your opening move is to spit on them. Then you ignore them a while, make them wait, and when they finally feel like shit, you might start resolving their problem. People will behave with complete bad faith and then smile at each other and pretend nothing happened. It's very inefficient. You waste time and energy with a lot of shouting, a lot of useless talking.

I've noticed that Romanians like foreigners they have to speak to in English. Once you can speak Romanian they find you much less interesting. Once you've been absorbed by the country to the extent that you can actually function on your own and speak the language, they're not so fond of you. Most foreigners here, they don't speak the language. It's advantageous for a Romanian to relate to someone like that, through English, and basically be their intermediary, or guide in a sense. I found when I was living in that shithole Titan on the tenth floor of this block, people weren't interested in me because I was a foreigner.

They were quite right. I was not interesting at all. I could speak Romanian. I was living in a poor part of town. Clearly I didn't have much cash. The question must arise, why was I living voluntarily in the sort of place no Romanian would particularly want to live. Obviously I was stupid or crazy. You hear these foreign guys talking about how popular they are with Romanian women. I wasn't popular at all. No I wasn't. Why would I be? Obviously I was a defective foreigner. There was a curiosity. What are you doing here? Why are you here? And you'd try and answer the question and say, I don't want to earn money, there's something else I want to do, I'd like to learn how to write. At that point you'd be lucky if they ever talk to you again.

When I was living in Titan my friends were people I knew in the area and we didn't even go into the centre very often. It was a frustrating time in many ways, the four or five years I spent there; it was claustrophobic, a feeling of being trapped, it wasn't a feeling of even participating in the city.

I wrote the story *In the Neighbourhood* when I knew I was going to be leaving. I knew I'd seen a place that was unusual and certainly wasn't being registered in writing by Romanians. Most of all, for myself, I wanted to have a record of that time.

I gathered characters from the block. A lot of them were descriptions of my neighbours, a lot of the incidents were the day-to-day happenings of the place and I compressed it into a day, using different characters. Even broke myself into several different characters to do that. I just had to figure out where and how they intersected, so it became quite an unusual story in the sense that nothing really happens, just the everyday kind of thing – a pipe breaks and has to be fixed, causing a bit of chaos, and people run around and bump into each other.

My biggest challenge over the years has been getting through the winters. In order to enjoy Bucharest you have to leave it, frequently. It saps you, this town, it takes a lot of energy from you. You see people from Bucharest who've gone off abroad and their first couple of days back they're bitching about the city and you think to yourself, Jesus, I used to be like that. They become foreign to this place very fast, because it is a strange city. I don't know any in Europe like this, that's been vandalised the way it has been by the last dictator, where people never discuss repairing the damage. Basically he's put a motorway through the centre and cut off walkable communication between the different parts of town.

This is something I started to examine in the last story I wrote; we're still in the shadow of this man every time we walk through the city. It's like somebody was insane, had a dream and turned it into reality. He said, 'I'm going to build a dream palace,' and he did it. So we're walking through a mad person's dream, that's what it feels like to me. We walk through it daily, and most people don't even think about it. I feel it. I live now in one of the blocks that was constructed in what was the old Jewish part of town, after he bulldozed it. I see the occasional old building that survived and realise this is only 23 years old, this is younger than me, this piece of vandalism. The conception of human life that the buildings themselves express is to me nightmarish, and I don't get used to it, I've never got used to it. I feel it every time I look out the window.

Do people talk about those times of dictatorship?

When I came in '96 no one wanted to talk about it. People were just too sick, too sick of what had happened and the ongoing reality of it, the ongoing disappointment. Somehow that caused a reticence or inability to discuss plain things plainly. Writers, artists, didn't want to take it on. People became accustomed to secrecy and silence. Everybody snitching on everybody else. When the South Africans dismantled apartheid they had a Truth and Reconciliation Commission. They said, 'We're not going to prosecute anybody for what they did in that time but we want everyone to talk about it openly, to find out what happened.' I imagine this helps a society to heal, to speak openly about things; at least it allows a problem to be confronted.

This never happened here. Now, neighbours snitching on their neighbours is the least of it. We're talking about people being thrown into prison, people who were tortured, people who were harassed for years, and they know who did it. We know who the police were at this time, we know who were generals in the *Securitate*. But they didn't become convicts in 1990s, they became the political class, so it was immediately in their interest not to make their crimes an issue. Their take on it was: what's done is done, that was a different system, we all lived under it, we were all shits. Some people were bigger shits than others though, some profited from persecuting others in a style that can only be described as criminal. We can thank NATO and the European Union for facilitating these people, instead of confronting the fact that crimes were committed here. And the people who committed them shouldn't be in positions of power. The EU and NATO legitimated the hold on power that these people have.

Asta este! I say it myself. It's a verbal shrug in the face of all the shit you can't change. Frustration is an interesting thing. You know, when you've been here as long as I have, you accumulate not days or weeks or months but years of complaining about things that don't suit you. Recently I decided I didn't want to do that anymore. There's no point complaining, there's no point bitching, there's no point getting angry about things.

I decided simply to try and live more positively, because talking doesn't change anything. You should forfeit complaining that reality doesn't suit you, unless you are willing to act to alter the situation. I think it's healthier. I have had a positive experience recently, helping this candidate Nicuşor Dan. I was one of his many volunteers, in a very humble way, I simply helped collect a few signatures. I talked to other people about him, got them collecting signatures. Back in the winter I did an interview with him to find out something about him. Gave him a little publicity that way and informed myself. You have to be willing to do something positive, to extend a hand to somebody who wants to do something good.

In Ireland people are troubled by a lot of trivial things. You see rich people imagining that they're poor. You hear people saying in Ireland that the country's destroyed, that it's a mess, that nobody's got any money. To hear them talk, you'd think it's Burkina Faso. Ireland is still one of the richest countries in the world, by spending power. Look at the UN Human Development Index – it's near the top. I tend to find it too orderly. You become accustomed to haphazardness, chaos. Places where things don't work are necessarily more spontaneous, whether it be India or Egypt or Romania, so I've kind of got knocked towards chaos. You find yourself feeding off that kind of stimulation. In an urban environment anyway. I find northern European cities too quiet. Where are all the people? Why is nothing happening? You walk down the street here, there's always something on.

I don't make plans. I'm focused on the week or two ahead. I see no point in thinking about things a year down the road. No, I'm quite happy here today. Home? Home is just off Piaţa Unirii, in this block.

Leaving Romania, What Would You Miss?

The buzz, I'd miss the buzz, yeah. Romania's got something that other places don't have, and it's hard to put your finger on it. You've got so many different cultures here going back centuries. The country is so diverse. Yes, I'd miss that a lot.
Mike Ormsby.

A sense of mission. That's what I'd miss.
Leslie Hawke.

The creative chaos and liveliness, the unpredictability. Some say that Romania is a spectacle, a theatre, and it's very entertaining; living in Romania is never dull. And I agree.
Johan Bouman.

The chaos. And the logic that is different from what I grew up with, and is difficult to articulate, but has its own sense of reason.
Andrew Begg.

The bottles of free country booze – wine and *ţuică* – people keep giving me.
Philip O'Ceallaigh.

The can-do attitude; the space and the mountains; Romanian hospitality and my Universal red tractor.
Duncan Ridgley.

That sense of freedom that continues to prevail in some parts of the country.
Craig Turp.

My lifestyle here. I like having the freedom – I'm not tied down, I haven't got a nine-to-five job – and the adventure and the excitement.
Judy Faint.

The two Easters, wonderful sites, and my friends who come from such mixed experiences, people I'd never have known living at home in NYC.
Andrew Littauer.

It's difficult to get bored here. There's a constant challenge of living. Every day is different and in Romania the plan always changes. You never know what's going to happen.
Colin Shaw.

The language. I like to have fun in it. Somebody here once told me you're as many personalities as languages you know. And I think that's true. In Romanian I'm a different person.
Peter Hurley.

The country itself! Romania is so beautiful…
Gianluca Falco.

The space I have here: only fields and a little stream nearby, and sometimes there's cattle and sheep and horses and dogs. It's very good to see the sunrise in the summer time. I'm always awake early.
Frans Brinkman.

Mainly the informality of the way of living, and the sensation of moving things, creating changes.
Franco Aloisio.

I'm going to leave Romania for the next two years for an international project, and I'll miss most the warm people, the nature, and the restless but very interesting everyday life.
Israela Vodovoz.

My garden, which is slowly taking shape and which does indeed teach me that the four seasons here are not 'hot and hotter', as in Texas.
Nancy Rice.

These relationships that are much closer here. In Romania people are more sincere.
Egle Chisiu.

Jutka with her fantastic facials.
Jerelyn Taubert.

This joy I see when people are sharing a meal together. The adventure of Romania, that everything still isn't very organised yet.
Sonja van Zee.

The natural world and the feeling that I found here, an ancient situation that is no more in Italy, an old Europe. This I think I lose.
Italo de Michelis.

The pace of life, so much easier than the UK, and the warmth of the new friends made here.
Paul Davies.

The mountains, the forests, the space and the wilderness. A lot of space to go out, go off on my own and not see anybody for three days.
Greg Helm.

I don't want to even think about it, but I do, because it might happen in the next few years. I would miss my sincere, true friends; the architecture; the closeness to nature and the land.
Carolyn Litchfield.

The easy familiarity and sense of community, and relaxed open way you can communicate with people here. Even dealing with grumpy people at the post office is quite fun sometimes. Usually the human being will come out.
Rupert Wolfe-Murray.

A very kind people; I am thankful for the unreserved welcome I received from all Romanians, anytime and anywhere, a very special experience indeed; a beautiful, largely intact natural landscape and excellent conditions for escaping 21st century stress.
Rob Rosinga.

The social aspect as well as the accessibility of people and places. And the energy and vitality of the people and the endless celebrations. But most of all, the human scale of the place, and the sense of peace and calm and creative inspiration it brings.
John Ketchum.

The friendships.
Liria Themo.

The whole kaleidoscope of it all really. There are so many restrictions and yet there are so many freedoms. It's a country full

of contradictions. I'd miss everything, the bad as well as the good, because it's what makes it go.
Ian Tilling.

Contributor Contacts

Andrew Littauer

APT
andrewlittauer@aol.com
www.apt.ro

Colin Shaw

Roving Romania
rovingrom@gmail.com
www.roving-romania.co.uk
Tel: 0040 (0) 724 348 272
Mobile: 0040 (0) 744 212 065

Craig Turp

craig@craigturp.com

Duncan Ridgley

www.somewheredifferent.com

Egle Chisiu

eglebag@yahoo.it
Tel: 0040 (0) 729 244 718

Franco Aloisio

Fundaţia Parada
Strada Bucur 23, Sector 4, Bucharest
www.paradaromania.ro

Gianluca Falco

Hieroglifs Translations
gianluca.falco@hieroglifstranslations.ro
www.hieroglifstranslations.ro
Tel: 0040 (0) 372 701 748
Mobile: 0040 (0) 726 356 051

Contributor Contacts

Greg Helm

fprotcophelm@clicknet.ro
Tel: 0040 (0) 741 119 769

Ian Tilling

Casa Ioana
Şoseaua Olteniţei 39-41, Sector 4,
Bucharest 041294
office@casaioana.org
www.casaioana.org
Tel: 0040 (0) 21 332 6390

Israela Vodovoz

'Casa Livisra', Vişeu de Sus, Maramureş
www.livisra.ro
Tel: 0040 (0) 765 252 325

Italo De Michelis

San Gennaro Restaurant
Str. Petöfi Sándor 15, Miercurea Ciuc,
Harghita, 530210, Romania
italodemichelis@yahoo.com
Tel: 0040 (0) 266 206 500

Jonas Schäfer

Valea Verde Transylvania
jonas@transcarp.com
www.discover-transilvania.com
Tel: 0040 (0) 265 714 399

Leslie Hawke

Asociaţia OvidiuRo
leslie.hawke@ovidiuro.org
www.ovid.ro
Tel: 0040 (0) 213 158 806

Mike Ormsby

www.nicoarobooks.com
www.childwitch.com

Paul Davies

Everyone's Child Romania
pdaviesro@yahoo.com
merriel.jovetic@btopenworld.com

Peter Hurley

Asociația Interculturală de Tradiții
www.traditia.ro
www.facebook.com/PeterHurley.official
https://twitter.com/PeterHurley13

Ricardo Alcaine

GIS Group
www.gisgroup.ro/english/
Tel: 0040 (0) 213 005 604

Rupert Wolfe Murray

wolfemurray@gmail.com
www.wolfemurray.tumblr.com
www.productive.ro
Twitter: @wolfemurray
Mobile: 0040 (0) 745 801 896

Scott Eastman

www.eastmanphoto.com

Count Tibor Kalnoky

Count Kalnoky's Guesthouses
Miklosvar nr. 186, Jud. Covasna
k@transylvaniancastle.com
www.transylvaniancastle.com
Tel: 0040 (0) 742 202 586
Fax: 0040 (0) 267 314 088